Steve McQueen: Interviews

Conversations with Filmmakers Series

STEVE MCQUEEN
INTERVIEWS

Edited by Geoffrey Lokke

University Press of Mississippi

The University Press of Mississippi is the scholarly publishing agency of
the Mississippi Institutions of Higher Learning: Alcorn State University,
Delta State University, Jackson State University, Mississippi State University,
Mississippi University for Women, Mississippi Valley State University,
University of Mississippi, and University of Southern Mississippi.

www.upress.state.ms.us

The University Press of Mississippi is a member
of the Association of University Presses.

Any discriminatory or derogatory language or hate speech regarding race, ethnicity, religion, sex, gender, class, national origin, age, or disability that has been retained or appears in elided form is in no way an endorsement of the use of such language outside a scholarly context.

Copyright © 2025 by University Press of Mississippi
All rights reserved
Manufactured in the United States of America

∞

Library of Congress Cataloging-in-Publication Data

Names: Lokke, Geoffrey, editor.
Title: Steve McQueen : interviews / Geoffrey Lokke.
Other titles: Conversations with filmmakers series.
Description: Jackson : University Press of Mississippi, 2025. | Series: Conversations with filmmakers series | Includes bibliographical references and index.
Identifiers: LCCN 2025019215 (print) | LCCN 2025019216 (ebook) |
 ISBN 9781496858818 (hardcover) | ISBN 9781496858825 (trade paperback) |
 ISBN 9781496858832 (epub) | ISBN 9781496858849 (epub) | ISBN 9781496858856 (pdf) |
 ISBN 9781496858863 (pdf)
Subjects: LCSH: McQueen, Steve, 1969—Interviews. | Motion picture producers and directors—Interviews. | Motion pictures—Production and direction—Interviews. | Motion picture producers and directors—Great Britain—Interviews. | Black people in the motion picture industry—Interviews.
Classification: LCC PN1998.3.M3784 A5 2025 (print) | LCC PN1998.3.M3784 (ebook) | DDC 791.43092/2—dc23/eng/20250615
LC record available at https://lccn.loc.gov/2025019215
LC ebook record available at https://lccn.loc.gov/2025019216

Authorised GPSR Safety Representative: Easy Access System Europe - Mustamäe tee 50, 10621 Tallinn, Estonia, *gpsr.requests@easproject.com*

British Library Cataloging-in-Publication Data available

Contents

Introduction   vii

Chronology   xiii

Filmography   xxi

Buster Keaton Routines as Art Installations? Don't Laugh . . .   3
    Jonathan Jones / 1999

Driven to Abstraction: Steve McQueen   6
    Sabine Durrant / 1999

Interview Transcript: Tricky   10
    Steve McQueen / 2001

Interview with Steve McQueen   32
    Hans Ulrich Obrist and Angeline Scherf / 2002

Life in Film: Steve McQueen   39
    Steve McQueen / 2007

Steve McQueen, Director: Intimacy and Distance   41
    Fabien Lemercier / 2008

Steve McQueen on Film   44
    Armelle Leturcq / 2008

You Use Your Body to Die: An Interview with Steve McQueen   48
    Zachary Wigon / 2009

Steve McQueen: Q&A with the Director of *Hunger*   52
    Chris Tinkham / 2009

The Human Body as Political Weapon: An Interview with Steve McQueen   57
    Gary Crowdus / 2009

Sex Addiction and the City: Steve McQueen on *Shame*   66
    Jamie Dunn / 2012

Interview: Director Steve McQueen on *12 Years a Slave*   70
    Matthew Toomey / 2014

Steve McQueen and Donna De Salvo in Conversation   73
    Donna De Salvo / 2016

Steve McQueen and Dr. Cornel West on Paul Robeson, Art, and Politics   93
    Cornel West / 2016

Steve McQueen on *Widows*, Viola Davis, the Politics of Chicago, and More   122
    Gregory Ellwood / 2018

Interview: Steve McQueen Q&A   127
    Simon Grant / 2019

Every Story Has Already Been Told: Steve McQueen Interview and Portfolio   131
    William J. Simmons / 2020

Transcript: In Conversation with Steve McQueen   136
    Paul Gilroy / 2020

"These Are the Untold Stories that Make up Our Nation": Steve McQueen on *Small Axe*   147
    David Olusoga / 2020

"Sometimes the Present Erases the Past, and Sometimes the Past Erases the Present": Steve McQueen on His Cannes-Premiering *Occupied City*   159
    Nicolas Rapold / 2023

Interview with Steve McQueen and Bianca Stigter about Their Documentary *Occupied City*   165
    Susan Kouguell / 2023

Additional Resources   171

Index   177

Introduction

Steve McQueen is the rarest of filmmakers, one as committed to avant-garde cinema and lyric forms of documentary as he is to crafting his wide-reaching and acclaimed historical dramas. (He is also a celebrated photographer, sculptor, and installation artist.) Tellingly, McQueen only turned to narrative features decades into his storied career. And it is likely this devotion to wildly different modes and methods of film, media, and historiography, inspiring and frustrating one another as he moves from work to work, that makes McQueen both a restless and deeply humane artist.

McQueen, who was born in London in 1969 to West Indian parents, is still best known for his landmark drama *12 Years a Slave* (2013). An adaptation of Solomon Northup's 1853 memoir, the film depicts a Black farmer, musician, and free man who was kidnapped into slavery. *12 Years a Slave* is the final installment of a trilogy of sorts, three exacting studies of very different men harboring violent obsessions, each portrayed by the Irish German actor Michael Fassbender. *Shame* (2011) follows the everyday life of a sex addict living in contemporary New York, while *Hunger* (2008), McQueen's feature-film debut, reimagined the final weeks in the life of the Irish militant and prisoner Bobby Sands before his death during a high-profile hunger strike. (Fassbender subsequently played a plantation owner in *12 Years a Slave*.)

McQueen's films appear to ask questions of each other: "What makes a martyr?" for instance, is one that reverberates throughout not just *Hunger* but the artist's entire oeuvre—a political question outlined in a fractious and seventeen-minute cross-examination, filmed in one unbroken take, between Sands and his priest.[1]

Others might recognize McQueen as a fixture at major museum and cultural exhibitions for the last three decades. His short films and works for video are often presented on loop, works clearly influenced by Andy Warhol's early experiments in filmmaking—a debt that McQueen frequently acknowledges.[2] These films seem to explore the edges or test the limits of his chosen medium. When does a film stop being a film? What is beyond the frame? Why should an image move? (McQueen's *7th Nov.* [2001] and *Running Thunder* [2007], among other audio-visual projections, consist solely of still images.) His sculptures *Broken*

Column (2014) and *Weight* (2016), which contemplate the carceral state and institutional violence against Black bodies, lead viewers to consider why one should make a film at all.

Understandably, McQueen is lauded as one of the great living Black filmmakers, which somehow has the ring of a wild understatement. His films, from a minute-long provocation such as *Catch* (1997) to his four-and-half-hour epic *Occupied City* (2023), are almost always arresting works of art that demand sobering self-reflection by its viewers. Still, McQueen never loses sight of the sublime experience of scale that cinema can afford its viewers.

So he is a Baldwin, a Warhol, at times something of a David Lean. But his films, at least in my mind, do not ever defy belief, really; they are not beguiling, seemingly impossible things that feign some presence of anything approaching the divine. As he told Cornel West in their public talk at New York's Whitney Museum in 2016, what he wants, above anything else, is to be a *human being*—a desire and ethos that clearly resonates throughout his ever-growing body of work.

This book collects McQueen's occasional thoughts on life, art, and cinema made largely in conversation with journalists, critics, curators, and other artists. (I have also included an early essay by McQueen on, among other things, his love for the French director Jean Vigo.) In a way, this volume, which spans McQueen's career to date, is a kind of autobiography that documents McQueen's growth both as an artist and a public figure whose reflections on politics, history, and race often go hand-in-hand with his widely discussed films. (In 2014, the same year that *12 Years a Slave* won the Academy Award for Best Picture, Harvard University awarded McQueen the W. E. B. Du Bois Medal for "contributions to African and African American culture and the life of the mind.")[3]

For me, there is a noticeable difference between McQueen, say, on the cusp of winning the Turner Prize in 1999, an artist who was extraordinarily guarded about his work, and the open and generous not-quite-elder figure discussing *Small Axe* (2020) and *Occupied City* toward the end of this collection. When he was younger, McQueen's oft-repeated comment on this matter had to do with *showing evidence*: the art is evidence, art-speak—no doubt he got foretaste of what was to come at Goldsmiths and other schools—was not. It simply did not matter, at least at the time, what he had to say about his films, nor, did it seem, what critics might have had in mind.

One of the first pieces of commentary—I suppose it was more gossip than anything else, but the sort of gossip spread by writers at *The Guardian*—that I can recall reading about McQueen, amidst the wall-to-wall adulation for his first feature films, was that he was a very difficult and even willfully obstructive interview subject. Naturally, this was and remains an unfair construal or interpretation of his early interactions with the press. Some of the weak evidence that was presented included McQueen's brusque reaction to the hundredth critic talking to him about "the body": "McQueen has always claimed to have no idea what they're talking about. 'Well, everybody's using their body in a movie,' he objects. 'I mean, how are they not? I don't understand the point.' But the problem turns out to be the phrase 'the body.' He thinks it sounds pretentious. . . . When I suggest 'physicality' instead of 'the body,' he instantly relaxes, and agrees it's a recurring theme."[4]

From what I can tell, McQueen's former reputation had a lot to do with his (entirely admirable) suspicion of theoretical jargon. ("The body" is, of course, specious language and probably should not be used; among other things, there is no singular, monolithic body out there.) McQueen was also concerned about the imprecision of his off-the-cuff remarks; he often seems stymied by the precision of his art in light of the fluency with which he could communicate using a movie camera. So he used to take precautions: McQueen would have interviewers read back his statements to him, going on- and off-the-record, occasionally doubling back to rehabilitate previously stricken remarks. Which in hindsight seems more than anything like a young artist anxious to curate the reception of his work. (And perhaps, his own art-speak was evidence of something after all.)

Accordingly, I imagine McQueen's younger self would have found the public format of his more recent conversations, often delivered before large audiences, to be a particularly galling exercise: revealing some of his inchoate reasoning, working through his thoughts aloud, (occasionally) stumbling over his remarks. McQueen eventually addressed the question of his hastily misapplied and unearned reputation when he appeared on *Desert Island Discs* after the radio host, Kirsty Young, remarked that he was not at all the irascible figure she had been led to expect.[5] McQueen surmised that his treatment by the media was a product of the same sort of racial profiling and corollary double standards he has encountered throughout his life.[6]

Yet there is continuity between the McQueens young and old, as he still refuses to give interviewers what they want to hear. These moments of friction or even dialectic are especially enlightening for those hoping to better understand McQueen's motivations, artistic process, and practice across different modes and media. Take, for instance, a short exchange between the artist and William J. Simmons, a scholar of film and photography, included in this volume. In his long preface to their conversation, Simmons praises McQueen for complicating or even dispelling a number of critical assumptions about Black artists, "whose cultural output is frequently aligned with a documentary status."[7] Simmons puts this question of truth and documentary to the filmmaker, asking how he relates to the mode or "genre" as a whole. McQueen responded: "Every film is a documentary. That's the only way I can answer that question."[8]

Years on, McQueen extends this reading of his artistic practice when discussing *Occupied City*, a film based on a book written by his wife, the Dutch critic and filmmaker Bianca Stigter. The documentary film consists of contemporary footage of Amsterdam—where McQueen has lived since the late 1990s—filmed before, during, and in the direct aftermath of the city's COVID-19 lockdowns. The film's narration, delivered with little perceptible emotion, recounts official acts of persecution and harassment by the Nazi state as well as Dutch acts of resistance and, perhaps more harrowing, countless acts of despair. The contemporary footage typically bears no trace of the violent occupation from decades earlier. With a runtime of over four hours, this quasi-encyclopedic work has a curious effect on many viewers. As the film critic Nicolas Rapold told McQueen, he was not able to focus to both the images and the words; they seemed to counteract each other, demanding him to focus on one over the other or simply letting the film wash over him. McQueen intimates that this was his intention: "Sometimes the present erases the past, and sometimes the past erases the present."[9]

These related notions, that each of McQueen's films is a historical document making direct claims about the past, a work that has the ability to both erase the historical record and be, in turn, erased by the viewer or the individual staging—in McQueen's words, "what happens in the room"—is part of what gives his oeuvre its particular charge, interweaving McQueen's acute interest in the materiality of his own work with his pronounced commitment to directly engage with historical narratives and his place within them. McQueen makes this connection plain in his evolving installation *End Credits*, which vocalizes every phoneme, mark, blemish, and crease of the FBI's files amassed against the performer and activist Paul Robeson. We also cannot take all of it in, but we still, like the Austrian writer Elfriede Jelinek intimates in her sprawling and divisive "speak-trash" novels and plays, must root ourselves within that shifting morass and discern, against all odds, the truth, despite a corrupting discourse and channels of reception.[10]

As I was for my previous book of conversations with Gaspar Noé, I am deeply grateful for the opportunity to edit volumes for this invaluable series, and value getting to work once again with Emily Snyder Bandy and her colleagues at the University Press of Mississippi. Likewise, this collection would not have been possible without Steve McQueen, and I would like to thank him and his associates at Thomas Dane Gallery, Marian Goodman Gallery, and Lammas Park for their kind permission and assistance throughout the editing process. I also feel especially indebted to the Whitney Museum of American Art, New York, whose 2016 programming for *Open Plan: Steve McQueen* are substantial contributions to this book. Last, but not least, I would like to dedicate this collection to the late

James H. Cone, an immense scholar and pioneering figure within Black liberation theology, whose courses inspired a number of my first publications.

GL

Notes

1. This much-discussed scene from *Hunger*, a prolonged debate about the nature of vanity and martyrdom, is evocative of words between the martyr Thomas Becket and the final tempter in T. S. Eliot's 1935 verse drama *Murder in the Cathedral*. Notably, the Irish playwright Enda Walsh, who cowrote the screenplay with McQueen, writes vernacular, poetic dramas that hearken back to the high modernism of W. B. Yeats and J. M. Synge. For a discussion of the influence of 1930s verse drama on subsequent playwrights, see Geoffrey Lokke, "T. S. Eliot and the Group Theatre," in *The Routledge Companion to Absurdist Literature*, edited by Michael Y. Bennett (New York: Routledge, 2024), 87–97.
2. McQueen says his all-time favorite films are Jean Vigo's *Zéro de conduite* (1933), Warhol's *Couch* (1964), and *Singin' in the Rain* (1952), alongside any number of films by the Taiwanese director Hou Hsiao-hsien. Letterboxd, "Four Favorites with Steve McQueen and Bianca Stigter," February 9, 2024, https://www.tiktok.com/@letterboxd/video/7333726216693828907.
3. Hutchins Center for African & African American Research, "W. E. B. Du Bois Medal Recipients," https://hutchinscenter.fas.harvard.edu/people/w-e-b-du-bois-medal-recipients, accessed July 25, 2024.
4. Decca Aitkenhead, "Steve McQueen: My Hidden Shame," *The Guardian*, January 4, 2014, https://www.theguardian.com/film/2014/jan/04/steve-mcqueen-my-painful-childhood-shame.
5. Steve McQueen, interview by Kirsty Young, *Desert Island Discs*, September 12, 2014, https://www.bbc.co.uk/programmes/b04hml41.
6. Consequently, McQueen has paid no mind to rumors surrounding actors whom are supposedly "difficult" to have on set. Mike Ryan, "Steve McQueen on *Widows* and Why He Ignored a 'Warning' that an Actor Was 'Difficult' to Work With," *Uproxx*, September 11, 2018, https://uproxx.com/movies/steve-mcqueen-interview-widows-michelle-rodriguez/.
7. William J. Simmons, "Every Story Has Already Been Told: Steve McQueen Interview and Portfolio," *Framework: The Journal of Cinema and Media* 61, no. 1 (2020): 59.
8. Simmons, "Every Story Has Already Been Told," 65.
9. Nicolas Rapold, "'Sometimes the Present Erases the Past, and Sometimes the Past Erases the Present': Steve McQueen on His Cannes-Premiering *Occupied City*," *Filmmaker Magazine*, May 25, 2023, https://filmmakermagazine.com/121446-sometimes-the-present-erases-the-past-and-sometimes-the-past-erases-the-present-steve-mcqueen-on-his-cannes-premiering-occupied-city/.
10. See my discussion of Bertolt Brecht, Elfriede Jelinek, and the representation of mass media, satire, and truth. Geoffrey Lokke, "Speak-Trash: Irony for Exterminators," *PAJ: A Journal of Performance and Art* 42, no. 3 (2020): 125–31.

Chronology

1969   Steve McQueen is born in London to West Indian parents. His mother, who is originally from Trinidad, lived briefly in Grenada before moving to the United Kingdom. His Grenadian father subsequently worked as a builder for Transport for London. McQueen grows up in Ealing, West London, and later attends Drayton Manor High School. Although he initially struggles in classroom settings, McQueen soon demonstrates a clear talent and passion for drawing.

1989   McQueen enrolls at the Chelsea School of Art.

1990   McQueen transfers to Goldsmiths, University of London. He would later recall that his formative influences during this period were films by Jean Vigo, Andy Warhol, Jean-Luc Godard, and Ingmar Bergman.

1992   McQueen completes his student film *Exodus*, which depicts two Black men in trilby hats carrying potted palm trees across an East London street. McQueen eventually includes the footage in his first US show at Marian Goodman Gallery in 1997.

1993   McQueen graduates from Goldsmiths with a BA in Fine Art (first-class honors). He debuts *Bear*, a silent avant-garde film that features two naked men wrestling, McQueen being one of them. (One of his actors had failed to show on the day of the shoot.)

1994   McQueen leaves an MFA program at New York University's Tisch School of the Arts after one year. He had attended NYU in order to work with the director Jim Jarmusch, among others, but found the school's methods of instruction to be antithetical to his sensibilities.

1995   McQueen screens an experimental film called *Five Easy Pieces*, studies in motion and repetition that includes slowed-down footage of a bouncing woman and five hula-hooping men shot from above.

1996   McQueen is awarded the ICA London Futures Award. His film *Just Above My Head*, which takes its name from James Baldwin's final novel, has the artist's head lingering at the bottom of the frame before disappearing from view entirely.

1997   McQueen participates in Documenta X in Kassel, Germany, where he debuts *Catch*. The film consists of McQueen and another person tossing a camera between one another, which produces disorientating landscapes of greenery and sky. McQueen moves to Amsterdam, which becomes a primary place of residence with his wife Bianca Stigter and their children. (Stigter, a cultural critic and filmmaker, is the daughter of K. Schippers, a well-known Dutch poet.) They will eventually split their time between London and Amsterdam. McQueen also debuts *Deadpan*, a silent, black-and-white film that repurposes a Buster Keaton stunt in which the artist remains standing, unscathed, as a house collapses around him.

1998　McQueen outfits an oil drum with three cameras and rolls the makeshift device through the streets of New York City. The result is his twenty-two-minute film and installation *Drumroll* in which McQueen projects the footage from the cameras on three screens side by side. McQueen's photograph series *Barrage*, named after the French word for "barrier," captures dampened, tied-up bundles of rags McQueen found in gutters throughout Paris. His short film and installation *Something Old, Something New, Something Borrowed, Something Blue* is projected on the floor of a gallery and shows the artist's hand desperately, purposelessly clawing at the ground.

1999　McQueen wins the prestigious Turner Prize awarded by the Tate Gallery, London, for his work in film and video, beating out shortlisted artists including Tracey Emin with her found object (and critical bête noire) *My Bed*. McQueen's black-and-white film *Cold Breath* shows the artist playing with and tugging at his nipples soundtracked by breathy noises for eighteen minutes. Other works from this year include *Current*, which fades between still images of the Limmat River in Zurich, and *Prey*, a film that slowly reveals a reel-to-reel tape recorder—emitting a series of eclectic, rhythmic sounds—to be connected to a small weather balloon.

2001　McQueen's installation *7th Nov.* pairs a single 35mm color slide, which resembles a scarred body lying in a morgue, with testimony delivered by McQueen's cousin Marcus in which he recounts how he accidentally killed his own brother. The video *Illuminer* depicts a figure (McQueen) lying in the dark, a black silhouette against white bed sheets. The audio is from an off-camera television report detailing American soldiers' final day of training before their deployment to Afghanistan. McQueen also films the Bristol rapper and producer Tricky in the studio as he rehearses the song "Girls" for his 2001 album *Blowback*. McQueen also interviews Tricky at length for the art magazine *SHOWstudio*.

2002   McQueen is named Officer of the Most Excellent Order of the British Empire. He participates in Documenta XI and presents his documentary diptych *Caribs' Leap/ Western Deep* as a single installation. *Caribs' Leap* features scenes of beachfronts in Grenada with intermittent images of bodies falling through the sky, while *Western Deep* is a noisy, chaotic descent into the depths of a South African goldmine. McQueen also stages *Once Upon a Time*, a sequence of 116 color slides, each of them photographs chosen by NASA in the late 1970s to be housed within the *Voyager II* space probe, which McQueen pairs with sounds of people speaking in tongues.

2003   McQueen participates in the Venice Biennale in June. Two months earlier, the United Kingdom commences military operations in Iraq as part of the Second Gulf War. McQueen is subsequently named an "Official War Artist to Iraq" by the Imperial War Museum.

2004   McQueen premieres *Charlotte* in which the British screen legend Charlotte Rampling is shown in a close up—just her eye—and bathed in red light; McQueen proceeds to prod her naked eyeball with his forefinger.

2005   McQueen debuts a film called *Pursuit* for which the artist walked around an Amsterdam park at night wearing a jacket adorned with white lights. His makeshift garment magnifies his position and movement, giving viewers the sense of being followed in the dark. McQueen also premieres his light box (with color transparency) *Mees, after Evening Dip, New Year's Day, 2002*, consisting of a photograph showing a trembling figure wrapped in a towel by the water's edge.

2006   McQueen's photograph *Untitled (Fingers)* shows the artist's fingers forming a T-shape atop a wooden table. Elsewhere, he renders his photograph *Portrait as an Escapologist* into a wall-sized poster that consists of 150 offset prints of the image. McQueen's photograph, a self-portrait, re-creates a historical image of a Dutch escapologist taken in 1926.

2007   McQueen unveils *Queen and Country*. Inspired by his time in Iraq, the work is an oak cabinet filled with 160 facsimile postage sheets that depict the British war dead. His proposal to enter his stamp designs into circulation is rejected by the Royal Mail. McQueen participates in this year's Venice Biennale, where he debuts his film diptych *Gravesend/ Unexploded*. *Gravesend* documents the extraction and refining of coltan, a black mineral used in electronic devices. *Unexploded*, shown on a small monitor in the same room, portrays an unexploded bomb in a crater that McQueen had come across in Basra. McQueen also

	creates the film *Running Thunder*, a static image of a dead horse that presages a sequence in his upcoming feature film.
2008	McQueen's feature-film debut *Hunger*, cowritten by McQueen and the Irish playwright Enda Walsh, is released to wide acclaim. Starring the Irish German actor Michael Fassbender, the historical drama depicts the final weeks in the life of Bobby Sands, an Irish militant who died as part of the hunger strikes he led at HM Prison Maze (Long Kesh Detention Centre) in 1981. The film garners McQueen the Caméra d'Or, an award for first-time directors, at the Cannes Film Festival among other accolades.
2009	McQueen participates in the Venice Biennale, representing the United Kingdom, and debuts *Giardini*, a split-screen film that documents the titular municipal gardens. He also announces that he will be directing *Fela* for Focus Pictures, a biopic on the Nigerian musician Fela Kuti. (McQueen eventually abandons the project.) He debuts a film called *Static*, an aerial portrait of the Statue of Liberty and its raised torch.
2011	McQueen is named Commander of the Most Excellent Order of the British Empire. McQueen's second feature film *Shame* is released. The erotic melodrama, which portrays a sex addict living in New York City, stars Michael Fassbender and Carey Mulligan as the fractious siblings Brandon and Sissy Sullivan. *Shame* debuts at the Venice International Film Festival and garners awards throughout the year, many of them for Fassbender's performance.
2012	A large-scale survey of McQueen's career is held at the Art Institute of Chicago. In March, McQueen replaced the lightbulbs of all 275 streetlamps in Amsterdam's Vondelpark so that they would emit blue light, the resulting work being his installation *Blues Before Sunrise*.
2013	The Schaulager, a museum in Basel, Switzerland, presents a wide-ranging exhibition of McQueen's oeuvre. He once again participates in the Venice Biennale. In August, McQueen debuts his historical drama *12 Years a Slave*, an adaptation of the 1853 memoir by Solomon Northup. Born a free man in New York, Northup was kidnapped into slavery while visiting Washington, DC, in 1841. The film stars Chiwetal Ejiofor as Northup alongside Lupita Nyong'o, Michael Fassbender, Paul Dano, Benedict Cumberbatch, Alfre Woodard, and Michael K. Williams. *Lynching Tree*, a photograph that McQueen would later mounted in a lightbox, is taken while filming *12 Years a Slave* on the outskirts of New Orleans.

2014	McQueen receives the W. E. B. Du Bois Medal from Harvard University, an award given "in recognition of contributions to African and African American culture and the life of the mind." At the Oscars, McQueen wins the Academy Award for the Best Motion Picture for *12 Years a Slave*. (John Ridley also wins for Best Adapted Screenplay and Lupita Nyong'o wins for Best Actress.) The film, widely considered to be a cultural landmark, likewise wins top honors at the Golden Globes and the BAFTA Awards. McQueen announces his attention to make a feature-length film about the life of Paul Robeson in collaboration with the singer and civil rights activist Harry Belafonte. The project, however, does not materialize before Belafonte's death in 2023. McQueen films the pilot for a six-part television series entitled *Codes of Conduct*, which explores a young African American man's engagement with New York high society. Actors Devon Terrell (in the lead role), Paul Dano, Helena Bonham Carter, and Rebecca Hall are all attached to appear in the HBO production. McQueen debuts his first sculpture, *Broken Column*, a truncated pillar of Zimbabwe granite that acknowledges the premature deaths of marginalized Black persons worldwide.
2015	McQueen participates in the Venice Biennale. He also directs a nine-minute music video for the Kanye West song "All Day" that features the rappers Theophilus London and Allan Kingdom alongside Paul McCartney. The music video debuts at the Fondation Louis Vuitton as part of Paris Fashion Week. McQueen and West subsequently appear together at screenings of the work.
2016	In February, HBO cancels *Codes of Conduct* despite McQueen having started work on the second and third episodes. McQueen receives the Johannes Vermeer Award, a Dutch state prize given to exceptional artists working in the Netherlands. An iteration of McQueen's evolving installation *End Credits*, first developed in 2012, appears at the Whitney Museum of American Art, New York. The work projects and vocalizes redacted versions of the files that the FBI had amassed against Paul Robeson throughout the activist's life. As well, McQueen contributes a sculpture called *Weight* to an exhibition at Reading Prison in which a prison bed is veiled by a gold-plated mosquito net.
2017	McQueen holds solo exhibitions at Boston's Institute of Contemporary Art, the Whitworth in Manchester, England, Miami's Pérez Art Museum, the Museum of Modern Art in New York, and the Art Institute of Chicago.

2018	McQueen premieres his feature film *Widows*, a Chicago-based heist drama with an ensemble cast that features Viola Davis, Michelle Rodriguez, Elizabeth Debicki, Cynthia Erivo, Colin Farrell, and Liam Neeson. The film, cowritten by McQueen and the thriller novelist Gillian Flynn, is an adaptation of the ITV television series by the same name. McQueen films a one-minute commercial for Chanel's fragrance Bleu de Chanel starring the French actor Gaspard Ulliel.
2019	The presentation of McQueen's *Year 3* begins at Tate Britain. For the evolving exhibition, McQueen invited every Year 3 pupil in London—seven- and eight-year-old children—to be photographed with their classmates. Tens of thousands of students eventually participate in the project. *Year 3* photographs are also featured on 617 billboards across London.
2020	McQueen is knighted by Queen Elizabeth II in her New Year Honours and named Knight Commander of the Most Excellent Order of the British Empire. A large-scale survey of McQueen's work is featured at Tate Modern. In November, McQueen debuts *Small Axe*, a five-part film anthology streaming on BBC One and Amazon Prime. Each of the films portray West Indian culture, politics, and everyday life in Britain between the 1960s and the 1980s. *Mangrove* depicts the brutal acts of police espionage and misconduct that led to the trial of the Mangrove Nine, a group of Black activists prosecuted for inciting a 1970 riot. *Alex Wheatle*, an intimate character study, follows the early life of the titular novelist who was imprisoned for his role in a subsequent London protest. *Red, White and Blue* portrays the real-life story of Leroy Logan, founder of the Black Police Association, and his attempts to reform London's systemically racist police force from within. *Education* depicts the classification of West Indian children as "educationally subnormal," segregating Black students from the wider school population. Perhaps the most surprising of the films is McQueen's lightly sensual and joyous film *Lovers Rock*, which drifts in and out of its framing narrative to re-create the physicality, exhilaration, and romance of an all-night house party. The *Small Axe* films were shot and released during and in the wake of the Black Lives Matter protests organized after the murder of George Floyd, an African American man, by a white police officer in Minneapolis. John Boyega, who starred as Leroy Logan in *Red, White and Blue*, delivered a widely discussed speech at one of the London demonstrations.
2021	McQueen announces his work on *Blitz*, a film set in London during the Second World War. Actors Saoirse Ronan, Elliott Heffernan,

	Leigh Gill, and Stephen Graham are attached alongside the English musician Paul Weller in his acting debut. BBC One airs McQueen's three-part documentary series *Uprising*, codirected with filmmaker James Rogan. The series depicts three events in 1981 that redefined race relations in the United Kingdom, including the New Cross house fire, the Black People's Day of Action, and the Brixton riots.
2022	A large-scale survey of McQueen's work is held at Pirelli Hangar-Bicocca, Milan. McQueen debuts his installation *Sunshine State*, a two-channel video projection shown on both sides of two screens. The work includes high-definition images of the burning sun as well as footage of Al Jolson taken from *The Jazz Singer* (1927). McQueen's production company Lammas Park releases Bianca Stigter's *Three Minutes: A Lengthening*, a short documentary that interrogates several minutes of archival footage depicting a Jewish community residing in Poland before the ravages of the Holocaust. The film is narrated by Helena Bonham Carter.
2023	The Serpentine Gallery in London shows McQueen's *Grenfell*, a film and installation in response to the 2019 Grenfell Tower fire that claimed over seventy lives. McQueen's four-hour documentary *Occupied City* subsequently debuts at the Cannes Film Festival. Based on Bianca Stigter's 2019 book *Atlas of an Occupied City, Amsterdam, 1940–1945*, the film pairs affectless accounts of the German occupation of Amsterdam through voiceover with contemporary footage of the city shot during and between the COVID-19 lockdowns.
2024	McQueen debuts his installation *Bass* at Dia Beacon, a museum located in upstate New York. In a sprawling, garage-like space, lighting slowly shifts between different colors as a bass-heavy soundscape, conducted by McQueen, is played throughout. *Blitz* premieres at the BFI London Film Festival in October.

Filmography

EXODUS (1992–1997)
Director: **Steve McQueen**
1 minute, 5 seconds (continuous play) / color

BEAR (1993)
Director: **Steve McQueen**
Cast: Vernon Douglas, **Steve McQueen**
10 minutes, 35 seconds / black-and-white

FIVE EASY PIECES (1995)
Director: **Steve McQueen**
7 minutes, 4 seconds / black-and-white

JUST ABOVE MY HEAD (1996)
Director: **Steve McQueen**
9 minutes, 35 seconds (continuous play) / black-and-white

DEADPAN (1997)
Director: **Steve McQueen**
Cast: **Steve McQueen**
4 minutes, 35 seconds (continuous play) / black-and-white

CATCH (1997)
Director: **Steve McQueen**
Cast: **Steve McQueen**
1 minute, 54 seconds (continuous play) / color

DRUMROLL (1998)
Director: **Steve McQueen**
22 minutes, 4 seconds / color

SOMETHING OLD, SOMETHING NEW, SOMETHING BORROWED, SOMETHING BLUE (1998)
Director: **Steve McQueen**
2 minutes (continuous play) / black-and-white

PREY (1999)
Director: **Steve McQueen**
6 minutes, 25 seconds (continuous play) / color

COLD BREATH (1999)
Director: **Steve McQueen**
10 minutes (continuous play) / black-and-white

GIRLS, TRICKY (2001)
Director: **Steve McQueen**
Cast: Tricky
14 minutes, 47 seconds / color

ILLUMINER (2001)
Director: **Steve McQueen**
15 minutes, 13 seconds (continuous play) / color

CARIBS' LEAP/WESTERN DEEP (2002)
Director: **Steve McQueen**
28 minutes, 53 seconds, 12 minutes 6 seconds [*Caribs' Leap*]; 24 minutes, 12 seconds [*Western Deep*] / color

ASHES (2002–2015)
Director: **Steve McQueen**
21 minutes, 31 seconds / color

CHARLOTTE (2004)
Director: **Steve McQueen**
Cast: Charlotte Rampling, **Steve McQueen**
5 minutes, 42 seconds (continuous play) / color

PURSUIT (2005)
Director: **Steve McQueen**
14 minutes / Color

GRAVESEND/UNEXPLODED (2007)
Director: **Steve McQueen**
18 minutes, 4 seconds (continuous play) [*Gravesend*]; 54 seconds [*Unexploded*] / color

RUNNING THUNDER (2007)
Director: **Steve McQueen**
11 minutes, 41 seconds (continuous play) / color

HUNGER (2008)
Production companies: Film4, Channel 4, Northern Ireland Screen, Broadcasting Commission of Ireland, Wales Creative IP Fund
Producers: Laura Hastings-Smith, Robin Gutch
Director: **Steve McQueen**
Screenplay: Enda Walsh, **Steve McQueen**
Cinematography: Sean Bobbitt
Editor: Joe Walker
Cast: Michael Fassbender (Bobby Sands), Liam Cunningham (Father Dominic Moran), Liam McMahon (Gerry Campbell), Stuart Graham (Raymond Lohan), Brian Milligan (Davey Gillen), Laine Megaw (Mrs. Lohan), Karen Hassan (Gerry's Girlfriend), Frank McCusker (The Governor), Lalor Roddy (William), Helen Madden (Mrs. Sands), Des McAleer (Mr. Sands), Geoff Gatt (Bearded Man), Rory Mullen (Priest), Ben Peel (Riot Prison Officer Stephen Graves), Helena Bereen (Raymond's Mother), Paddy Jenkins (Hitman), Billy Clarke (Chief Medical Officer), B. J. Hogg (Loyalist Orderly), Ciaran Flynn (Twelve-Year-Old Bobby), Aaron Goldring (Young Bobby's Friend)
96 minutes / color

GIARDINI (2009)
Director: **Steve McQueen**
30 minutes, 8 seconds / color

STATIC (2009)
Director: **Steve McQueen**
7 minutes, 3 seconds / color

END CREDITS (2012–2022)
Director: **Steve McQueen**
774 minutes [video], 4,025 minutes [audio] / black-and-white

SHAME (2011)
Production companies: Film4, UK Film Council, Alliance Films, Lipsync Productions, HanWay Films, See-Saw Films
Producers: Iain Canning, Emile Sherman
Director: **Steve McQueen**
Screenplay: **Steve McQueen**, Abi Morgan
Cinematography: Sean Bobbitt
Editor: Joe Walker
Cast: Michael Fassbender (Brandon Sullivan), Carey Mulligan (Sissy Sullivan), James Badge Dale (David), Nicole Beharie (Marianne), Alex Manette (Steven), Lucy Walters (The Subway Lady), Elizabeth Masucci (Elizabeth), Amy Hargreaves (Hotel Lover), Hannah Ware (Samantha), Robert Montano (Waiter)
101 minutes / color

12 YEARS A SLAVE (2013)
Production companies: Regency Enterprises, River Road Entertainment, Plan B Entertainment, Film4
Producers: Brad Pitt, Dede Gardner, Jeremy Kleiner, Bill Pohlad, **Steve McQueen**, Arnon Milchan, Anthony Katagas
Director: **Steve McQueen**
Screenplay: John Ridley
Cinematography: Sean Bobbitt
Editor: Joe Walker
Cast: Chiwetel Ejiofor (Solomon Northup/Platt), Michael Fassbender (Edwin Epps), Benedict Cumberbatch (William Ford), Paul Dano (John Tibeats), Garret Dillahunt (Armsby), Paul Giamatti (Theophilus Freeman), Scoot McNairy (Merrill Brown), Lupita Nyong'o (Patsey), Adepero Oduye (Eliza), Sarah Paulson (Mary Epps), Brad Pitt (Samuel Bass), Michael Kenneth Williams (Robert) Alfre Woodard (Mistress Harriet Shaw), Chris Chalk (Clemens Ray), Taran Killam (Abram Hamilton), Bill Camp (Ebenezer Radburn), J. D. Evermore (Chapin), Christopher Berry (James H. Birch), Rob Steinberg (Mr. Parker), Bryan Batt (Judge Turner), Tom Proctor (Biddee), Jay Huguley (Sheriff), Storm Reid (Emily), Quvenzhané Wallis (Margaret Northup), Dwight Henry (Uncle Abram)
134 minutes / color

CODES OF CONDUCT ["PILOT"] (2016)
Production company: HBO Entertainment, See-Saw Films, RSTV
Producers: Iain Canning, Matthew Michael Carnahan, Steve McQueen, Alan Poul, Emile Sherman, Russell Simmons, Bergen Swanson, April Lamb, Jessica Levin
Director: **Steve McQueen**

Teleplay: Matthew Michael Carnahan, **Steve McQueen**
Cinematography: Sean Bobbitt
Editor: Jay Rabinowitz
Cast: Joe Carr (Limo Driver), Kale Browne (Paul Rotmensen), Andrew Casanova (Food Truck Guy), Dwelvan David (Bouncer), Steve Ferrarie (Secret Society Couple), Brad Heberlee (Young Dad), Dillon Mathews (Subway Passenger), Kaitlyn Raymond (Waitress), Lynette Scire (Secret Society Couple), Robbie Sublett (Charles Farnham), Devon Terrell (Beverly Snow), Jack Tynan (Club Goer)
[Unreleased] / color

WIDOWS (2018)
Production companies: Regency Enterprises, Film4, New Regency, See-Saw Films, Lammas Park, TSG Entertainment
Producers: **Steve McQueen**, Iain Canning, Emile Sherman, Arnon Milchan
Director: **Steve McQueen**
Screenplay: Gillian Flynn, **Steve McQueen**
Cinematography: Sean Bobbitt
Editor: Joe Walker
Cast: Viola Davis (Veronica Rawlings), Michelle Rodriguez (Linda), Elizabeth Debicki (Alice), Cynthia Erivo (Belle), Colin Farrell (Jack Mulligan), Brian Tyree Henry (Jamal Manning), Daniel Kaluuya (Jatemme Manning), Jacki Weaver (Agnieska), Carrie Coon (Amanda), Robert Duvall (Tom Mulligan), Liam Neeson (Harry Rawlings), Jon Bernthal (Florek), Manuel Garcia-Rulfo (Carlos), Garret Dillahunt ("Bash" Babiak), Lukas Haas (David), Matt Walsh (Ken), Kevin J. O'Connor (Bobby Welsh), Jon Michael Hill (Reverend Wheeler), Coburn Goss (Jimmy Nun)
130 minutes / color

GRENFELL (2019)
Director: **Steve McQueen**
22 minutes, 2 seconds / color

MANGROVE (2020)
Film for the anthology series *Small Axe*
Production companies: BBC Studios, BBC Films, Turbine Studios, Lammas Park, Amazon Studios, EMU Films, Six Temple Productions
Producers: Anita Overland, Michael Elliott
Director: **Steve McQueen**
Screenplay: **Steve McQueen**, Alastair Siddons
Cinematography: Shabier Kirchner

Editors: Chris Dickens, **Steve McQueen**
Cast: Letitia Wright (Altheia Jones-LeCointe), Malachi Kirby (Darcus Howe), Shaun Parkes (Frank Crichlow), Rochenda Sandall (Barbara Beese), Nathaniel Martello-White (Rhodan Gordon), Darren Braithwaite (Anthony Carlisle Innis), Richie Campbell (Rothwell Kentish), Duane Facey-Pearson (Rupert Boyce), Jumayn Hunter (Godfrey Millett), Jack Lowden (Ian Macdonald), Sam Spruell (PC Frank Pulley), Alex Jennings (Judge Edward Clarke), Samuel West (Mr. Hill, Prosecuting Barrister), Gershwyn Eustache Jr. (Eddie LeCointe), Gary Beadle (Dolston Isaacs), Richard Cordery (Mr. Croft), Derek Griffiths (C. L. R. James), Jodhi May (Selma James), Llewella Gideon (Aunt Betty), Thomas Coombes (PC Royce), Joseph Quinn (PC Dixon), Tahj Miles (Kendrick Manning), Michelle Greenidge (Mrs. Manning), Joe Tucker (Court Officer), James Hillier (Chief Inspector), Stephen O'Neill (The Magistrate), Ben Caplan (Mr. Stedman), Stefan Kalipha (Card Player), Jay Simpson (Duty Officer), Doreen Ingleton (Mrs. Tetley), Akbar Kurtha (Dr. Chadee), Shem Hamilton (Benson), Tayo Jarrett (Linton), Tyrone Huggins (Granville), Tahj Miles (Kendrick Manning)
128 minutes / color

LOVERS ROCK (2020)
Film for the anthology series *Small Axe*
Production companies: BBC Studios, BBC Films, Turbine Studios, Lammas Park, Amazon Studios, EMU Films, Six Temple Productions
Producers: Anita Overland, Michael Elliott
Director: **Steve McQueen**
Screenplay: **Steve McQueen**, Courttia Newland
Cinematography: Shabier Kirchner
Editors: Chris Dickens, **Steve McQueen**
Cast: Micheal Ward (Franklyn Cooper), Amarah-Jae St. Aubyn (Martha Trenton), Kedar Williams-Stirling (Clifton), Shaniqua Okwok (Patty), Ellis George (Cynthia), Francis Lovehall (Reggie), Daniel Francis-Swaby (Bammy), Alexander James-Blake (Parker B), Kadeem Ramsay (Samson), Romario Simpson (Lizard), Jermaine Freeman (Skinner), Marcus Fraser (Jabba), Saffron Coomber (Grace), Frankie Fox (Eddie Marks), Dennis Bovell (Milton)
68 minutes / color

RED, WHITE AND BLUE (2020)
Film for the anthology series *Small Axe*
Production companies: BBC Studios, BBC Films, Turbine Studios, Lammas Park, Amazon Studios, EMU Films, Six Temple Productions
Producers: Anita Overland, Michael Elliott

Director: **Steve McQueen**
Screenplay: **Steve McQueen**, Courttia Newland
Cinematography: Shabier Kirchner
Editors: Chris Dickens, **Steve McQueen**
Cast: John Boyega (Leroy Logan), Nathan Vidal (Young Logan), Steve Toussaint (Ken Logan), Joy Richardson (Mrs. Logan), Corey Peterson (Philford), Neil Maskell (Inspector Willis), Stephen Boxer (Chief Inspector), Calum Callaghan (PC Beck), Conor Lowson (David), Assad Zaman (PC Asif Kamali), Antonia Thomas (Gretl), Liam Garrigan (Greg Huggan), Tyrone Huntley (Leee John), Jaden Oshenye (Young Leee), Nadine Marshall (Jesse John), Mark Stanley (Ed Harrigan), Seroca Davis (Hyacinth)
80 minutes / color

ALEX WHEATLE (2020)
Film for the anthology series *Small Axe*
Production companies: BBC Studios, BBC Films, Turbine Studios, Lammas Park, Amazon Studios, EMU Films, Six Temple Productions
Producers: Anita Overland, Michael Elliott
Director: **Steve McQueen**
Screenplay: **Steve McQueen**, Alastair Siddons
Cinematography: Shabier Kirchner
Editors: Chris Dickens, **Steve McQueen**
Cast: Sheyi Cole (Alex Wheatle), Asad-Shareef Muhammad (Young Alex Wheatle), Robbie Gee (Simeon), Johann Myers (Cutlass Rankin), Jonathan Jules (Dennis Isaacs), Elliot Edusah (Valin), Khali Best (Badger), Fumilayo Brown-Olateju (Dawn), Dexter Flanders (Floyd)
66 minutes / color

EDUCATION (2020)
Film for the anthology series *Small Axe*
Production companies: BBC Studios, BBC Films, Turbine Studios, Lammas Park, Amazon Studios, EMU Films, Six Temple Productions
Producers: Anita Overland, Michael Elliott
Director: **Steve McQueen**
Screenplay: **Steve McQueen**, Alastair Siddons
Cinematography: Shabier Kirchner
Editors: Chris Dickens, **Steve McQueen**
Cast: Kenyah Sandy (Kingsley Smith), Sharlene Whyte (Agnes Smith), Tamara Lawrance (Stephanie Smith), Daniel Francis (Esmond Smith), Josette Simon (Lydia Thomas), Naomi Ackie (Hazel), Ryan Masher (Joseph), Jairaj Varsani

(Sajid), Tabitha Byron (Sheila), Roshawn Hewitt (Baz), Aiyana Goodfellow (Nina), Nathan Moses (Ashley), Jo Martin (Mrs. Tabitha Bartholomew), Kate Dickie (Miss Gill), Stewart Wright (Mr. Baines), Jade Anouka (Mrs. Morrison), Adrian Rawlins (Headmaster Evans), Nigel Boyle (Mr. Hamley)
63 minutes / color

UPRISING (2021)
Three-part documentary television series
Production companies: Turbine Studios, Lammas Park, Rogan Productions
Producers: Joanna Boateng, Nelson Adeosun
Directors: **Steve McQueen**, James Rogan
Cinematography: Charlie Laing
Editors: Brett Irwin, Esther Gimenez
177 minutes / color

SUNSHINE STATE (2022)
Director: **Steve McQueen**
30 minutes, 1 second (continuous play) / color and black-and-white

OCCUPIED CITY (2023)
Production companies: Lammas Park, Family Affair Films, Film4, A24, Regency Enterprises
Producers: **Steve McQueen**, Bianca Stigter, Anna Smith-Tenser, Floor Onrust
Director: **Steve McQueen**
Screenplay: Bianca Stigter, **Steve McQueen**
Cinematography: Lennert Hillege
Editor: Xander Nijsten
Cast: Melanie Hyams (Narrator) [English-language version]; Carice van Houten (Narrator) [Dutch-language version]
266 minutes / color

BLITZ (2024)
Production companies: Apple Studios, Regency Enterprises, New Regency, Working Title Films, Lammas Park
Producers: Tim Bevan, Eric Fellner, **Steve McQueen**, Anita Overland, Adam Somner, Arnon Milchan, Yariv Milchan, Michael Schaefer
Director: **Steve McQueen**
Screenplay: **Steve McQueen**
Cinematography: Yorick Le Saux
Editor: Peter Sciberras

Cast: Elliott Heffernan (George), Saoirse Ronan (Rita), Harris Dickinson (Jack), Benjamin Clementine (Ife), Kathy Burke (Beryl), Paul Weller (Gerald), Stephen Graham (Albert), Leigh Gill (Mickey Davies), Mica Ricketts (Jess), C. J. Beckford (Marcus), Alex Jennings (Victor Smythe), Joshua McGuire (Clive), Hayley Squires (Tilda), Erin Kellyman (Doris), Sally Messham (Agnes), Devon McKenzie-Smith (Ken "Snakehips" Johnson), Celeste (Anita Sinclair), Peter Rogers (Bus Driver)

120 minutes / color

Steve McQueen: Interviews

Buster Keaton Routines as Art Installations? Don't Laugh...

Jonathan Jones / 1999

From *The Observer*, January 31, 1999. Reprinted by permission. Copyright © 2023 Guardian News & Media, Ltd.

The filmmaker and artist Steve McQueen is trying to set up a stepladder against a wall he has constructed in a narrow corridor as people squeeze past. It's pure slapstick. He mutters to himself, he swears. "It's a vicious wall," he says.

McQueen is a funny, serious man. In the film *Deadpan*, showing in his current exhibition at the ICA (until March 21), he restages Buster Keaton's famous routine in which the silent comedian miraculously remains standing as a house collapses on top of him. The episode is repeatedly restaged until the joke is transformed into something somber, monumental. McQueen stares ahead so stoically that you wouldn't dream of laughing.

You wouldn't dream of mocking his name, either. He's *the* Steve McQueen and that's funny and serious too. He has a huge international reputation, confirmed by an exhibition at the Museum of Modern Art in New York in 1997. His first major one-man show in this country is so strong that it may even be able to save the ICA's tarnished honor. As an artist and filmmaker, McQueen is probably unique in British art. (He will make a feature film if he ever gets an idea, he says.) His films are screened in art galleries, in installations that thrust the image forward into space. Yet they are real films, not the work of an artist playing with film.

When artists turn to film they are usually drawn to its trashiness. McQueen is different. Monochrome and silent, his films strip away a hundred years of history. They depict men wrestling and embracing, a woman on a tightrope, and a white woman and a Black man in a strange, unresolved drama.

His ICA show is a trip through the story of cinema, culminating in his latest film in glorious widescreen color, a Manhattan musical called *Drumroll*.

Talking to McQueen can be disorienting. He backtracks and tells me not to put things in, even to cut out individual words, as if editing his conversation on film. At the end, he gives me a review of the beginning, middle, and end of the interview, and takes back his "censorship." There's a restlessness in McQueen and in his work. He swears a lot, too. McQueen, thirty this year, trained in art at Goldsmiths, where a whole generation of young British artists have been nurtured. He didn't like it. "Black students were a mystery to the staff. In a tutorial they'd talk about carnival or African bollocks." Race is a tantalizing dimension of his work. It seems to change the meaning of a Buster Keaton routine when a Black man takes the role, but precisely how the meaning is changed is difficult to say. McQueen loathes the nationalism of the British art scene. He prefers New York, or his current home, Amsterdam. He left Goldsmiths with a First and a memory of seeing an Andy Warhol film in which two men lie suspended in one another's orbit "like two magnets." He decided to study film at New York University.

"I hated NYU because it was like a Chinese circus school," he says. "You come out and you can do the splits. You're learning their language of film, and I wanted to find out my language of film." He found himself appalled by what it meant to be a professional filmmaker, learning to use a camera the same way as everybody else. "I understand the formal aspects of film. But I want to have something else." The film that most haunts him is Bob Rafelson's *Five Easy Pieces*, in which Jack Nicholson plays a blue-collar drifter hooked up with waitress Karen Black. At the end, Nicholson leaves her and we find out he's a scion of a rich family and a classical pianist. "We read it back again, and it becomes something else." McQueen constantly returns to such double takes. He admits to making works then leaving them for a year, in one case five years, to see how they grow. His first films were tiny marvels of structure. One of them was called *Five Easy Pieces*.

In *Bear*, his 1993 film of two men wrestling or flirting, the masculinity of Martin Scorsese's *Raging Bull* is opened to erotic possibilities; this and all McQueen's films are short, yet they break the rules of the "short."

McQueen says he wants his films to be sexier, "funkier," more physically present than conventional cinema. Then he worries about the word "funky." "'Funky' is part of Black artists' terminology. Funk means sweat, body odor, sex—not the sense it has when white people say, 'Hey! Funky Black guy!'" Throughout our meeting, McQueen urges me to focus on his work, while communicating a personality so strong that of course I want to write about him. The exhibition opens with a chrome roundabout nestling in a pink room. Nearby is a brick wall topped with jagged glass. It is a menacing wall, designed to keep out the children on the roundabout. *Drumroll* is his most astonishing film yet, made by rolling an oil drum fitted with cameras through the streets of Manhattan. On three screens the pedestrians, trash, and skyline of New York twist and dive—a "whirlwind,"

McQueen calls it—in which the city is turned inside out. "My work is like the drumroll," he says. "It goes on, it goes on, it goes on." McQueen, like American video artist Bruce Nauman and Turner Prize–winning "film appropriator" Douglas Gordon, is pioneering a new art of the moving image.

This is not cinema, but something else: a pleasure on a grand scale, like monumental sculpture or heroic painting in which the gallery becomes filled with the physical presence of a projected image. What McQueen does looks like the future of art. Slapstick always did have a lugubrious intensity, embodied in the stone-faced Keaton. In a world where irony in art is all-pervasive, McQueen offers slapstick as another model for art, in which the comic becomes inseparable from the critical.

He reflects on his own weightiness. "I am not a person who makes T-shirts," he says, but quickly adds: "Don't print that," regretting his jibe against the young British artists who have designed clothes which are on sale in the ICA shop.

He means it, though. "I see what other artists are doing and I say, 'But this is work! It's serious!'"

Driven to Abstraction: Steve McQueen

Sabine Durrant / 1999

From *The Guardian*, November 22, 1999. Reprinted by permission. Copyright © 2023 Guardian News & Media, Ltd.

To reach Steve McQueen's Turner Prize entries at the Tate, you have to walk through the rest of the shortlist first. Past Tracy Emin's bed, with its throng of onlookers, ears cocked for the rude bits in her confessional movie next door; through the Wilson twins' wraparound Las Vegas, fruit machines clanking, roulette wheels humming; across the busy space given over to Steven Pippin's fisheye washing machines, past the bored guard to three dark, empty rooms.

In one of them, you can see *Deadpan*, a film installation in which a barn wall collapses, again and again, around a standing, impassive man. Next door, in *Current*, a bike lies under some imperceptibly shifting water. In *Prey*, a small tape recorder is lifted up above a field by a white balloon. They're beautiful to look at, these films, and funny, and it would be quite peaceful standing there watching them if it wasn't for Emin shouting "Slag, slag, slag" in the distance.

McQueen, the hotly tipped favorite, is the cool, quiet man of this year's Turner competition. In his work and in person, he doesn't seem the sort to push himself forward. No Japanese performance artists have spread-eagled themselves across his projection screens. No fish, or cattle, have died for his art.

He is the current scene's outsider. He lives in Amsterdam, where he knows nobody and nobody knows him and "I can walk down the street in my flipflops without anybody caring."

He has few friends in the art world: "I don't like it. I don't like groups. I just get bored."

He doesn't like "being pushed" into having shows. He disapproves of the cult of personality. "I believe in evidence," he says.

He rarely gives interviews, but here he is in a café in Soho, a stocky, diffident man of thirty with a bear-like hunch to his anoraked back and a beetly expression across his eyebrows. He is all anxiety at first. What kind of croissant, he's asking himself, what kind of croissant? He'll have plain. Plain. No, almond. Almond. Black tea. No, not black, with milk. Ordinary tea. Ordinary tea, please. He's very polite he dabs his mouth with a napkin between sugary bites but he's on edge, he's on edge. He says everything twice. He has a repertoire of inarticulate noises: a click, click, click with his tongue on the roof of his mouth when he's thinking hard; a "brrrrr" with his lips, to accompany a shake of the head; a lot of "da, di, da, di das" for et cetera, et cetera, and a "n'yuh n'yuh," which seems to express approval.

He clicks his fingers a lot too. "Let's start. Okay. How do we start this thing? Brrrrrr." He claps his hands together twice. He pours out some tea with a lot of clattering of pots. "Okay," he says. "It just takes time. Like everything else you have to warm up." He sweeps his hand over his head. "This is desperate: 'Steve's not very talkative.' Okay. It happens. It just takes time. Don't worry. What was the question again?"

It turns out he doesn't like talking about his work. He likes reading about it even less. "When you read something in the papers, it's like, what is that like? But when you go to see it, it's, like, *Oh*." He relates with some eagerness how the tape recorder in *Prey* was the type used by the FBI and the CIA and how they found this Cuban defector, "hm, hm, hm, hum," he hums conspiratorially to help them use it; and how a stunt coordinator trained him to stand still for *Deadpan* ("Every time, it was like, 'Take your time, Steve, take a deep breath'"); and about the day he found the bike at the bottom of a river in Zurich. "And I knew it was right. It just hit me: boom!"

But try and pin down what he does with it all, he says, and you end up chasing abstractions. So descriptions of his films sound loopy? "Totally. Totally," he says. "N'yuh, n'yuh."

He is often described as a Black artist, which irritates him. "I'm not interested in this, this, or this," he says, pointing at his skin, his nose, his lips, his hair. "To make art from a Black perspective, that's what you focus on. When you don't, people scratch their heads. If he or she is not illustrating themselves, what are they doing? It must be the media. It must be film about film. Or painting about painting. Well, people wouldn't say Miles Davis makes jazz about jazz. It ain't there. If I film certain things in a certain stereotypical way, they say it's irony. They love that shit! I'm not interested. It bores the hell out of me. It's, like, *next*!"

His mind is whirring all the time, spinning with the ordinary matter that makes up his art. "Things happen, you know. I plant things in my brain and what happens is certain answers that are coming out are to questions that I asked myself, like a year, two years, ago. So basically I'm in '97 right now in my head." He pauses for some calculations, adjusts his little gold-rimmed glasses. "'99 . . . '98 . . . yeah, '97. Only now do I get the answer." So what questions is he busy asking himself at the moment? "Well, I'm looking at this chair now and if I look at it again in two years' time, it's like, oh yeah! You can't see it now. You see it later."

And what answers? "Phew," he says, and thinks for a while. Then he makes a clicking noise as if to say, Okay, let's go for it. "One question just got answered the other day that was about sex basically. There are the obvious images of sex, but how do you represent that? Not just the in-and-out business because put that in a film, that's not interesting at all. It's the circularity of . . . of . . . of *sex*" (he says that last word in a low voice as if suddenly reminded of his audience). "It's a ball, it's complete in some way and how do you go from that realization to make something interesting?"

And how do you? "That is what is so damned difficult," he says. There's a silence. "I should be generous. I should be generous," he says. "It's just more talk."

Oh, tell me, I say. "Alright," he says. "I have a lazy eye. I was the guy in the class with the patch over his eye! That was me, remember? That was me. Anyway, the sex situation and the lazy eye situation, they're two of the ingredients in my new work." Later, he tells me that Joyce's *Ulysses* comes into it too.

McQueen is an Ealing boy. There was quite a crowd of them back then: Jamiroquai, the Brand New Heavies, it was a "situation of possibilities," he says now. His mum was a nurse, his father worked for London Transport. (His parents like his work, though seeing him naked in *Bear* took "a lot of explanations and explaining.") School was terrible, but he could draw and that got him into Goldsmiths. He got a First there, but it was only when he got to New York, with a place at Jim Jarmusch's NYU Graduate Film program, that things "really exploded" for him. "Over here, there's a choice: yes or no. Over there, there's yes, no, possibly, maybe I don't know, could be. . . . A big mixture that's just wonderful, of people, cultures, ideas, situations; things coming together to make something else, which is the key to all this stuff."

He knew he had "to get out" of Britain, "a place for happy amateurs," but he ended up in Amsterdam because he fell in love with a Dutch woman he met at a football match (Ajax versus Atletico Madrid in the European Supercup Final). They have a sixteen-month-old daughter called Alex McQueen. He doesn't have a studio, spends a lot of his time at home, Hoovering, washing-up, "having it all in your head and just looking."

He tries to avoid international travel because it mucks up his digestive system. He meets collectors if he has to, though there aren't many who can accommodate his work. He sells about three pieces a year. He describes himself as "comfortably off." "I'm not a domestic artist. I am not an interior designer." He doesn't like having things on his walls, though his girlfriend has some stuff, "including one Man Ray thing."

He recently took part in a book-reading club. "I'd rather just get on with things really," he says, rearranging a daffodil that he'd just knocked out of its vase. "All the candy floss that comes with it, it's nice but what I'm interested in is doing it. I'm interested in evidence. I mean, Toni Morrison's books, or Miles Davis's records, or Bach's records, that's evidence. Bach could be a dickhead, but what's left, the music—wow, fantastic. Miles Davis, he was a right womanizer, bisexual, all kinds of stuff he denied. What a wanker. But the music! I'm not putting myself forward with them, but what I'm saying is interviews, biographies, the talk . . . fuck that. It's the work. It's the work." And he frowned down at the remains of his pastry as if seeing it for the first time.

Interview Transcript: Tricky

Steve McQueen / 2001

From *SHOWstudio*, March 20, 2001. Reprinted by permission. Copyright © Steve McQueen. Courtesy of the artist and Thomas Dane Gallery.

Steve McQueen: Well, the first thing I want to say to you.... I think, I mean how do you feel you're doing, exactly? You're doing what you want to do, and that's amazing . . . and what's so amazing about it to me is an artist to get financially rewarded for it. I mean, that is amazing.

Tricky: I feel so lucky and blessed. It's good, it keeps me humble, because I wake up every day and it's like I feel I'm lucky to have a record deal, even though you get a lot of acclaim and things, I still feel like I'm lucky to have a record deal. And to do what I want is I'm so lucky, and it's all by accident, really. I fumbled my way into Island Records and they wanted to sign me but I was this mouthy young kid and said, "These are the conditions," you know; I doubt you're going to get any radio-friendly music, but if you wanna sign me, and I was really lucky with the people I had. I had Chris Blackwell and Julian Palmer. A friend of mine at Island is Darcus Beese, and these people become friends of mine and they're the people who run the company. So I lucked out, and I think they were smart in that like Chris and Julian Palmer especially, the more extreme I was the more they could see. I gave them my mistakes, made people interested in me.

SM: Your mistakes are what I'm interested in, all the time. Whatever people want to call it, mistakes or whatever, that's it—and what interests me about your work is that you remind me of Miles Davis. Miles for me is a guy who just do what he want, turning his back on the audience, writing what he wants to write, but also being so influential. But also he's got these followers and what I mean by that is he changed music about three times and you've changed it once already—and how old are you?

T: Thirty-one.

SM: Yeah, thirty-one, and you've changed it once already, and he's like changed it three times, so we'll see. The next odd sixty years or so you'll keep going. You know, I'm not an interviewer; I can't do that interview shit. I'm just so fascinated in how, you know, when you're in a studio, when you're at home, what you're thinking about, how the sounds come out, the images, et cetera.

T: Basically, keyboards. I muck about—I'm just like a kid playing around. I love playing with keyboards and stuff, and before you know it you've got a sound you like, and I'll record it. And then I'll play with a different sound, and I'll record it on top. I love playing with sounds. I love listening to sounds, and I'm still really.... I really do love what I'm doing. When you're making music you don't think about anything else. You spend three hours or so and for that three hours you're lost. It's a beautiful getaway, you know, from getting away from everything.

SM: I also want to, just coming back, you left London, you left Bristol, you left Britain basically, and you're living in New York now. Why did you leave?

T: Um . . . I got bored. I loved London, you know. When I first got here, I loved London. It was exciting, but with my success, and I was going to certain clubs and hanging out with certain people, and, you know, it wasn't me. It really wasn't me. Like all of a sudden you're in a club and you're surrounded by producers, producers, directors, producers. It's like I got a bit lonely, surrounded by people who liked me because I was Tricky. I felt like I had to run away.

SM: But when you talk about your music and what you said before, what you're saying, I can just feel this kind of knowledge when you speak of this situation. You're kind of rounded, you know, you're aware, you use your nose, your senses, more than anything else. I hope I do it—it gives you an edge. You go with the feel.

T: That's exactly what happens. When I'm recording, say, whoever I'm recording, say like a vocal, I write words and it'd be this length and, you know, I'd give the words to the singer and then listen to it, and there would be a chorus in there. You'd hear a chorus. There'd be one part of the vocal that would stand out, and I'd see that as a chorus. I'd just think chorus. Everything happens. I just feel it rather than direct the music. I let the music direct me. Music is—I know it sounds mad, but it's magic. You know what I mean. Like, you know, just to sit back and listen to something, and it'll tell you what it means. It'll speak to you. A melody will be there. You've just got to follow the music.

SM: Tell me about your instrument, your voice. I'm fascinated by your voice, your singing voice. Can you tell me a little bit more about it?

T: Like a year ago, I can remember someone said to me once, "Watch my voice." 'Cause from Massive Attack it's got a lot different—you know, it's gone down. But when I was a lot younger I used to go out with this girl. We were about fifteen, and we were playing around and she put her fingers down my throat, trying to make me be sick. You know, we were drunk, and she cut my throat. I went to see a throat doctor. I got a lump in my throat. I can leave it or take it out, but he said if I take it off, I will be able to sing like hit top notes, like opera. I asked a few people round, and they said don't do it. I'm a frustrated singer—I've always wanted to be able to sing.

SM: You sing beautifully, and that's not wank-talking people. Really beautifully.

T: The grass is always greener. So I'll listen to people like Bob Marley or John Lennon or Prince and I get gutted 'cause I'd love to be able to sing a song like that. But everyone around me is like saying, "Don't do it, don't do it." So I'm not going to bother. Maybe like when I'm forty or something.

SM: What, like change your voice? That's mad. That's a fantastic idea.

T: Yeah, it would be a different career. Because I've just found a different career, it's weird. I've had a thing called candida. When I did *Maxinquaye*. I'm asthmatic. I've been given from a young kid courses of antibiotics and steroids, and after a while it just breaks your immune system down, so things like sugar, milk, can't be digested any more, and you develop this thing called candida. It makes your moods—you go real dark. You know, they say eight or nine schizophrenics in hospital are starting off with candida, but society really don't know enough about candida, so instead of treating it with diet, they treat it with medication. And it's like a certain medication . . . there's this thing called dorphins . . . endorphins, and it's like a relaxing drug the psychiatrist gives you, and it was made up by Hitler, invented by Hitler's peoples. It's kind of like a controlling thing, and they say there's more chance of getting raped on a psychiatrist's bed than in any street in New York, know what I mean? A lot of dark stuff.

SM: Shit . . .

T: 'Cause you know, it's drug dealing, innit?

SM: Absolutely.

T: Like, I haven't had an asthma attack since I controlled my blood.

SM: And you found that out in the States?

T: Not just because of the States. I found out from being a person from having no money to having money.

SM: Precisely that, paying . . .

T: Pay for a doctor and then, all of a sudden you go to a. . . . When you're getting health for free, they're just giving antibiotics and steroids, but when you're paying for doctors they're saying to me, "How many years have you been using antibiotic steroids? This is not good for you." So with my candida my music got darker, so I've been making music in a state of madness. I did go to a state of madness—I wanted to jump out of a window a year and a half ago. And now I'm controlling it all. I did *Maxinquaye* and then *Pre-Millennium Tension* when I started getting sick, I went down. And now I'm coming out. It's almost like I've had two careers. I'm lucky—it's like the *Maxinquaye* thing, and then there's the dark side, and now I've got better and my music's changing again.

SM: Sure. Would you say the political of that was your third album, the one that you . . . I've forgotten the title . . . Tricky.

T: *Angels with Dirty Faces.*

SM: That. Because a lot of people said that was like hard and dark and . . . but it was brilliant.

T: I thought it was the blues.

SM: Yeah, total.

T: I thought it was the blues. It's funny, like . . . some people, a lot of people, loved *Maxinquaye*, and those people can get into *Pre-Millennium Tension* and *Angels*, and there are people who are really into *Angels*, and some people say my best album is *Nearer to God*. And I kind of like that, like everybody's got their own . . .

SM: Yeah, yeah.

T: And that's down to . . .

SM: Sure, sure. I thought that your last album is fantastic . . . it's sort of . . . it seems sort of total reckless confidence . . .

T: Yeah, I really felt like that I really don't care, it's like . . . it's mad. I used to think that when you go to the industry, you're led to believe that success is videos, cars, such like that. It's like, I've got a house with two acres of land that my daughter runs around on, and I mean, that's success. So when I realized I've got a beautiful kid, that's success. Know what I mean? So I realized what success is—success is being happy. Do you know what I mean? You can have as many cars as. . . . But success is definitely about being happy, and I realized that over the last year. So I just feel stronger; I can do what I want. I don't need your chart success; I don't need to be at the top of the charts for you to tell me I'm successful. It's like, it's funny, I mean, I was nominated for six Brits, and the same year, the same year I went to America, I was nominated for eight Brits. But I'm a lot happier now than I've ever been. So it's like "I don't need to top the charts; I know I'm successful, because I'm happy."

SM: I think that . . . when I read that you'd left the country, I thought, this guy's very bright, he's doing something at the right time for the right reasons. Sometimes you just need that distance. I find now that living in Amsterdam . . . I travel a bit, and I don't basically . . . you know, I'm back in London once a month or once every two months, see my mum and things, whatever, that you get a real understanding of who you are to a certain extent, and also where you come from. And also to a certain extent you get a sense of Britain and British people and English people and London people and all that kind of. . . . Everyone's kind of, like I say, how fucking small-minded we are.

T: Oh definitely. And people don't like you to say that in England.

SM: No.

T: But I feel I can say that because I'm English and I'm talking about myself.

SM: Exactly.

T: And I'm totally . . . we are small-minded. It's like crazy, it's just so . . . people in America, you can have a dream and you can become anything and do anything you want. Your dreams can come true—but only to a certain degree in England until someone stamps on it; know what I mean, your dream just gets trampled on and you wake up to reality.

SM: And also the class system here, you know, people go on about it and all that, but it is in effect big-time still.

T: It is big-time. See, in America you've got money, that wipes out all class systems for me. And I'd rather have it like that, to be honest with you, in some ways. And it's like here, I know this is mad, I was in a place yesterday, and when I first went in, you know, there was only three Black guys in there, and it's not even a racial thing but it's a class thing. If I'd been with three Black guys and three white guys it'd be the same thing. And I just noticed no one was interested in us at all. I don't mean . . . you go out and you look at people . . . I'm not saying socialize but kind of getting more spiritual. I could see these people walking towards us and kind of looking at us like. . . . But then people found out who I was.

SM: Well, this happens to me very often. In certain areas it becomes like that, yeah. But tell me about . . . I'm interested in how people see you. I mean, you're a Black guy . . .

T: Yeah. But it's funny, I've only ever felt I was a Black guy since I've been in the music industry. Before I entered this industry. . . . Because I grew up with a very mixed-race society in a mixed-race family. But when I entered this industry, I realized I was Black for the first time ever—it was ridiculous, but I realized what racism was.

SM: You mean at school, you didn't realize what racism was?

T: Oh, only stupid things like someone might call you a name and you'd have to fight them or something.

SM: What, teachers, the system, stuff like that?

T: No, it was very strange. I mean, I come from a place called Knowle West and very old-fashioned things like this part of Bristol was so old-fashioned, so it was like everyone was in the shit, and because you were so in the shit . . . everyone was busy because they didn't have no money. And if you got all of Knowle West, and there wasn't a rich part. So everyone was poorer, and these guys would just go out drinking and fighting. And it didn't matter who it was with, and it was really weird because like it was crazy, because I grew up in a white community, there was only about five Black families, and I didn't really experience any racism. I know this sounds ridiculous, but I didn't experience any racism. But then when I got into the music industry, that was a different thing, because it was white people telling me it existed. But, you know, I remember on *Maxinquaye* thinking like these bands in the charts now, I was saying to Julian Palmer—he'd say, "These bands sound like you," and I'd say, "Julian, if these bands sound like me, how come I get into the charts but I don't get radio play?" And he'd go, "It's because you're Black, Tricky." I say, "What are you talking about?" He goes: "'Cause you're Black. Massive Attack, it helps because they've got a front boy who's white. And stuff like that, Portishead, they're white."

SM: Listen, it's like when Hendrix did it all . . . the whole Black band, what was it called, that band? I can't remember. People were trying to put him away, saying, "You've got to have your white drummer and your white bass guitar." When Hendrix went Black, it was fine, because he was so powerful, popular, avant-garde and all Black. So therefore in that situation it becomes a fear, there's a real fear of that—I don't know why that is.

T: Yes, it's really weird—I've only just started selling to Black people.

SM: So you think being in America, you think that helped?

T: Definitely. Because there's a stronger Black community there. The community there has got respect, the Black community has money.

SM: But do you think your music changed when you went to the States?

T: I think it's definitely changed, but not because of . . . just because it's a different environment. So I don't think there's a change . . . I've got a new song that sounds a little bit Hispanic and I mean, I've been hanging out with Hispanic kids, Black kids, Asians, it's like being a kid again. I grew up . . . I remember I must have been like fourteen, and in my little firm of friends there were like Asians, we had two Greek boys, there was an Italian boy who went to a Catholic school, you had Pakistanis, Black, a couple of kids half-caste, so it's like it is now, I see kids of all colors and races . . .

SM: That's the beautiful thing about America, New York, at least for me, because you know I can speak to this girl and her mother's from Ireland and her father's from Venezuela, and you know, this guy comes from Russia, these mixes, and it's just wonderful.

T: It breaks down racism.

SM: And also you learn more, you learn more about each other, certain cultures and situations, in a very kind of round way.

T: That's the future of society, that's the future of England, that's how England's going to have to be.

SM: It'll have to be. I mean, London maybe. It's weird how resistant . . .

T: The main cities kind of do that—all these different people are coming to the big cities, and in the smaller towns it doesn't happen so much. But I think London's going to have to, it's going to go that way . . .

SM: Has to.

T: ... because people are mixing race. And it's like wild, it's like in Newark, round a corner of Newark there's a Black community and an Indian section, and in a place called West Orange y'got Indians and Black people living side by side like it's nothing.

SM: Don't people want you back here? People in general, do they want you back?

T: I felt like that one time, and now sometimes I feel like I've been forgotten about almost. That's why I was really complimented about this.

SM: Really?

T: In the press there was a bit of "Tricky's betrayed England," and you know what's mad is I love England, because one of the reasons I'm successful in America is because I'm English, and that makes me different straight away. So I've never really left this place, I just had to get out for a while. It's like it's really weird—you know, you get nominated for a Brit. And it's so uptight, English people are so uptight with themselves.

SM: Like Bowie, he went to LA, he went to Berlin, he just bought a place ... he's just come back. But I think Bowie's had his time, and that's that. He's more of a ...

T: He's a good man and everything, but like I said his changing things has been done. His time has come. And I think they've seen it as a big kind of "fuck you," almost. And what's mad is I think if I'd stayed here the press would have crucified me.

SM: I think you're overestimating a bit because people will always.... That last album got a lot of good reviews, which I was pleased about. And surprised.

T: People think I have a problem with the English press, but I love the English press. Because they're the people who made me. Obviously, I don't like some people in the press but the English press have said some of the nicest things ever about me. So how can I not like the English press—they really set me up.

SM: What do you think of people like Wu-Tang Clan. Have you met RZA?

T: Yeah, I've met RZA, a few times. He's a good guy—he's like real.

SM: Because I think you two are pretty close.

T: There are similarities as well, definitely. I know he does what he wants and with no compromise. He's a very quiet guy. I mean, to me, I always used to call him the Mozart of hip-hop. Because his music sounds to me very classical, you know? It's like ... his way of doing things is a bit different to mine. I mean, I can produce, but I have to hold some things back ...

SM: What do you mean?

T: Like he produces for hundreds of people, but I can't do that. I mean, I want my music to be heard, but it's almost like not too much because it waters it down almost? It's weird ...

SM: I understand. It's like Prince stretched himself.

T: Yeah, yeah. I don't want to be stretching myself, but I know the urge—you want to release.

SM: So have you learned from that? I remember reading you wanted the album to . . . I'm so pleased that you said that.

T: Yeah, I've learned a lot. Just chucking music out makes you less focused in a way.

SM: Total. Absolutely.

T: I like the fact that every one of my albums is different—whether people like it or not, everyone is different to each other. So I think that's more important than bringing out loads of stuff so I just want to make my albums do different things every time and keep learning. Every day you can learn something, and whatever, I'm just into learning, I just want to learn and travel and visit people in different countries talk. I mean, I could be in Israel, I'll be sat in dinner with the Israeli record company and I'll get a song from what the A&R girl said—she'll say something and, you know, you're in a crazy setting in the middle of Israel, and this girl says, "I was brought up in a kibbutz," in Israel, you know, and to me this just sounds like a song, and I'd take and write that down. . . . You know, I'm always taking things out of people's mouths. They say things, and a lot of people lose what they say: they talk so fast they forget about it. And I just hear songs in people's words.

SM: Do you know what really interests me about your work as well, which other people . . . which hasn't been given any real volume. You have a really . . . a tenderness, a real gentleness, a real . . . I'm trying to think of words very quickly but I can't . . . a real beauty, a real gentleness, a real . . . like Miles Davis, he could be crazy, he could be aggressive, but when he blows it's so pure, it cuts a fine line. It's like a straight line—it doesn't go this way and that way, it's just straight, and it's so beautiful.

T: What it is, is honest . . .

SM: Tender.

T: Yeah, and I'm the sort of guy that . . . I could be working in a big studio and I come outside and see someone begging on the streets, and I feel so bad and I feel guilty and like driving through that area—obviously, I live in good areas, I've got a family, and I live in good areas. I live with Italians and Jewish people, but I drive through a certain area and you just feel so sad for everybody . . .

SM: But what I meant is love, whatever that love is, personal relationship love . . .

T: I've got a lot of love in me, yeah. My friends, I mean. . . . Everything I love, I love to extremes. I'm quite extreme. So I'm so extreme with my friends. I'll do anything for them. And my family, I love them so much. I've got quite a bit of love in me.

SM: Quite a bit of love in you?

T: I was brought up by all women. There was never any men in my life.

SM: That's wonderful. I was brought up with mainly women, and I think you definitely have a very feminine situation.

T: Definitely. I've been taught everything, every lesson by women, and not many by men, because the men in my family sort things with their fists, and you learn that quick when you're at school anyway, and there's nothing else to learn. So these men figures just become fighters, and everything that was taught to me was taught to me by women, how to behave, how to act in society, how to treat people; I was always pushed into saying "please" and "thank you" and stuff for my nan and stuff. And every kind of lesson I've learned is from a woman, and the men have been, you know, distant. I've been disciplined by a woman, and I've been loved by a woman. And sometimes the parents share these responsibilities, but not in my family, so it's the woman disciplining me, love me, taught me, and so on.

SM: Sometimes your songs sound like a caress, sort of someone caressing someone's body.... It's very beautiful.

T: I know I've always wanted to touch people's souls rather than their ears. I always want to touch people's souls.

SM: You do that very successfully. But what do you think about Europe right now? Do you have time to see these places or is it a case of "Next!"?

T: Certain places like Israel you make time, because it's so different, but you do get a lot of time on your hands, and then you get lazy, and if you're tired you don't want to leave. But I do try to make the effort to try go to places where the people from the country go. But when I'm in Paris it's so much like England that you don't bother, and it's a little bit . . . Paris is a really good place for selling music, but when I go into a shop and buy something, people are so rude.

SM: How does it feel to be recognized, because you are Tricky and all that? How does that feel—if you were in town, like Soho now, would it be easy?

T: No, because you get what you want . . . I mean, you can attract a certain amount of attention. If you're just walking around . . .

SM: It's like a tap, you can turn on and off?

T: Yeah. If someone recognizes you, you go, "All right, how you doin'?" and just walk on. And sometimes I can walk through a place and no one would know—I'd just have my head down, and I'm just going to get somewhere . . .

Yeah, you can do it. And it's really easy to do, especially as it's like, where did I go the other night? I went to this crap club called 10. And sometimes being recognized is a disadvantage, but you've got this security guy at 10, not really security, but more like a guest list guy and he just didn't want to let us in. And there's no one in there! And then someone said who I was, and he said, "Never heard of you," and I know he had, because I could see it in his eyes; he didn't want to let me in. So sometimes it's a disadvantage. It all depends what reasons: sometimes it's a compliment when people recognize you, and sometimes it's total disrespect because they're just seeing someone they've seen on TV, and people just stare at you. I'm not into being stared at, and if I'm sat in a café or something, and someone's just staring and staring, it means I have to ask them, "Excuse me, what are you looking at?" I'd rather they just say, "All right, mate?," then that's it.

SM: I want to go back again, further back—whether you feel uncomfortable about it, I'm not too sure—and talk about Massive Attack.

T: Yeah. No, I don't feel uncomfortable at all, man.

SM: Okay, good. I listened to their album recently again, and I just think that you on those albums are so . . . somewhere else.

T: I was totally . . . that is it exactly.

SM: And I listened to all these chats that you and 3D and D were doing, some chats and stuff, and I was listening to these things and. . . . Age was a big part in this because you were far younger than them, you were far more . . . and it showed. They were in this definite sound system, chatting on a mic, and you were somewhere else.

T: Yeah. Yeah. I had a more punk-rock attitude.

SM: I wouldn't call it white-influenced, because it's my influence as well. You talk about the Specials, you talk about whatever punk band, whatever rock band was going on in the late seventies, early eighties, whatever. These things were definitely coming out in you.

T: Yeah, and it was frustrating for me, because I was in Massive Attack doing certain lyrics, and they'd say, "You can't put that down."

SM: What lyrics, for example?

T: I had these lyrics, like kind of Jamaican English stuff, using words like "bloodclot," and stuff like that, and we talked on the street. Or certain things you say with your friends. And it was like . . . there was competition with me and D. And I didn't know I was in the competition at the time. But within his mind there was . . . know what I mean? And at the same time he was pushing me forward, because I can remember . . . when I was real young, when we were doing interviews like with cameras, he'd push me to the front and tell me what to say, like, "Talk about this." But I couldn't really bring anything towards the music. I found the music kind of like . . .

SM: Soulless. Like "let's do another album."

T: Yeah, totally soulless. Like, manufactured, soulless, and neither here nor there. I'd rather do an album that everybody hated, but really said, "I hate this because this is too angry." Do something, make something happen.

SM: This is what I mean, because when I hear . . . why I'm totally an admirer of your work is that I feel that if you died tomorrow, the last album that you'd put out, God forbid, that is like, he'd just pushed it to the limit.

T: See, yeah, it'd be horrible to die and not know you've had that opportunity and you've played it safe. Which I know Massive Attack has done, they've played it safe.

SM: Yeah, it's so obvious.

T: And it's like, how can you live with yourself when you've got that opportunity to do everything?

SM: I think this stuff we won't put in, I don't think it'll be good for us. We can talk about it, but it's just not in. But this 3D guy, is he the leader of the group?

T: 3D's the leader—well, he wasn't. It's really weird—Miles and Claude started off as the leaders, and then as they disappeared, he kind of took over, because it became businessy, and no one else wanted to deal with the business. As soon as the record deals started, he's the one who got a relationship with the record company guy, he's the one who wanted Nellee Hooper to come and mess the album up. I mean, I'm not a fan of Nellee Hooper, and it's no disrespect to the man, because I don't know the man. But as a producer, I don't respect that, you know? And I think they just made one compromise after another.

SM: I want to talk about Björk, because I feel that at a certain point she was excellent, at the same point you were excellent. In fact, you were together at that excellent point in time—apparently; I read in the papers that you were together.

T: Yeah, it's true.

SM: But now I . . . I think she's looking for a way to go, and she really doesn't know what to do. And she's got a fantastic voice, but it's almost like it stopped before it started. Why is that? It's kinda interesting, because you keep on going on.

T: I think some artists . . .

SM: Is it money?

T: No. I think some artists are always looking for that new. Instead of doing what they do, they're always going for the next thing. I don't look for the next thing, I just make my music, and I'm lucky that my music becomes the next thing. So I'm never looking for anything—I just go in the studio. I'm not looking for. . . . I don't make jungle, I don't make hip-hop, I don't make rock, I make music.

SM: I make my own.

T: I make my own art. And, like, it's harder for a singer. Björk . . . her talent is her voice, but then she's got to go and choose producers. So what she's gotta do is choose almost what's *now*. So straight away you're compromising. So I think after a while it gets harder to choose what's now. It's harder to go and pick off the tune and say "yeah."

SM: Absolutely. I think that's very perceptive, very sharp, that's it, that idea. But how do you feel about people like D'Angelo, for example?

T: I think what he's doing now is a big mistake, trying to do that Marvin Gaye, pretty-boy stuff. I liked it when he first came out, because he was a guy with a sweet voice, but he was on that street-boy tip and he's just a normal geezer. Now, he's got his top off in the video, and it's all that . . . he's manipulated by sex. I think it's more about D'Angelo than the music, man. But if that's what people want—but . . .

SM: I think it's just what people advise. What's interesting to hear what you say about these other artists from your own perspective and your own ideas is that you very much control what you do—and that's very rare.

T: And visually as well, see. I control my side visually as well as musically. And I know . . . it's just simple to me—I try to keep it honest. Me doing a video like that, like Maxwell or D'Angelo, is just not very honest. It's almost like, who are you trying to kid? Who are you trying to fool? This is so old.

SM: Also, I feel . . . I'd call it brave, the way you appear in the sexual side. You're very open about that, and it's real sex. It's not porno.

T: No. No.

SM: It's not gels and soft lights, it's what sex is, and sex is fluid, sex is teeth, sex is, you know, a bit rough, a bit whatever, a bit not so . . .

T: You know, all this stuff comes into it, and what D'Angelo becomes is a starred artist, it's all about the way he looks.

SM: That's right, the body. And also the Black male bodies, the glamorization of that . . .

T: That stereotype of. . . . That's why I've always loved being skinny. I've always loved being skinny.

SM: I'm trying to love being fat right now, but . . .

T: I think it's just about loving yourself. And I think courage, getting in front of that camera and like . . . I don't need . . . I need my music, so I can take my top off in front of the camera. My music is going to speak afterwards, so that's not the last thing you're going to see, my visuals are not the last thing you're going to see. I feel like there's music to back that up, you know what I mean? So I don't need this super . . .

SM: Tell me about the visuals, your videos that you're making for your album. What are they like, because I haven't seen any?

T: They're all just a waking dream state, like listening to music and . . . even when I'm listening to someone else's song, I dream a video in my head. Like I'm listening to the Specials and Prince, and I'll pretend it's my song, and I've got a video. And with the music comes the visuals, and a lot of the time as I'm writing music, the visuals come as well, and a lot of the time if I'm working with a good director like Stéphane [Sednaoui], I let him put his ideas in. But the music takes you all the way.

SM: There was one really great video I saw of yours—it's the lyrics from the Massive Attack album which you took and redid and where you're shaking your hand . . .

T: Yeah. That's Stéphane. That's his ideal. And I was so amazed how he said the record made him feel a certain way, and he it made him feel like that in the video. And I was amazed at how he took the music and translated that, know what I mean? I'm totally into letting a director do exactly what he wants. If I trust someone, I don't even have to be involved, you know?

SM: Well, that's obvious. So that's interesting what you said about Björk, but that is the answer.

T: Yeah, everybody's looking for new. To go forward you have to go backwards sometimes. It's like the same with the Rolling Stones. The reason I know this is there's been a fear in me since *Maxinquaye*. I look at artists and think, "How can artists be so good, and then be so terrible?" And I'd rather not do the music if it comes to that. So I know exactly what I'm going to do when I get old. I'm going to become a blues artist, because blues and reggae artists are the only artists who seem to grow old gracefully, you know? And when you're a Rolling Stone chasing the next thing, and you're fifty, sixty years of age in tight underpants and that, but you see these blues guys, they just stand on stage and do a guitar solo and sing a song, and they don't look embarrassing at all. And it's like . . . so I used to think, this used to be my nightmare, my music ending one day. So I totally had to think about why, and I've been thinking about it for years, many, many years. And just realized it's because you can't chase it, you can't chase for the new thing. It's like, when I made *Maxinquaye*, everyone started making dark music. But it don't sound dark because you're trying to sound dark. I didn't mean for *Maxinquaye* to be dark or *Pre-Millennium* to be tense, that's just how it is.

SM: I think people are on drugs, you know. I think a lot of people are on drugs.

T: A lot of people are on drugs, definitely.

SM: Absolutely. But also in that kind of other way, because when you say that album was dark, for me, it was like rubbing my hands together on some gravel. It felt real, it felt urgent, it felt necessary . . .

At this point, the Steve McQueen interview tape runs out, though the Tricky tape continues for a few minutes. Because Steve McQueen's questions from this point on are only being picked up by Tricky's microphone, they are sometimes inaudible or indistinct, so apologies for any omissions. Normal service will be resumed for the second half of the interview.

T: Yeah. Yeah.

SM: [*Tape indistinct.*]

T: Yeah. And it's because . . .

SM: [*Tape indistinct.*]

T: It used to be the music industry, right? And now it's just the industry. And this is why I stand out like a sore thumb. I'm very lucky. There's so much manufactured music around, that there's not many artists . . . there's no artists who are real and who get through any more. Except me. I'm like in the wrong place, I've got my foot in the door.

SM: [*Tape indistinct.*]

T: Yep. They want their product—and you know, they're having quotas like if you don't sell five thousand records, five hundred thousand records, you're not really a priority on the label any more. So, you know, like . . .

SM: Tell me about Island—are you still with them?

T: No, I've left Island now. And I really had a good time at Island, but it changed. I had a brilliant time at Island.

SM: It got sold, didn't it?

Tricky: Yeah. And I had no complaints until it got sold. And when it got sold, all of a sudden I started changing my way of thinking. Like, what do I need to do to get on the radio? And I've never thought like that. So I just needed to get off, and they're good people, so they let me go. And they're real cool people, man. And I had a real good time there, but I had to get off of there. So I was trying to get off, so it's all been quiet for me over here as well because I haven't been doing any press in England or anything, because I've been trying to get off the label for about a year. And it's taken about a year to get off the label. I've had to give them another album and serve a certain time in my contract and all this rubbish.

SM: [*Tape indistinct.*]

T: They still let me go one album early, though, which is cool. And they're sensible, because when a relationship breaks down, it's like, what are they gonna do, man? They know I'm not going to give them anything.

SM: You seem really happy.

T: I am really happy at the moment, yeah. It's like everything's making more sense to me. I've got a label and I've got these kids who I've known for years, and within a year from being on the dole they're going to France and doing Canal+ and doing gigs in front of two thousand people and that. And they're number two in the charts in France and number three in another chart and number six . . .

SM: What is in France—what has France got with hip-hop? It's like a big industry, people making money. What's going on in England? What is it?

T: It's crazy—it's like . . . it just seems that there's no support for hip-hop here. There's no general real support. And I don't know why that is, it's crazy. I think a lot of it was you've got too many English guys trying to sound American, and like . . .

SM: Yeah. This is what I was reading about . . . exactly, go on.

T: . . . and in America where they've got millions of apples everywhere, why are you going to buy a watered-down product? And in England, there just don't seem to be a mass for it. People ain't got it. I don't think people have done it smart enough, on a big enough scale. Like for hip-hop in this country, you need the majors—you need to be on a major, man, and you need a major to put money into you. And majors don't put money into hip-hop.

SM: [*Tape indistinct.*]

T: No. I think . . . the odd one, maybe, but not a Black artist, a male artist like me who's not really a singer. So . . .

SM: So who is?

T: Mark Morrison.

SM: Mark Morrison. And who else?

T: There's what's-her-name, that girl . . .

SM: [*Tape indistinct.*] . . . right. Okay.

T: I know I'm the first Black guy in this country to be on the front of *The Face* magazine and *NME* and *Melody Maker*, which is crazy.

SM: Were you the first on *NME*?

T: I think English Black guy.

SM: That's right, forgive me, yeah.

T: I think Public Enemy has done it.

SM: Yeah. Yeah.

T: And Mark Morrison, he sells a lot more records than me, and he's not been on the front of any of these magazines. And I think they find him more of a threat than me.

SM: You reckon?

T: Well, not a threat as in the obvious threat like gold chains . . .

SM: No, I think they know you're more of a threat but basically . . . I think with Mark Morrison, the situation where, you know, people will die out. Sorry about that, but it's like [*recording indistinct*]. It's like it's a tree, and it's not even that high yet, and it's growing. And it's like when it first blossomed, you know, it's like magical—but now, people are a bit scared of it. But it's become a bit like . . . I'm sorry, I'm going 'round in circles. But no, but it's true. And I think the situation is that you've already changed music once. You're on your own, you've changed music on your own, and you're thirty-one years old and you've changed music already. I think it's good.

T: Yeah, I feel like I've got a lot more stuff to do. I'm really excited about my new album. People are going to be shocked, especially in England, because I know they're going to expect something, and this is like . . . it's kind of like . . . it's real . . . it sounds the most contemporary . . .

SM: It was interesting when you said that, you know, you don't care what anyone thinks about you—it shows.

T: Yeah, I'm not worried if I'm liked at all. You know, in any way at all. I could go to a club and you could know who I am and you don't have to like me because I don't really care what you think about me.

SM: Are you in a privileged situation?

T: God, I'm the luckiest guy . . .

SM: Meaning that, you know, you could do that, I mean, some people have employees and so forth and whatnot and have to make them like them, you know, sort of smile . . .

T: Yeah. I am privileged. Totally privileged. And sometimes I behave in that way. Because I can be quite rude. Especially in social circumstances. Especially with famous people as well, I can be very, very rude because I won't play that game of, just because you're, say for instance you're Maxwell, like I've had situations with Maxwell—Maxwell asks this girl what's wrong with me.

SM: What, in front of you?

T: No. I was outside this club and Maxwell stood next to me, and I didn't say anything to him. I didn't talk to him because I don't know him. And he said to the girl . . . he was kind of looking at me, as if to say "talk to me." But I don't want to talk to him. So he's kind of saying what's wrong with me, have I got problems, have I got a problem with him because I don't talk to him? And I said to the girl, "Why should I talk to him? Because he's Maxwell? Because he's on MTV, and stuff like that?" That's not enough of a reason for me to go socializing with someone.

SM: There's a very famous story about Miles Davis. I think me personally, you definitely are . . . you definitely come from that vein.

T: Well, that's a major compliment. And what's mad is that people have said that I'll do my gigs with my back turned and I've never seen a Miles Davis gig, though.

SM: Let me tell you a true story about that. One day, I think it was Mick Jagger comes and knocks on Miles Davis's door, rings the doorbell. Miles come out from his bed, opens the door, and there's Mick Jagger and says, "What the fuck do you want? Who are you?" Slammed the door, went back to bed. He said, "Just because he's fucking someone . . . he think he can come and knock on my door—I don't know him! Who's he?"

T: Yeah. And that's how I feel about it. Artists are very uninteresting people.

SM: Totally.

T: I've met a lot of artists, and I'd rather hang out with someone from a different profession. Like whatever, anything, from villain to whatever, wall painter and decorator. Artists are very . . . it's almost like we live in a celebrity age now, as well as not much music. And it's like . . .

SM: I suppose it's not much art.

T: Yeah, not much art. Celebrities take themselves from video sets and award ceremonies, and they take it out on the street. Kids look like . . . they dress like they're in their videos and walk around and want attention. So it's a total celebrity age, and artists really ain't got much to say because all they do is take all the time. All they do is taking. So I just always get let down so I don't even bother any more—I just get let down.

SM: Do you mean take off you? Take things off you?

T: No, like all they do is seem to take from society and give little back. And some of these might do charities up the yin-yang, but basically kind of like . . . you get a lot of attention as an artist, so going out and demanding more is ridiculous. So, like, I get a lot of attention. I do a video and get a lot of attention. So I go to a club and I don't want a big deal made about me. I don't need loads of people around me. I don't need a special event.

SM: What, you don't have your entourage?

T: I don't need to be announced and all that stuff. I was out somewhere last week with my manager, and the club owner come over, and my manager said, "Yeah, you can take a picture of him," and I'm going, "What are you doing? I don't want to be in a club taking pictures." I'm an observer, I can sit in the club and just watch everything. You know what I mean, I'm a real observer, like—

SM: Undercover!

T: Yeah, you know what I mean—just watching anything. And it's like, artists are just mad constantly—they want attention, they want to be the center of attraction all the time. I don't need that. So I'm insecure in different ways.

SM: Total. But is there anyone who interests you—or not interests you, but someone you have some kind of affinity with or for?

T: I respect Gary Oldman a lot. Because when I met Gary Oldman—I met him a few times and talked to him a few times. And normally, he's like the biggest actor in the world, he's the best actor in the world. And he keeps his feet on the ground. He's so normal and so real, and that's why he's a great artist, I think—he's like so real. And he's like . . . and all that he's done must have touched him, but he doesn't show it. It just doesn't show. So I've got a lot of respect for him because he was like so normal with me, so normal and cool. He's got a real good vibe about him. You just look at him and it's Gary Oldman, the biggest actor in the world, the best actor in the world. And it's like, he's just so normal . . .

SM: I bumped into him once. In New York, years ago. And I think he was doing his . . . movie and I didn't know him, but I said "Gary! Gary!" And he turned 'round—he don't know me, I was just some sort of geek—and "I just wanna say, you know, mate, enough respect, give credit where credit's due, nice one." And he looked at me like this . . . [*stares*] . . . and he goes, "Nice one, nice one."

T: He's intense, isn't he? He's intense.

SM: I'm telling you, he was like he was in South London, and some geezer had said, "Gary!" and he turned round and he really kind of knew, you know, whose manor are you from? And then he kind of like clicked back and "I'm in New York, I'm going to get a taxi, this guy's just saying hello, and that's it." But . . .

T: He controls the situation, yeah, he definitely controls the situation when someone comes up. The vibe I got off him—and it's only spending a short amount of time, I didn't hang out with nobody on that set, but . . . I couldn't stay in my room and sit in my room and just do nothing. So I'd hang out in the corridor, I was hanging out with the security guy, sat down talking to him, smoke cigarettes, and Gary Oldman would come out and go, "You want a cup of tea? Come in!" So I'd go out and hang out with him. So I ended up spending. . . . Thank you, man.

[*McQueen pours a cup of tea.*]

T: So I hanged out with him a lot. But the vibe I got . . . I don't even know him. Even though I hanged out with him quite a bit, you can't get to know someone like that. But the vibe I got from his eyes sometimes—it was a person who's given a lot . . . I'm not saying he's not worried about dying, but his eyes seemed to say that it was all just daily motions, getting up.

SM: I get the impression he's very disenchanted with the industry he's in, and he's an extraordinarily talented actor. I get the impression that he's a bit disenchanted because he wanted to do *Nil by Mouth*, he wanted to write, he ended up doing a really great film. But it's a kind of disenchantment with his real talent. I'm not saying he's not a talented director, but, you know, the talent which sort of feeds him, but he has a disenchantment with it, I feel.

T: It's really weird with actors, what I've seen with actors is, like Al Pacino after *Scarface*, he didn't leave himself with much. That is such a great . . . he put every ounce of his soul in that, and he didn't seem to be left with anything else. I don't see that in music so much.

SM: No, because I think with actors, they're part of the vehicle, they're a tool for the director. And maybe that's why he wants to direct, he wants to control a bit more. And that's why, you know—actors are a weird bunch of people.

T: It's a horrible job, man.

SM: Total. You give yourself in a way that . . .

T: I didn't enjoy doing it at all. I really didn't. The bonus was I met Gary Oldman, that was the bonus. But apart from that I really didn't enjoy doing it. Too much waiting around, too much doing nothing, and even when you're doing something, you're doing nothing. I've got nothing in common with what I was doing, the words I was saying, they meant nothing to me.

SM: Yeah. They approached you—they wanted you for that film?

T: Yeah. Just got a phone call to my management one day saying, "Will I be in this Luc Besson movie?" And I was thinking *Nikita, Professional*.

SM: Yeah, wicked, yeah, of course.

T: I never thought it would be like this, to be honest with you.

SM: How was Brucie baby?

T: I was totally noninterested in him, didn't want to meet him, not interested at all. I don't know if he's a nice guy or not, you know what I mean? But I didn't want to take the time to find out. I was totally like, no passion to meet him at all.

SM: I want to move onto something that I want to ask you—there's a movie that's just come out called *Ghost Dog: The Way of the Samurai*. Have you heard about this movie?

T: I've heard about it, yeah.

SM: It's with Forest Whitaker, and RZA has done the score, a really beautiful score. And the movie. . . . I know you'll like the movie.

T: Yeah, I've been told I'll love the movie.

SM: And Forest Whitaker is just crazy in it. But what I want to ask you is, have you ever and will you ever . . .

T: Does he play a samurai?

SM: He's a professional hitman who follows the way of the samurai.

T: So he don't use swords, then?

SM: He practices with a sword. He actually assassinates with modern-day technology, but he uses the way of the samurai, so it's basically Eastern culture with a contemporary way of life and a contemporary way of killing people. And it's just so. . . . Forest Whitaker is for me on a par with Gary Oldman—get those two in a film, you'll really make something happen.

T: I love his . . .

SM: I think he's got his own company, actually.

T: I think his directing in his films is . . . I think he's a genius. Definitely.

SM: What I wanted to ask you is have you ever thought of doing a score for a film?

T: I've been asked a few times. It's not that I haven't been interested . . .

SM: You don't feel it's yours?

T: . . . it's just that . . . I'm quite lazy in some ways as in, somebody asks me and I'll say to my manager, "Yeah, yeah, I'll think about it," then I'll never think about it, and it's just gone. Then I'm in a studio and doing my thing.

SM: You're such an artist in that way, in some ways. It's kind of like, forgive me for being so direct, but what I wanted to ask you is . . . I'm doing this sort of bigger movie . . .

T: You're doing a movie?

SM: Yeah, a Channel 4/BFI collaboration. Have you ever heard of Zadie Smith? This girl called Zadie Smith?

T: No.

SM: She's a young Black writer, a very beautiful, very interesting girl. And we're cowriting this thing, and she's great. But what I wanted to ask you, in some ways, is the whole idea of . . . have you ever thought of a theme and variations on a theme? Because you did it once, you obviously did it on the last album, unless I'm going crazy, you did it on *Ladies*, you did a rock version and the sort of hip-hop version.

T: Oh, the Public Enemy thing on *Maxinquaye*, you mean?

SM: No, the last album. Why can't I remember titles right now? The one with the guy who raps really fast . . .

T: "I Like the Girls"?

SM: That's bad. That's just rockin' bad.

T: Only now and again you get a concept, but mostly it's all freestyle words, and then . . . Mad Dog likes girls. I like girls.

SM: Obviously.

T: Because he writes a lot of lyrics about girls, I just thought of that old Beastie Boys song, "I Like the Girls," so I kind of took that and used that as a chorus. So now and again I get concepts, but I'm not really a concept man. But actually I just did an album, and there is a concept to it—it's political, it's about racism, know what I mean?

SM: What album's that?

T: I haven't even got a name for it yet, but it's the album I would have done if I'd have stayed in Bristol. I would have started off as a rapper, and if I'd started doing music earlier, if I'd started doing music before I entered Massive Attack my music would have probably been more hip-hop based. But because . . . then again, I don't know, because I was listening to the Specials before hip-hop, so I don't know if that's true. But it would have been more on a rap thing, see? So this is like the album I missed, and it's about racism and English politics—a lot about England.

SM: What title is it gonna be?

T: I don't know. I haven't even thought of a title yet.

SM: I'm seeing this sort of . . .

T: It's very street as well, very street and very dirty-sounding, very street. It sounds very English, very, very English.

SM: More of that! What is it with us—or at least me, I'm not and I am, I'm not and I am nationalistic?

T: Oh, I am and I'm not, yeah. It's the same with racism, I am and I'm not.

SM: Someone said to me, "Are you an artist or are you a Black artist?" And I say: "Sometimes I am, sometimes I'm not, sometimes I forget."

T: Sometimes you're forced to be. I've never thought of myself as a Black artist, but I've been forced to be a Black artist. In England it's crazy, though, they gave me this thing where . . . this is where I was very lucky, being very . . . not anything. The English press just wrote about me as an artist, and Black, white never had anything to do with it.

SM: No, and you escaped that, and that's a thing which—I think that's the key to it. What is that? I mean, you escape it and other people don't, and what is it? What is Black?

T: I think you can fall into the trap. Black is what a record company tells you to be. It's like diamond rings, diamond bracelets, cars, women in videos. The record company, the industry tells us that's what's Black and people follow that. Like, I wear dresses, I wear lipstick, I wear make-up, I don't usually follow the same format for videos, so no one can trap me. It's not rap, it's not singing . . .

SM: This is exactly what I try, you know. I tend to try to be a wet piece of soap, so as soon as they've got me, they're off, they think they've got me, but . . .

T: Yeah. You just do another thing. You know, it's weird, when I was going out with Björk, I started getting, you know, like the *Sunday Mirror*, *The Sun* press, tabloids—they'd call me "Black rapper." And that's them making me Black, it's them making me be a rapper, because I'm Black, they're calling me a rapper. The people from *The Sun* have probably never heard my music.

SM: I should ask her this question to Björk, but unfortunately she's not here and I want to ask it. Because she's from, like, Norway, how does she feel about the situation of the Black music industry in England or Britain. Was there any . . . ?

T: I don't think . . . with some artists it don't really affect them, they're not really aware of them.

SM: They're not interested and why should they be?

T: And I know she likes good artists, whether they're Black, white, yellow, but I don't think it really matters to her. It's crazy, like it don't matter to me. I'm lucky, in a way, because I sell records to all people, kind of.

SM: It definitely doesn't matter to me, but what you say about the record industry is that it does sort of . . .

T: Oh, definitely. Especially more in America as well. It's crazy. I've been there like four, five years nearly now, and they've . . . someone phoned me up the other day, and I'm in this hip-hop magazine and . . . was on TV and said I influenced him, and they just accepted me there, but they've accepted me as a Black person. And what's mad is that when people like . . . heard me, and these people found out about me, I wasn't in the Black community. I'm still not in any community, but the Black community found out about me later there, and it was just white press who used to write about me, and the Black press didn't really . . . I didn't exist to them. But now it's like they've just found me, and it's almost like it keeps me a new artist all the time, all these different. . . . They say I've changed music, but what music? White music, Black music?

Interview with Steve McQueen

Hans Ulrich Obrist and Angeline Scherf / 2002

From Steve McQueen, *Speaking in Tongues: 7 février–23 mars 2003, Musée d'art moderne de la ville de Paris*. Transcribed by Matt Price. Reprinted by permission.

Angeline Scherf: Steve, you occupy a specific place in contemporary art today, not only due to the sophisticated nature of your installations, but also because, for the most part, the human being in its individual and collective, rational or irrational dimension is at the heart of your work.

This exhibition brings together a new work, *Once Upon a Time*, based on the NASA *Voyager* mission in 1977, and three films centered on monologue, in one way or another. Let's start by discussing *7th Nov.*, with which the exhibition starts. The spectator is immediately plunged into an extremely tense, totally overwhelming world.

Steve McQueen: The person you hear speaking is my cousin Marcus. You see a portrait of his head projected on the wall. The piece is a monologue, in which he talks about an incident that happened a while back. He shot his brother by accident. It's a monologue, but unwritten and spontaneous. Marcus has a certain kind of talent. He's one of these people who looks interesting even if he's eating cornflakes! He has a certain way of speaking that is very engrossing. It draws you in. In the work, there's an avalanche of words, an avalanche of emotions. He basically tells his story directly into a microphone. Through the way he speaks your imagination pictures everything.

Hans Ulrich Obrist: To what extent did you plan the work, the length, the way that it was recorded and so on . . .

SM: I just let it happen. It was a situation where all he needed was the frame. I just had to put him in a situation where I could record the story. I didn't know how long it would last. It lasted as long as it needed to last, which was about twenty-four minutes, I think. He has a way of speaking whereby he can go on and on with descriptions.

AS: So he didn't prepare it at all?

SM: I imagine he's told the story a thousand times to different people—parts of the story at least. I imagine it to be like a musician who improvises. You practice "My Funny Valentine" sixteen times, or all the time perhaps, but every night you improvise with this song, so it is different. Marcus knew he was being recorded, but after the first two or three minutes, you leave the conscious situation behind you and go into the unconscious, and you're interested in bringing something out of yourself that you can translate and give images to through language.

AS: You often speak of the documentary filmmaker Jean Rouch as a reference. Is [cinéma-vérité] important for you? It seems to always be there in your work.

SM: Anything in this room could have attention drawn to it, and many artists have done that. I guess Jean Rouch wanted to bring reality into the cinema space, something unplanned. Once the audience was there, they were brought into that, startled—they didn't feel they were in a cinema anymore.

HUO: With Rouch, there is also the notion of feedback and participation. When working with the other, filming or photographing someone else, there is the idea of it being an intermediary, of being a vehicle for feedback. One of the things he developed, injected into the economy of the people he worked with, was the sense of them being coauthors.

How do you see this notion of feedback and collaboration?

SM: *7th Nov.* is similar to *Girls Tricky* (2001) in some way. I was with Tricky for three or four days, recording him, and at a certain moment something happened and that became the film; just like something happened when Marcus was speaking about this incident. At a certain moment, things just click. As far as collaboration goes, it is all about collaboration. If it's a painter painting a dead flower or any kind of artistic endeavor, it's all about collaboration.

AS: Yet *7th Nov.* represents an extreme situation: it is a first-hand account of a man who has committed a crime.

SM: It wasn't a crime: it was a tragedy.

AS: And we have the feeling that it could happen to anybody.

SM: And it's not alien to anyone. It's not a freak show here. It's all about humanity. We know tragedy from Shakespeare. The question here is how that is articulated and the humanity that exists in it. Just like Tricky, how one works one's way out of a situation, breaks through a barrier to arrive at a peak.

AS: You also reach a generic dimension.

SM: I imagine it's like prayer in a way, like Buddhist chanting or some other ritual of meditation, in order to get higher, to get above it. You break out and you get into the unconscious. You start at one point, you end up at another point, and then you come back down again. When Tricky finishes the song in the piece, he says something like, "That one feels like the best one yet. We'll do another one, if we have to." He seems to go out of himself and then all of a sudden, he's back in control of himself again. It's similar with Marcus in *7th Nov.*, when he says, "It's difficult, it's difficult," because through the journey he's gone back to where he started.

HUO: This leads us to the question of other levels of consciousness, and it is something that comes up in your work, and in many pieces this leads to a sonic dimension, to sound. In *Once Upon a Time*, the work realized for this exhibition, you use "speaking in tongues."

SM: It relates to the ideas of meditation that I mentioned before, and to the improvisation of jazz. Speaking in tongues has nothing to do with entertainment, but everything with a state of mind, and the whole idea of that translating orally was fascinating for me. And the fact that it didn't make sense at a certain point—one couldn't recognize what one was saying. That is great. It is a wonderful thing to contemplate. It is unconscious sound made directly through human beings. I went to Toronto to speak to William Samarin, a linguist specialized in the subject. He let me use his archive of recordings.

AS: Is speaking in tongues a postsymbolic communication, as Jaron Lanier calls it, which allows beyond language?

SM: Beyond language is not far off. Think of Beckett for example. He uses half sentences, and goes backwards, or think of Joyce. People like Toni Morrison very much come into the loop. I was interested in these writers, especially Beckett, who tried to put everything on the head of a needle. If the writer manages to transcend what I'm reading so that it becomes something about what is happening in your head, then that's great. But it's very rare. Toni Morrison's last book, *Paradise*, starts with the line: "They shoot the white girl first."

Throughout the book, you don't know who's Black and who's white—it's fascinating. But the funny thing is, we want to be told, and we take that for granted. It's marvelous, holding a mirror up to ourselves.

The idea of language going beyond text is of course also true for songs and poetry—poetry's not meant to be on the page. It's meant to be read aloud as part of what we do. It's alive, more physical, more of the body as such.

HUO: *Speaking in Tongues* is, by the way, the title for the exhibition.

SM: "For anyone who speaks in tongues does not speak to men but to God. Indeed, no one understands him." The Bible goes on and on about speaking to God, and the people who speak in tongues not actually understanding what they're saying, so they're being used as a mobile phone in a way, teleporting messages from God. So basically you're lost. You just take off, and that's very much what I'm interested in—us as a vessel.

HUO: Speaking in tongues has been used to describe two very different phenomena—glossolalia and xenoglossia.

SM: Xenoglossia means you suddenly seem to speak a language you had never studied or even heard of before. Glossolalia means you speak a language that did not exist before, or no one has ever heard before. The phenomenon is not strictly Christian. It exists in a lot of cultures.

AS: One thing I'm interested in learning about, is how far control is an issue for you and your work?

SM: It's very much controlled because you instigate it. Like whirling dervishes, you spin, then get closer to God. You do it because you know how to do it—there's an apparent out-of-control-ness, but you're totally in control of it. You have to get out of control to be in control. That's what improvisation is. It's controlled chaos. After a while it takes on its own momentum, but it needs to be wound up a bit to get into a certain state. *Once Upon a Time*, by the middle you are somewhere else, lost. And then you come down again. The same thing happens with Tricky's music. As far as Tricky is concerned, it's a situation where there is a certain amount of planning—there's a rhythm and a bassline, and on top of that you improvise, putting down certain lyrics in the song. It's interesting to think about intimacy in relation to whirling dervishes because I did this piece called *Five Easy Pieces* [1995], in which five people were filmed hula-hooping from above. I said, "I don't know what they're doing—they could be masturbating!" Maybe they're masturbating to get closer to God! Like in a hotel room with the TV on!

AS: So that's the meaning of *Illuminer*?

SM: Maybe. No, I wouldn't say that. But in a hotel room, on your own, the first thing you do is put the TV on. This isn't about being an artist who travels, none of that nonsense. This is about being in a small room on your own, with that little box in front of you, watching TV. You're taken away from yourself a little bit. There's no domestic situation there—it's just you, the bed, and the TV. The idea of isolation and language is important: it relates to Marcus because of what happened to him; the isolation of Tricky behind the glass, and the isolation of the guy in his bedroom, in a hotel room with the TV on.

HUO: Everything was spontaneous; nothing was planned?

SM: Nothing was planned at all. It was weird. I don't know what came over me. Panic, maybe. I do trust a lot in things. I thought, "Okay, let's do this." So I set it up, put the camera on the tripod on top of the TV, and looked through the lens to see where I was. It was a very strange situation. There was this military thing on TV and it just happened. Maybe the passivity of my situation in that bed, totally passive, contrasted with the activity on screen.

AS: And at the same time, being alone in a hotel is a bit disturbing. One thinks about one's life, a bit like a tightrope walker looking at the void. It's a strange, almost timeless, sensation.

SM: Yes, you're quite right, time does stop.

AS: How did you come up with the title, *Illuminer*?

SM: To illuminate in the sense of the illumination of minds, but also because I was being illuminated by the television. If the television had been off, you'd have just seen black. My existence was only there because the TV allowed my existence to be there. My presence was "given" by the screen. And what was being projected onto me and allowed me my visibility was violent; it was an assault in a way.

AS: If it had been an entertainment program, maybe nothing would have happened.

SM: That's the key to this for me. The documentary was about Special Forces training to go to Afghanistan, and was very energetic. The program had been voiced-over again by a French narrator. So you've got this American guy speaking, with this French voice over the top. It's kind of weird that they didn't take the American voice out. They were both going on at the same time.

HUO: The pixels try to focus on the image and break through the darkness. Could you tell us some more about pixelation and why this work was filmed with a digital camera, while most of your works are not?

SM: There's a certain sense of directness of action, which can help to take down barriers that are in one's mind when trying to make a piece. The fact of the matter was that as soon as I picked up the digital camera I knew that it would fight the blackness to try to make sense of it all. That's what they do. There's an auto-focus facility on Sony cameras—it's kind of interesting because it's a hindrance and a help at the same time. The camera was using that auto-focusing to work overtime: through the flickering of the TV screen in the darkness it would have to bust a gut to get things into focus.

HUO: So it's an experiment?

SM: I think everything's an experiment. It's not particularly perfectly rounded; it's what it is, and in that way it is very human. I like the iris. There is a human quality to the gaze, looking at me on the bed. There's a voyeurism to a certain extent, and the digital camera takes on the presence of the human eye. It's working all the time; it's not just a static picture.

AS: *Once Upon a Time* is connected to the conscious/unconscious issue. It's a portrait of humanity compressed into one hundred and sixteen images that you confront with another form of knowledge, glossolalia, which is indecipherable.

SM: For me the images in *Voyager II* are all about our so-called "knowledge." It was launched by NASA in '77, so is very much biased towards Western knowledge to a certain degree. It's all about what we apparently know. With the sound, for sure, it's all about what we don't know, or "nothing." The idea of sound meaning nothing or sound that we don't know anything about is very interesting, coming from us to the situation where these images are there of what we "know." Just to put the two together leaves an ingredient missing. We're having this conversation while the work is in progress, which is unusual. I think we're living in limbo. We're not living in the past, we're not living in the future; we're living in between. I'm trying to create a zombie situation: not dead, not alive. Not a passive zombie, but a conscious zombie. So limbo is what I'm interested in.

HUO: There's a song by Brian Ferry about limbo. . . . How do you see this limbo space?

SM: It's like reading a book—you only understand the book as far as the last words you've read. Each time you turn the page, you're somewhere else. It's a journey. And there's a beginning, which will be our immediate past, and the future in front but we can't see it.

Every word we say has gone. So when interesting things happen, it's immediate, and is just there, and it reinforces your presence. There is a relationship with the image. If it's not in drugs and rock 'n' roll, it's in something else.

HUO: Could we talk a little about the genesis of the *Voyager* project? It was somehow triggered by the book *Murmurs of Earth*. During *Voyager I*, as documented in that book, the plan was to gather relevant information (whatever that means) and send it, as if it was a bottle, into outer space.

SM: With *Voyager II*, what interests me is the whole idea of the physical distance of the project—it will be the furthest man-made object away from Earth. I was always interested by the idea of the images of *Voyager* in relation to it actually being in outer space. I also like the idea of holding up a mirror to ourselves—a reflection of ourselves not for us, but for alien intelligence. It leaves out poverty, war, nuclear bombs, religion and so on. So it's a weird quasilook at ourselves. It's absurd and intriguing. That's something I wish to investigate further. The idea of the past interests me as well—the time when it was made and launched, and yet it has this special relationship with the future, and even with the present. I like those three aspects. The present is only one view on the project. Some of these images are dated to the early seventies. Nothing dates beyond 1977. And then there is the thought that it will travel into the future, and we're living in the middle somehow.

AS: Why did you want to transform documentary images into a film?

SM: "Fiction" and "journey" were the two starting points for me. Looking at the *Voyager* images was not like looking at the earth that I know. It felt to me more like a fantasy.

AS: There is a drawing that is supposed to represent all of humanity—the one with the father, the mother, and the baby in the womb—and also a star and lots of things going on that are meant to transmit a lot of information.

SM: There's also a map to show where we are, the solar system, where the probe was launched. It is a lot of information indeed, but it is used to construct a fairy tale for outer space.

HUO: A precedent to this sequence of still images is Eames, the great exhibition of Ray and Charles Eames. They did a lot of experiments with multiscreens, such as the famous Moscow '59 screen.

SM: With *Once Upon a Time* there is only one screen. There is a sense of being drawn to the light. The images are right at the end of a long corridor. From afar, it is like a painting. It is the only frame in the corridor. You have a different relationship as you walk towards it.

It's almost like tunnel vision, which is exactly what I want: right between your eyes. A tunnel, a physical focus, echoed by the back wall, by the frame and by the side walls.

AS: Will this be the first time that you have used archive images?

SM: Yes. I feel those images belong to all of us. They have been sent out to represent "us," so they belong to us. Ownership is ours.

HUO: I have an interview here with Tricky in which he speaks about peace and rage. It moves between the two. In terms of the exhibition, this would be quite a dramatic start.

SM: I was not sure it would be dramatic. Nothing has been conspired to create drama. It has not been written to create drama—it's not dressing-up, it's not pretend; it's a situation where people are recounting a situation that has happened to them. It's real. It's a part of life. All three people in these pieces are dealing with circumstances beyond their control. As I say, if it's raining, all you can do is wear a fucking raincoat, though you can choose the color.

Life in Film: Steve McQueen

Steve McQueen / 2007

From *Frieze*, September 12, 2007. Reprinted by permission. Copyright © Steve McQueen. Courtesy of the artist and Thomas Dane Gallery.

Steve McQueen's recent films Gravesend *and* Unexploded (Handheld) *were commissioned for the Italian Pavilion of the Fifty-second Venice Biennale.* Queen and Country, *his response to the Iraq War, was premiered at the first Manchester International Festival this year and will be shown at the Imperial War Museum in London this autumn. He is currently shooting his first feature film—commissioned by Channel 4 Films—which focuses on the Troubles in Northern Ireland. An exhibition of new work will be on view at Thomas Dane Gallery from October 8–November 10, 2007. He lives and works in Amsterdam.*

Zéro de conduite (*Zero for Conduct*, 1933) by Jean Vigo had a massive impact on me. It's just forty-five minutes long and depicts a rebellion in a French boys' boarding school. The film says everything: it's inventive, it's magical, to some extent it is sexually ambiguous, it's political, it's bizarre, and it has a great narrative at the same time. All these ingredients add up to something that's huge, almost too big. But there's also the fact that it's so magnetizing, beautiful, and wonderful to watch—you want to look at this film. You're always thinking on different levels, not just about the images, but what is happening, and the psychology of the characters.

There's a slapstick element to the film, a real sense of comedy that drives it. I think at the time *Zéro de conduite* was made, to create anything of that subversive nature, there had to be an element of humor to carry people along. However, it was banned for years by French censors and didn't get a general release until 1946.

The influence of *Zéro de conduite*, which I saw for the first time in 1990, is as much about a period in my life as it is about my understanding of art. Going to New York and coming across the Whitney Biennial in 1993, I felt that anything was possible if you did it rather than thought about it. At Goldsmiths, where

I was studying at the time, there were certain ways of doing things, of talking, which put limits on how you approached making art. When I went to New York, I realized that London was a dot on a white piece of paper at that time. Seeing *Zéro de conduite* gave me a sense of permission, and in some ways it was the first movie that allowed me to think that things were possible. To some extent, your imagination is limited when you look at something and you're not making work yourself. You're trapped, because it's all about the effort to actually do it. Say you have to lug a load of boxes up the stairs: if you think about it, your feeling is, "Oh fuck, I can't do that"—if you just do it, you're involved.

While I was at Goldsmiths, a film enthusiast came in—unfortunately I can't recall his name—and brought with him a bunch of film reels, including Andy Warhol's *Couch* (1964), in which one of Warhol's superstars lies on a couch with another lying along the top of the backrest, just looking at him. He shot it at the average speed of twenty-four frames a second, but he projected it at a speed slower than the average heart rate. When it was projected, the film pulsated—it was incredible.

Couch and *Zéro de conduite* were the two films that really did it for me. I think that's where it started and, in a strange way, where it stopped. It's one thing having, for instance, nice images on your studio wall that influence you when you're just beginning as an artist or filmmaker, but when you go about getting into a situation where you begin to make work yourself, it's a different kettle of fish altogether. It's all about doing it—the physicality of making films. What you see at the end is never the same as the situation of how it was done, yet that process is very important. It's all about making a lot of mistakes and being brave.

I used to go and watch a film at least twice: the first time for fun, the second time to look at it closely. If I liked it, I'd see it three or four times. But the last thing I want to do right now in my life is spend time in cinemas. I hate going to them. Nowadays, I'd rather go and see something live—a concert or dance, jazz, or contemporary music—because when I'm in a cinema, I often feel that I'm wasting time watching something old and stale, shot two or three years ago, and that I should be doing something else instead.

The connection with the idea of "filmmakers" and "film" doesn't mean anything to me. Exhibitions just about painting, sculpture, or film ghettoize the whole thing. It's nonsense. I also feel a connection with musicians. For example, I like Tricky very much—he has his own sound and is amazing, but he never got his dues. Because he has asthma, there's a lot of strange breathing that can be heard in his work. This connects back to Warhol's *Couch* and projecting below the heartrate; there's a really direct physiological effect, a kind of physical angst, that's being explored in both artists' work.

I shoot films, but I do other things; at the end of the day it's got to be about the ideas, not one particular medium.

Steve McQueen, Director: Intimacy and Distance

Fabien Lemercier / 2008

From *Cineuropa*, October 23, 2008. Reprinted by permission.

Born in London in 1969, Steve McQueen has, over the past ten years, become a leading international figure in contemporary video art, amassing awards and distinctions. We met in the Paris offices of MK2—the French distributor of *Hunger*—with this lively character, who is as talkative as he is observant, as he retraced for us his film debut.

Cineuropa: When did you first hear about Bobby Sands's hunger strike?

Steve McQueen: I was eleven, and at that age the idea that someone would voluntarily stop eating seemed very strange to me. Every evening, Bobby Sands's picture appeared on television along with the growing number of days since the start of his hunger strike. Emotions ran high that year as it was also the time of the Brixton riots and my whole world literally opened up during that period.

C: Why did you choose this subject for your debut feature?

SM: I believe it's the most important event to have happened in the UK over the past twenty-seven years, for this type of situation continues to occur all over the world today. But it was more the human situation than the political context that interested me. I wanted to explore that strong impression it gave me at the time and find out more. I thought it was a very powerful subject for a film. My decision to make a film about it didn't stem from wanting to find a wider audience than for my work in contemporary art, but because the subject required a complex narrative approach.

C: What type of research did you carry out before writing the screenplay?

SM: My coscreenwriter [Enda Walsh] and I did a lot of research. We viewed archive material and went to Belfast to talk with former prisoners, prison guards, and the priests who used to visit the inmates. It was necessary in order to re-create the somber atmosphere of the early 1980s. The interviews were also essential for beyond the historical event I wanted to capture the details: Was it raining that day? What kind of rain? As a visual artist, these details bring me closer to the story.

C: Why did you create such an unusual narrative structure, with the delayed appearance of the main character?

SM: What matters is how you tell a story. I believe the way you work visually leads to narrative creation. Sometimes, there's no need for a "once upon a time" approach. You can do things differently and stop when you want. All that's necessary is that the images and story reach a conclusion, in one way or another.

It's like using the camera as a fingerprint, like blindfolding someone, pushing him into a room and leaving him to find his own way out. He reconstructs the story alone as he goes along, thanks to his senses. The only thing we can do in the traditional field of filmmaking and narration is play on the form. We can't create this form because it already exists, but we can subvert it.

C: The film's rhythm is particularly striking.

SM: I had this idea that when you go down a river, you start by floating on a current. The scenery drifts by and gradually becomes familiar. Then you arrive at some rapids where reality is thrown into turmoil. You no longer feel secure in your environment and need to reposition yourself, but every time you do so you're shaken up again. The third part is the waterfall, the loss of the sense of gravity. I knew all the contrasts and contours of the film, but as someone who doesn't know how to write music and has the melody in their head. It was in this frame of mind that I worked with my coscreenwriter, Enda Walsh.

C: Why did you use a long take for the lengthy dialogue between Bobby Sands and the priest?

SM: We owed viewers a full and in-depth conversation about the reasons to live and the reasons to die. We didn't cut anything, so it's like a discussion watched from the outside. For the two characters want the same thing, but differently. Up to this point, there is relatively little dialogue in the film, and this moment arrives a bit like a psychoanalysis session, like an avalanche of water in a hitherto parched environment.

C: How did you work on the film's strong visual style?

SM: More than the setting, it's the light that interests me for you can almost feel the walls with the tips of your fingers and feel the texture. The light can also give a certain depth. Working with natural light was fascinating for me, a real challenge, for the film's setting is similar to a castle or monastery with a single window as a source of light.

C: Did you intend for your film to be so original and "revolutionary" or is it simply an expression of your artistic nature?

SM: I wasn't aware that I was making a radically different film, otherwise I would undoubtedly not have made it. I didn't do anything different for the sake of being different, but because it was necessary for the film, to help recount quite an extreme story.

To come back to the lengthy scene of dialogue, I filmed it that way because if I'd used a series of shots and reverse shots, the characters would have ended up talking to the audience. I wanted these two men to speak to each other, in a very intimate way. At the same time, I didn't want their faces to be too visible, like silhouettes. The viewers thus sharpen their eyes and ears: they realize they're not supposed to be in that room. This dynamic of intimacy and distance makes the scene very powerful.

C: Was it easy to secure funding for the film?

SM: We were lucky because we shot the film in Northern Ireland, but we received funding from Northern Ireland, Southern Ireland, Wales, and England. It would certainly not have been possible to obtain funding from so many different sources if we'd shot the film anywhere other than Belfast. The shoot lasted three and a half weeks (with a two-and-a-half-month break so that Michael Fassbender could lose weight). This is apparently very short for a film shoot, but I wasn't aware of this. What's more, directors who complain even though they are lucky enough to be able to make films should be shot!

C: What type of films do you enjoy?

SM: Jean Vigo's *Zero for Conduct* is very meaningful for me. I used to go to the cinema a lot and I've seen all the classics. But when I think about how I'm going to film a scene, I don't think of Fellini, Scorsese, or Spielberg, but the best way for me to shoot.

C: Will you repeat this experience of directing films?

SM: I don't know. I hope so, but there's no hurry. My new work will be shown at the Venice Biennale from June to November 2009.

Steve McQueen on Film

Armelle Leturcq / 2008

From *Crash*, no. 48 (2008). Reprinted by permission.

British artist Steve McQueen brings to screen an intense first feature film, where the body itself becomes a political battlefield. Winner of the Golden Camera Prize at the last Cannes Film Festival, *Hunger* depicts the 1981 hunger strikes that took place in the Maze Prison in Northern Ireland. Steve McQueen also gives his first big break to Irish actor Michael Fassbender who takes on the difficult part of Bobby Sands, political prisoner and flag-bearer of the IRA.

Armelle Leturcq: You are already a successful artist. Why did you decide to direct a feature film?
Steve McQueen: When I was eleven years old, I learned about the history of Irish political prisoners and about their hero, Bobby Sands. That story really stayed with me. Much later, I realized I could make a 35mm film about it. I wanted this event to reach a wider audience, and the best way to do that was through storytelling. Because everyone understands stories. When you are a child, your parents tell you stories. I wanted to make a narrative feature film about this particular idea of the hunger strike. It's like poetry or a novel. Not everyone can get poetry, but everyone can get a novel because, ever since you were a child, you grew up in a narrative way.
AL: Is the character of Bobby Sands really famous in England?
SM: What is very strange is that this subject is not well known. It is not really spoken about, and it's not very much in the public culture at all. What I wanted to do was to reveal this subject so that people could live it again. The idea that someone would stop eating to be heard was very strange to me as a little boy. Since then, it's always haunted me.
AL: You remember Bobby Sands specifically?
SM: When you are eleven years old, you can't make sense of all the details, you can't get a sense of the whole thing. It was more the idea, the concept of people starving themselves that stuck with me.

AL: How did you manage to find all these details about prison life?

SM: I did research for four years. But you can only go so far with books and documents. What I was interested in was finding the information hidden between the words. So I interviewed prisoners. I also spoke to a prison officer. I just asked them questions so as to have an oral history, or a verbal document, about what everyday life was like in Maze Prison. So a lot of the information comes directly from prisoners and one prison officer.

AL: Why did you choose the actor Michael Fassbender to play Bobby Sands?

SM: Michael came for the audition. There were a lot of actors. We weren't just looking for anybody; we were looking for Bobby Sands. Michael had something different; at first I thought he was American actually (in fact, he is an Irishman of German origin). That was my first experience casting. I didn't know how to do it very well. All these actors were very nervous, but none of them used their energy with confidence. It was also looking for a good-looking actor. When I talked to Michael myself, I knew he was the one. It was a very difficult process actually.

AL: The movie was difficult to make, wasn't it? For Michael too, it must have been difficult. He had to lose a lot of weight.

SM: Yes, the hunger element had to be visible. People have these notions that, in the movies, people don't really get hurt. I think what Michael did was phenomenal. He has benefited from the movie. I think now he is working with Quentin Tarantino. I think he will become a star. What he has is very special; he can actually perform and deliver. I mean, he is a good actor. We shot for three weeks first, and then waited two and a half months for Michael to lose weight. Then we came back for three and a half weeks. It was a very short time slice. I thought it was normal; I'd never made a feature film before. Now, I realize that it actually was very short. When he came back, he was very fragile. What was beautiful was that he stayed focused but at the same time sensitive.

AL: There is a very long dialogue in the film between Bobby Sands and the priest who comes to see him in prison.... How long is this sequence?

SM: Twenty-two minutes and thirty seconds.

AL: Was there some improvisation?

SM: No. The text was very precise. I wrote everything. The only things improvised were the pauses. You have to go in with the right mindset. We, the entire crew, we moved in the same direction. We were conscious of what we were doing. We are a very fortunate crew. We did four takes.

AL: In *Hunger*, there are both big moments of silence and very long dialogues.

SM: It is a choice because I wanted to work with only the necessary. Generally in movies, there are sounds and words tossed around like confetti . . . people saying things like "one coffee, two sugar." For me, it's okay to stay silent and observe. When you watch a film, you use another person's brain to understand, to feel . . . I needed to show both extremes precisely. The two elements, the verbal and the physical. When you make a movie, you are between two cameras: the one on the shoulder of the cameraman and the one on your own shoulder. There, you feel like you are meeting the audience. So I tried to give two sensations at the same time, action and reaction. Everything became much more sharp with this style of shooting.

AL: Was it shot in the prison?

SM: We had the authorization to shoot in the Maze Prison, but in the end, the director's office denied us access. But we had an amazing art director who found this place next to the train station and it was awesome. All the doors and the gates looked like the real Maze Prison. Their dimensions were close to the actual prison. When you are in a three and a half by five-meter cell . . . you can't fit in there with cameras. The architecture dictates you into some sort of frame. And I couldn't say "action" whenever I wanted because we were in a train station and I had to wait for the train to leave.

AL: Did you analyze other films while making your own?

SM: No, I was more into the images. They make more sense to me. You don't necessarily learn from movies, you learn from life. You learn from art. You learn from looking at people in the street.

AL: But in film, there are a lot of rules to follow . . .

SM: You break them. Because there are no rules. . . . The only rule is "there are no rules in film." That's why I dropped out of film school after three months. When someone said to me, "There are rules," I was gone. You can't communicate with the audience with a frame of rules.

AL: Your film is not boring at all, even with a twenty-minute dialogue.

SM: I hope not. The only rule is to keep the focus. That's the only rule.

AL: How did you find the funds to finance the film?

SM: Channel 4 helped a lot, about eight hundred thousand pounds. The rest came from Ireland, Northern Ireland, and Wales . . .

AL: In the future, do you think you will be more involved in film or in art?

SM: What I love are the ideas. An idea could lead me to a painting, a poem, or a video. It all depends on the idea. It's the idea that counts.

AL: Is it difficult to find good ideas?

SM: No. Ideas just take time, whatever they are. What's important is how you execute them. Like in films. Lots of people went to see the movie but they all thought about it in their own way. It is not a big budget Hollywood film.

AL: What are your big influences in film?

SM: My biggest influence is life. Life makes me want to pick up a camera. The camera preserves things. I am not very interested in cinema. I am interested in what I can do with it as a tool. Not in the seduction of it. What it can do is much more interesting than what it is.

AL: As an artist, you will be representing England at the next Biennale in Venice.

SM: Yes, that's correct. It will be completely different from *Hunger*. I cannot talk about it too much because I am in the middle of it, though I am very excited about it. I am looking forward to it. In a way, it is great because people will see my work in Venice. Musicians and artists will see my work and love it, hate it.

You Use Your Body to Die: An Interview with Steve McQueen

Zachary Wigon / 2009

From *Notebook*, March 26, 2009. Reprinted by permission of MUBI.

As I wrote in my 2008 year-in-review piece here on *The Auteurs*, Steve McQueen's *Hunger* is one of the best films that I have ever seen. For the uninitiated, *Hunger* is a fiercely formal retelling of the 1981 IRA prisoners' hunger strike, led by IRA member (and later, elected MP in parliament) Bobby Sands. Steve McQueen's understanding of politics, and specifically how politics can effectively be dealt with by cinema, has moved the cinematic language forward. Filmmakers have been given a new set of tools with which to work, a new mode of understanding political cinema. I could elaborate on this theme further here, but it's best to let the man speak for himself; my interview with Steve McQueen more passionately (and perhaps more articulately) deals with my thoughts on the film than my own review. I sat down with McQueen last Friday, the day of the film's release, in the lobby of his hotel in the meatpacking district.

Notebook: How do you conceive of the relationship between bodies and physicality, and politics?

Steve McQueen: It's the whole idea of people incarcerated in a cell twenty-four hours a day, for four and a half years, and what they did to protest—using their excrement, using their urine, not washing. Using their body as a weapon—if that's all you have, what do you do with it? Maximizing your resistance as such. That was interesting for me to show, visually, because it had never actually been filmed. The only videotape which actually survived of it is ninety seconds of footage. Ninety seconds. So reconstructing this as film was very fascinating to me, and of course the political aspect was huge. Also the personal: What was it like to be naked in the cell for four and a half years? At what point do you get used to the excrement on the wall? At what point do you get used to waking up with maggots all over your body? The filth and the stench. These are the questions I wanted to raise, the images I wanted to look at.

N: Do you see a connection between the prisoners reverting to these physical means of protest, and the idea of politics, on an elemental level, being ingrained into your own body?

SM: I don't know about that, because often elements of physical struggle turn out to be violent. It doesn't always end up peacefully. Now, these were extremes, the front lines of the struggle between the British government and the IRA. When the words had been exhausted, they picked up guns and bombs and whatnot. When that was exhausted, and you're in prison, you're pushed to the absolute extreme, and you use your body as a weapon not only to protest, you use your body to die. It's an extraordinary situation, and I wanted to put a light on that because it had been brushed beneath the carpet for twenty-seven years.

N: It's interesting, that the body is the last resort.

SM: It's the ultimate. And it's unfortunate, you see it in the present day, people using their bodies for suicide bombs, which is quite different from a hunger strike. Regardless, they're using their bodies as a weapon. One has to talk. It's difficult to understand, really, but that's why I made a film about it.

N: Some have said that the film deifies Bobby Sands, say that the film is a deification of a terrorist. But the film does seem to grasp the concept of victims all, especially in that shot where you get the split screen of the beating, and the riot squad member crying—

SM: Well, you have lots of examples. You have Raymond, the prison guard. It's tit for tat. It's not about glorifying anything, just about showing a part of history that happened. Think of the conversation with the priest and Bobby. If people think, after that, that I'm portraying him as some kind of martyr, they should really see the film again.

N: I think that if there is anything that is really deified, or celebrated—

SM: I wouldn't call it celebrated—

N: Right—anything that the film is in awe of, let's say, I would say that it's not Sands, the man, but what he does towards the end of the film, the level of political commitment his actions espouse.

SM: Hmm. Well, I don't know if awe is the word I would use.

N: What would you say?

SM: It's a situation of—desperation, as well. The desperation, that someone would use their life in that way, in order to be heard. And you see it happening. As a human being, anyone you see who is ill, you want to help, of course. It's only natural. So there's all these conflicting emotions. Some might be in awe of it, but others might say, it's a desperate act. There's no straight yes, no straight no. Again, this film is not about right-wing and left-wing, wrong and right—it's about you and me. That's what's more important to me than anything else.

N: It was fascinating, the way that loftily discussing politics, talking about politics, was placed in such marked contrast with the actual physicality of the struggle. Specifically, the Thatcher speeches—the clips from those speeches felt so hollow when juxtaposed with seeing the physicality of the struggle.

SM: I think what had to happen was, you have to have . . . there had to be the reason why they were in prison. Her voice was the key. At the same time, I wanted it to come in as vapor, rather than a physical person. She was the lock and key of that prison. That was the doctrine of those times: we don't talk to terrorists.

N: Bearing that in mind, I thought it was interesting that the politics of the situation were very much backgrounded—vapor, like you said. Did you have to make a conscious effort to temper down the politics at any point?

SM: No, because it's not my job to do that. I was focusing on the human element, the elements that could grab an audience. What can grab an audience, and me, is the tactile elements of the everyday, of the prison officers and prisoners. That's going to bring you much closer than someone telling you what's going on and whatnot, in a kind of cold manner, as you said. What I wanted to do was give the audience the weight of those times, to say, "Here, hold this for an hour and a half." I wanted them to feel and experience that situation. Then, once that happens, you can work in a way that is much more effective.

N: How did you decide to begin with the prison guard?

SM: I wanted the audience to be led into the Maze. I wanted it to go from outside to inside. Having breakfast, putting on his clothes, checking his car for bombs, and also the prisoner being led into the Maze—so you get an idea of the rituals, the manners of that particular kind of institution. And then we end up with Bobby.

N: The film is so aesthetically, formally consistent. How did you arrive at your style for this film?

SM: Well, the architect of the Maze dictated the camera. Unfortunately, we couldn't film in the Maze. Well, I say unfortunately, but that really would have affected our crew and cast, so instead we constructed a set, with no breakaway walls, and that really dictated the camera. That kind of institution—the whole idea of how the prison was designed—it was a prison like a Russian doll, a prison within a prison within a prison. One thing, as far as the camera was concerned, was that there was only one source of light in the cell. That's interesting, in terms of how you can play with that. You work with what you have, and that's it. One cannot impose their intentions on the situation, one has to embrace the environment, accept it.

N: Even though you were working with what the environment gave you, there is a very specific style that had clearly been chosen.

SM: Yes, the choice to respect what you have. I didn't want to come up with some queasy idea to put something into a situation. It's the geography and the light—that's all we had.

Steve McQueen: Q&A with the Director of *Hunger*

Chris Tinkham / 2009

From *Under the Radar*, March 27, 2009. Reprinted by permission of Mark Redfern, senior editor and copublisher, *Under the Radar*.

When a film director has shot a seventeen-minute debate between a prisoner and a Catholic priest in an epic single take, as English artist Steve McQueen did for the centerpiece of his feature-length debut *Hunger*, it's only fitting that he would want to challenge you during a conversation. The scene, cowritten by McQueen and award-winning Irish playwright Enda Walsh, is one of the most enthralling discussions ever captured on celluloid. But without the subtler details of *Hunger* etched in my memory, I was at a clear disadvantage during my interview with McQueen, who had me backpedaling after just a few minutes.

Hunger is a daunting film that portrays the troubling events leading up to the starvation and death of IRA hunger striker Bobby Sands in the Maze Prison outside of Belfast, Ireland, in 1981. Though *Hunger* is expertly photographed and features an astounding performance from Michael Fassbender as Sands, viewing the film is at times a confounding experience and brutal on the senses. Aside from depictions of point-blank murder, hand-on-hand torture, body deterioration, and the dispersion of human waste throughout a cellblock, there is little dialogue in the film's first thirty minutes, which focuses on a prison guard and two inmates, neither of whom are clearly identified. An easy assumption is that one of them is Bobby Sands, but that's not the case.

Born in London in 1969, McQueen was eleven years old when Sands's final protest was television news. McQueen studied film for a year at NYU in 1993 before making a name for himself in the art world. In his 1997 back-and-white film *Deadpan*, he re-created a Buster Keaton stunt from *Steamboat Bill, Jr.* that involved a house collapsing around him. In 1999, McQueen won the prestigious

Turner Prize for *Drumroll*, his 1998 work in which he mounted three cameras on an oil drum, rolled it through Manhattan and projected twenty-two minutes of the footage on three walls of an installation. At Cannes in 2008, *Hunger* earned McQueen the Caméra d'Or, the festival's award for first-time directors.

Though courteous and accommodating before and after the interview, McQueen went on the offensive when my questioning suggested that his narrative method caused puzzlement. He responded with: "What's the question you really wanted to ask me?" A fast talker whose words have trouble keeping up with his thoughts, McQueen retracted a premature dismissal of one question once he comprehended it fully and other times broke into contrarian answers while questions still were being asked. I met with McQueen in Beverly Hills days before *Hunger*'s Academy Award–qualifying run in December.

Chris Tinkham: I wanted to ask about the amount of information that the film gives the viewer. When I say information, not only do I mean historical, but I also mean conventional storytelling components like character names. Did your prior film work set any kind of precedent for how much information you would give the viewer in *Hunger*?

Steve McQueen: It's a situation where, if it works, that's the only rule one has to go by. I don't know about conventional. What does conventional give you? I don't know. I don't know what conventional is; I'm not thinking that way. I'm just making something which I think works, and it's all about communicating with the audience. So it's about setting 'em up as far as the context of where we are, and then letting it go. It's human beings in a certain situation, and how we present it is in a way of how one can communicate with who is on screen. What I mean by that is it's all about what works. If it works, it works.

CT: If a viewer's sitting in a theatre and asking, "Who's that? What's his name? What's his significance?," should they just put that aside?

SM: Not at all. Far from it. I think I answer all those questions in the movie. Is anyone confused about who's who and what's what in the movie?

CT: I did not know that the boy watching over Bobby Sands on his deathbed was a twelve-year-old Bobby. I thought maybe he was Bobby's younger brother or a relative.

SM: Until you heard the kids saying "Bobby, Bobby!" and you had the context of him running in the woods. Again, construction of a movie is about holding back and giving, and you get rewarded if you trust the director. That's what the movie's about. It's all about how one can actually use film in a way that can engross people. Film's only 115 years old. It's still in its nappies. What we can do with a film and what we can actually communicate with a film is up for grabs.

CT: Going back to the twelve-year-old Bobby, I was wondering if that was a connection to your boyhood impressions of him, because he's close to the same age as you were when Sands died.

SM: I never thought of that, actually. I never thought of that at all. But it's a good one. Possibly. Interesting. No one's ever asked that question. No one's ever said that to me before. That's ten points to you. Good question. Very good, I'll use it.

CT: The scene between Bobby and the priest, did that evolve strictly from the writing—

SM: —from an idea I had. The whole idea of Connors and McEnroe in the Wimbledon final, two people doing the same thing but differently—one is a serve-volleyer, one's a baseliner—and that confrontation, reasons to live and reasons to die, and having that conversation where it's played out. And as far as information is concerned, all of it is there as well, to get more than you ever need in that. It's overflowing, it's coming out of your ears as such. And also, it's where the tension is. It's the ultimate conversation in life: the reasons to live and reasons to die.

CT: Did shooting the long conversation with a static camera influence the writing of it, or was all the dialogue set beforehand?

SM: Listen, it's all about the idea. Once you have the idea, you go for it. Then you have to shoot it how it's being dictated to you. You have to go in there with an idea of how you want the film to be. And it might change, that's the idea. That was the first scene that I wrote, of course [*laughs*]. So other things we did in the beginning sort of came to that. But that, in some ways, was the bridge from the life to the death. That was the bridge into the last part of the film, the last twenty minutes or such. And you can break them up into twenty-minute rolls if you want.

CT: Could the shot have gone on longer? Was the length of the scene influenced by the length of the film roll?

SM: Nah, no no. No. It was by total coincidence, for economic reasons as well. We used two-perf 35mm film stock, where it doubles the amount of time we have on the reel, 'cause ten minutes is one reel. When you use 2-perf, it maximizes the footage to twenty minutes. We're only the second film in recent times using the Arri camera modified for 2-perf to shoot in Europe. And they did that to sort of help people shoot more on film, because people were interested in shooting in hi-def, so they were trying to make it cheaper for them to do that, by modifying these cameras for 2-perf. And it's just a situation where the economy of means can help you, and that was it, really.

CT: Did you imagine different setups for that scene?

SM: Before going into that scene, you do think, "How can you shoot this conversation?" And then I came up with this idea because it was honest. It seemed simple but it's truly sophisticated at the same time, because often in this case, if you and I are having a conversation and we're shooting a film, there would be a camera on your shoulder shooting me, there would be a camera on my shoulder shooting you. You will not be having a conversation with me, you'll be having a conversation with the audience, and I will be having a conversation with the audience as well. In this situation, what one needed was action and reaction. You needed that tension; you need to keep that three-dimensional triangle going on. So therefore, it's similar to a tennis match. We're not doing that necessarily, but there is that sort of dynamism, where you could be agreeing with Bobby one minute or agreeing with the priest another minute. The balance is there, and that geography is there too.

So there is that sort of duel, but at the same time, I liked the idea of doing that and also backlighting them so you can't hardly ever see the fronts of their faces very well. I wanted a setup that was extremely intimate between those two characters, but at the same time pushing the audience back, the audience knowing that they shouldn't be there, so it's not clear for them. What happens is, their ears become very, very sharp, and their eyes become much more in tune. Their focus is heightened because also it's the first time there's been dialogue in the film. So everything is much more heightened. A part of your brain has been rested for a long time, and all of a sudden there's a cascade, there's an avalanche of words, and that's what makes it a tense, focused and—in some ways—exhausting conversation. Because it's happening in real time. There's this time for it to be awkward at the beginning, and then there's a sort of crescendo, and then you come down again, which is wonderful, because what we had before was film time, and this is real time. And the real time is given to this ultimate conversation about the reasons to live and the reasons to die. Everything's scripted; it's not improvised.

CT: What was the atmosphere like on set when you yelled cut?

SM: Amazing, because now it's apparently the longest scene on film. I think the longest one before that was *The Player*. It's seventeen-and-a-half minutes. When it was over, there was spontaneous applause. We did it in four takes. It was pretty amazing. Funny thing was, we were shooting next to a train station, so I didn't even have the power to say "Action!" when I wanted because we had to wait until the train left the station, knowing that there's too much noise in the room. What was wonderful about that was the actors didn't know when I was going to say "Action!" So there was that tension. They didn't know when it was going to happen, when we were actually going to go for it. And also, by the third take, the boom man had collapsed because he was holding it up. There was a beautiful tension in the room. Everything was vital; we didn't have a lot of stock, so there wasn't too much time to fuck up, excuse my language, to make a mistake. So there was that real tightrope energy in the room, and that obviously helped the performance because it is a very vital conversation. All that added to the atmosphere in the room.

CT: There's a scene when Bobby is on hunger strike and he suffers some spasms. He's nearly immobile but the camera begins to move about freely. It's quite a contrast, not only to the rest of the film, but also between camera and subject. What was the impetus for that move?

SM: Pain. Cramp. It's what you have when the muscles cramp. I think at that point he wanted to die, but you can't decide when you die; your body decides when you die. For me, that scene was all about a balloon trapped in a room, trying to get out. The camera for me was a balloon trapped in a room, trying to get out. And it wasn't ready to do that. It was bumping around in the room, but it couldn't get out because it was staying in that room until it was time for it to leave, which wasn't then. So it combined the camera movements with his pain and wanting it to end.

CT: In respect to Michael Fassbender's weight loss for the latter section of the film, was he asked to reach a specific weight, and was there debate about what would be appropriate?

SM: Yes. 58 kilos.

CT: Somehow you made a determination of what would be right.

SM: The doctors did. They projected his body-mass index and what would be safe, and that's what we did. He was under constant medical supervision.

CT: Before making the film, you spoke to many people who were tied in some fashion to the events in the film. Have any of them seen *Hunger*, and how has the response been?

SM: I hear they have and the reaction is overwhelmed. That's what I hear; I'm not too sure if that's true or not.

CT: After researching and speaking to those people, was there an urge to share everything you had learned or a struggle to streamline what you wanted to share?

SM: No. Everyone knows you can't do everything. It's a film. It's not a documentary, and even documentaries don't tell you everything. It's about how you get over the best impression of an idea through film. Conventional or unconventional, it's bullshit. It's what works with the audience. That conversation never happened, for example, but to me it was a necessity to be in the movie because you had to understand what the stakes were, but also why someone would be for it and why someone would be against it. As film is concerned, it's how you translate that to the audience in an experiential way. It's the only way you can have it, because film for me is that way. Similar—not as good as, of course—music is the ultimate. But it's kind of—it's not even close, actually, film, but it's as far as you can get, I suppose.

The Human Body as Political Weapon: An Interview with Steve McQueen

Gary Crowdus / 2009

From *Cineaste*, Spring 2009. Reprinted by permission.

Before receiving critical acclaim and festival awards last year for his debut feature film, *Hunger*—scheduled for a March 2009 theatrical release in the US—British filmmaker Steve McQueen was best known for his museum and art-gallery installations and exhibitions of short films and videos. Many of the earlier films—*Bear* (1993), *Just Above My Head* (1996), and *Catch* (1997)—are experimental in nature, minimalist in style, often silent, and characterized by unusual camera angles and points of view. The later works, more semi-documentary in format, explore historical and contemporary social issues, but in a resolutely nondidactic, non-explanatory, abstract style that aims instead at conveying a participatory, sensory experience of their subjects, such as *Caribs' Leap* (2002), on a seventeenth-century historical event in Grenada, *Western Deep* (2002), on South African gold miners, or *Gravesend* (2007), on coltan miners in the Congo.

Hunger, winner of the International Film Critics (FIPRESCI) Award and the Caméra d'or Award for Best First Feature Film at the 2008 Cannes Film Festival, impressively conflates those earlier films' interests in innovative aesthetics and social themes in an evocative re-creation of the 1981 hunger strike by Irish Republican Army prisoners at the British prison of Long Kesh, known as the H-Blocks, outside Belfast in Northern Ireland. This campaign, led by twenty-seven-year-old Bobby Sands, was the focus of worldwide media coverage, and, as McQueen explains in the following interview, made an indelible impression on him, as an eleven-year-old growing up in a West London neighborhood who was trying to understand the seemingly bizarre events.

After March 1976, when the British government's Northern Ireland Office instituted a new policy of "criminalization" during the ongoing conflict known as the "Troubles," the struggle of IRA prisoners for political status, to be recognized as prisoners of war and not as common criminals, intensified within the walls of Long Kesh. Their campaign began with the "blanket protest," since they refused to wear a prison uniform and demanded the right to wear their own clothes. This escalated into the "no wash" and "dirty" protests, the latter of which involved the smearing of their excrement on the walls of their cells. The prisoners' determined efforts to thwart prison discipline were met in turn by increasing harassment and physical attacks by the guards. As de facto political prisoners, the IRA inmates, who were generally despised by their captors as violent terrorists and murderers (although many of them, like Sands, had never killed anyone and had received unusually harsh sentences for relatively minor offenses) were routinely brutalized, almost as a means of retribution.

For viewers expecting a more conventional, expository narrative approach (such as Terry George's *Some Mother's Son* or Les Blair's *H3*), *Hunger* will be disappointing. Apart from a few basic facts about the Troubles and the struggle between IRA prisoners and the British government over political status, which are conveyed in some pretitle texts and a few overheard excerpts from radio newscasts and political speeches by Margaret Thatcher, the filmmakers are unconcerned about providing any detailed historical or political context for the events portrayed.

McQueen even refuses to describe *Hunger* as a "political" film, preferring instead to characterize his approach as "humanist." *Hunger* is a decidedly non-partisan work, not interested in scoring political points (unlike, for example, the tendentious approach of fellow British filmmaker Ken Loach's 2006 historical treatise on the Anglo-Irish conflict, *The Wind that Shakes the Barley*), consciously attempting to avoid any "simplistic notion of 'hero,' or 'martyr' or 'victim.'" McQueen has explained that his political aim with *Hunger* is "to provoke debate in the audience, to challenge our own morality." This the film decidedly does, whether it's to question the morality of a prison officer who routinely batters IRA inmates with his fists while they are restrained by guards, the morality of an IRA gunman who later assassinates that same prison officer with a bullet to the head, the morality of a riot-squad policeman who savagely beats defenseless prisoners with a wooden truncheon, or even the morality of starving oneself to death as a political tactic.

While *Hunger* will be attacked by some for romanticizing Sands as the film's "hero," any dispassionate viewer will note that the film is eminently balanced in showing empathy for both prisoners and warders. While it never excuses or rationalizes the prison guards' inhumanity, it does imaginatively reveal the corrosive effects—physically, emotionally, and morally—of their behavior on themselves.

While many of the film's historical references (e.g., the British government's duplicitous negotiations to end an earlier hunger strike, an ongoing IRA campaign outside the prison of assassinations of prison guards, et cetera) and visual details (e.g., the close-up of the "UDA," for Ulster Defence Association, tattooed on a guard's knuckles) will resonate meaningfully for British and Irish viewers, they will mystify the average, uninformed moviegoer. The deliberate choice by McQueen and coscreenwriter Enda Walsh to forego more specific social and historical contextualization could nevertheless be seen as enabling more universal implications for a wider audience. Many viewers, even in Great Britain and Ireland, for example, will readily relate the atrocities in *Hunger* to more contemporary prisoner abuses at Abu Ghraib and Guantánamo Bay. As screenwriter Jorge Semprun once explained his and director Costa-Gavras's decision to not specify the Greek context of the political assassination dramatized in *Z*, "Let us not try to reassure ourselves, this type of thing doesn't only happen elsewhere, it happens everywhere." Or, as McQueen himself noted in a recent interview in *Cahiers du cinéma* about the power of cinema to provoke broader debate, "A film can perhaps be the point of departure for something much bigger."

Ironically, for a film which otherwise utilizes dialogue very sparely, at the center of the neatly delineated tripartite structure of *Hunger* is an extended scene featuring an absolute torrent of words, an encounter between Hunger Strike leader Bobby Sands and a Catholic Priest, Father Dominic Moran, which provocatively broaches many of the key religious, historical, and political issues involved in the Hunger Strike. This remarkable, twenty-two-minute scene, most of which consists of one uninterrupted take, is powered by the performances of Michael Fassbender as Sands and veteran Irish actor Liam Cunningham as Father Moran (a fictional amalgamation of several real-life priests, including Father Denis Faul, a prison reform advocate and frequent visitor to Long Kesh, and Sands's neighborhood curate, Father Sean Rogan). Their conversation, which progresses from awkward small talk, to playful banter, to ideological challenge and counterchallenge, and, finally, to lacerating criticisms, is clearly the work of McQueen's coscreenwriter, the Irish playwright Enda Walsh.

This thought-provoking exchange goes a long way, in fact, to compensate for the sketchiness of these issues elsewhere in the film. In their fierce battle of wills, we can appreciate the decision of Sands—who felt personally responsible for the failure of an earlier hunger strike—to use his body, as the only weapon he has left, as a means of political protest against an intransigent British government led by the "Iron Lady," the recently elected Prime Minister Margaret Thatcher. We can simultaneously discern the validity of the arguments of the priest who, although he too supports the nationalist cause, sees the absence of any strategic political thinking in Sands's stubborn, self-indulgent decision essentially to commit suicide.

Although, politically speaking, the film focuses on "the body as site of political warfare," as McQueen has commented, it's also clear that his primary aesthetic interest is "to show what it was like to see, hear, smell and touch in the H-Block." *Hunger* is indeed most remarkable, in purely cinematic terms—especially through the all-encompassing visual perspective of its 2.35:1 widescreen compositions and creative use of sound effects, ambient noise, and a minimalist musical score—for conveying a visceral sense of what it must have been like, for both prisoners and warders, to live or work in the politically charged, savagely violent environment of Northern Ireland's most notorious prison complex. While *Hunger* doesn't stint in its frank portrayal of the barbaric atmosphere within the H-Block—including periodic beatings by the guards, the gruesome body cavity searches for contraband, and the vicious clubbings administered by a squad of riot police after a prisoner rebellion—the film is equally notable for its impressionistic details: the long stretches of boredom, maggot-infested cells, a furtive nighttime attempt to masturbate without awakening one's cellmate, the ingenious smuggling of messages and other items during prisoners' monitored meetings with wives, girlfriends or relatives, hallways awash in urine and cell walls covered in excrement that must be cleaned up by hazmat-suited prison workers, and the gentle medical ministrations of a hospital attendant during Sands's prolonged death watch.

In the last third of the film—which portrays Sands's hunger strike, his gradual wasting away, as his body consumes itself, and the agonizing death throes of his final days—*Hunger* strives for a visual poetry of sorts in its cinematic rendering of his failing eyesight and hearing and delirious episodes in which he hallucinates images of himself as a twelve-year-old boy (a poignant visual echo of a childhood reminiscence related earlier in his conversation with the priest). It's in moments like these that the humanist vision of *Hunger* truly comes to the fore, making a more universal statement about the human tragedy so often created out of these bitter, bloody, and intransigent political conflicts.

We spoke with McQueen about *Hunger*, focusing on its unusual narrative approach and its striking cinematic qualities, in September 2008, when the filmmaker was in town for screenings of his film at the New York Film Festival.

—Gary Crowdus

Cineaste: In preparing your screenplay, which deals with an incredibly complex series of historical events, you've explained that since you and your coscreenwriter, Enda Walsh, could not "tell everything," you need only "tell enough." A British or an Irish audience will be very familiar with these events, and will pick up on all the details and nuances, but were you concerned that a broader international audience might be somewhat clueless?

Steve McQueen: No, because as far as I was concerned it was about the essence, the essentials, and not to sort of tick off every box. One has to focus and narrow it down to get to the essence of it, and that's what I wanted to achieve. I think that by doing that more people can relate to it than by trying to convey the entire history of these past events.

C: What sort of research did you do for the film?

SM: I went to Northern Ireland two years before I met Enda, and did some research there. Later, when Enda came on board, we went back and did a week of intense interviews with hunger strikers and prison officers. You can't get that kind of information from any other source. I was interested in the information between the words. It was all about the details, such as guys waking up with maggots crawling on the floor underneath them, of how during the summer there were these horrible bluebottle flies all over the place, how it was freezing cold in the winter, or the details of living for four and a half years in a cell covered with excrement and awash with urine, and all the time surrounded by violence. You can't get that kind of information through books and I needed it and wanted it.

C: How did you conceive of the narrative structure?

SM: It's really a three-act structure. The only way I can describe it is that it's almost like floating down a river on your back. Basically you're initially taking in and familiarizing yourself with your surroundings. At a certain point it becomes a rapid, and your surroundings become fractured, the images become distorted. After that it becomes a waterfall, with a loss of gravity, through the slow death of Bobby Sands. That's the way I wanted to structure it. It's a situation where one has to be led in by a prison guard and then led out by Bobby.

While we were researching the film, we came across this comment by Godard that the only way one could film the Holocaust was through the eyes of a guard. Likewise, we wanted to find multiple viewpoints for our story in order to arrive at a better understanding of the situation, and not merely a stereotypical understanding.

C: One of the things that most impressed me about the film was the very spare use of dialogue, and in particular the avoidance of using dialogue for very obvious and clumsy plot exposition.

SM: I think viewers are much more intelligent than many screenwriters think. That's why, when I decided I wanted to work with somebody, I didn't want to work with a screenwriter but with a theatre writer. After many interviews, Enda Walsh was the one who came through because, for me at least, it's less about the narrative than it is about the abstract, which would have contained some kind of, for lack of a better word, truth.

In most movies, as soon as things start, dialogue emerges, and I wanted to have a movie where more or less the first forty minutes is in silence, so the viewers' other senses would come to the fore. In that kind of optimum situation, the brain isn't overloaded or overworked, so when dialogue does happen at a certain point, the viewer can focus on the dialogue in a very sensual and focused way.

C: In this regard, one of the film's standout sequences is the long, single-take dialogue scene between Bobby Sands and the Catholic priest, Father Dominic Moran. How long does that scene actually run?

SM: It's one seventeen-and-a-half-minute take of Bobby and the priest before we cut to a close-up of Bobby. We shot the scene on an Arriflex camera modified for two-perf film—you know, like Sergio Leone used for his Spaghetti Westerns. Usually 35mm film is four perforations per frame, but Arri—because more people are shooting on hi-def video and they want to encourage more people to shoot on film—modified this camera for us. It doubles the amount of footage on a roll, twenty minutes instead of the usual ten minutes, so we were able to film the dialogue scene in one continuous take.

C: How did you arrive at that aesthetic choice?

SM: Well, if we filmed this conversation we're having now, the camera would be shooting over your shoulder on me, followed by a reverse shot over my shoulder on you. In that case, you wouldn't appear to be talking to me but to the audience, and vice versa. What I wanted was a scene with two people who were having an intimate conversation with each other, where they were getting the action and reaction from each other. At the same time, we backlit them so their faces are virtually in shadow, so what happens is that the audience's ears become much more attuned, their eyes become much sharper, they lean in more because aesthetically we're pushing them away from a conversation about the reasons for choosing to die. When I first had the idea for the scene, I thought of it as like a Connors and McEnroe Wimbledon finals match, where both guys want the same thing but they play differently—one is a serve and volleyer and the other is a baseliner—so each has a way of how they want to win this.

C: How many takes did you do of the scene?

SM: We did four. It was amazing what happened in that room. Of course, the conversation itself was critical and essential to the story and the actors had rehearsed and rehearsed before that, but when the time finally came that they had to do it, the tension in the room really ratcheted up a couple of notches. The focus was intense, it was almost like a tightrope walker's situation; there was that amount of stress. But all that added to the performances in some way.

C: Was the character of the fictional priest based on Father Denis Faul, the Catholic priest at the H-Blocks during the hunger strikes?

SM: Well, we met Faul before he died, but we also talked to several other priests, so the character was actually an amalgamation of a number of priests involved in the events.

C: He really makes a variety of very strong arguments against Sands's decision to go on a hunger strike to death.

SM: Oh, absolutely. I mean, we had to go all the way. Both of them are nationalists but one wants the people for the church and the other wants the people for a kind of socialism.

C: Although the film is likely to be attacked by the Tory press in the UK as a glorification of IRA terrorists and hunger strikers, any dispassionate viewer will see that the film has as much empathy for the physical and emotional trauma that the guards, as well as the inmates, are undergoing.

SM: Absolutely.

C: I was particularly impressed, in this regard, with the scene where you focus on a young, obviously nervous and presumably more inexperienced member of the riot squad sent in to the H-Blocks. After joining in the brutalization of the inmates, including a particularly vicious beating and kicking, this young policeman is last seen, shaking and in tears, hiding in a corner away from the continuing violence. How important was that scene for you and why?

SM: It was very important for me because it showed the basic humanity of the situation. It's vitally important that we can reveal ourselves not just as brutes but as human beings in reaction to what we've done. Once you do something like that, it's not like you can just sort of walk away and forget about it. It resonates. It's almost like the frustration of it all—he has to get involved himself, he has to be one of the guys . . .

C: He plays the role but then he's repulsed by his actions . . .

SM: And by himself. So I felt that we needed to have this scene of him crying, after having kicked and beaten another person, in order to show these people as human beings, not as freaks.

C: Why did you decide to use the 2.35:1 aspect ratio, a widescreen format?

SM: It was Monet's water lilies. I was in Japan and I saw his paintings, and I rang my cinematographer and said, "It has to be this kind of frame, I see it now." What happens in that widescreen frame is narrative. What I mean by that is that it's so wide that when you put one thing in the frame, you've always got to put another thing in, and soon two and two becomes four. You always have to sort of put one thing in the frame with something else, so there's always this narrative going on within this full frame. There is also this linear situation, with the film going on at twenty-four frames per second and telling a story. But at the same time you can tell another narrative within frames, because the screen format is so wide that you've always got two or three things within the frame, which is just beautiful.

C: The soundtrack of the film is quite unusual in that it doesn't use a traditional melodic underscore but instead either ambient noise or a sort of astringent minimalism, which, especially toward the end of the film, tends to undercut any easy or manipulative sentiment.

SM: Well, that's my kind of thing. I want people to make up their own minds. I don't like music that makes the viewer say, "Oh, I should feel this now." It's not my cup of tea. Besides, the film is very lean. I don't want it to seem decorative or something that needs to be filled.

Sound in itself is music, and is enough to actually drive the film forward. I want people to become more aware of themselves while they're watching the film, and therefore the sound becomes a necessity. The sound of the police truncheons hitting the shields, for example, is based on a drumbeat. It's a violent, aggressive situation, and that sound raises your heartbeat, and it becomes this forward narrative drive—boom, boom, boom!—and it puts you on edge. So it's a question of how you play up the sound. Music sometimes can block a lot of things. Using sound can make people sensitive to themselves while they're watching the film, so it becomes a fuller experience, and more of a cinematic than a theatrical experience.

C: Films dealing with the IRA, such as Terry George's *Some Mother's Son* or, more recently, Ken Loach's *The Wind that Shakes the Barley*, tend to be attacked, especially by right-wing elements of the UK press, as "pro-IRA" movies. Do you expect, as a British filmmaker, to be criticized for glorifying the hunger strikers?

SM: I don't know if they will attack the film. I hope they will see the humanity of the situation. For me it's not about the politics. What's interesting for me about this film is not just about what happened twenty-seven years ago. It's also about what's happening now, to a certain extent, with Guantánamo Bay and Abu Ghraib. For me that's the main accomplishment. I think people, even those on the right, understand and realize that what happened in the H-Blocks was particularly shameful. I also think that if they see that the people who are looking after or guarding the hunger strikers are portrayed in a right and proper manner, then they'll understand the situation a little bit better.

C: One might say that the film's principal protagonists are Bobby Sands, as the leader of the IRA hunger strikers, and Margaret Thatcher, the "Iron Lady," as the leader of the British government. It could be said that *Hunger* dramatizes the unstoppable force meeting the immoveable object.

SM: Yes, it's two extremes.

C: Sands's position is conveyed primarily in the long dialogue scene with the priest, whereas Thatcher's position is conveyed in a few brief excerpts from radio broadcasts, including two of her speeches. Did you consider including some of her other more outrageous statements to heighten this conflict even more?

SM: No, I didn't think it was necessary. The two statements we use—about the denial of political status for the prisoners and how the hunger strike was an appeal to pity—were enough. I also liked how her voice almost came in like a vapor. And her voice, even without her image, is so strong, that it's enough. The fact that she's heard in the movie only twice, and we're having this conversation about it now, shows how strong and forceful and iconic that voice was.

C: There seems to be a very strong political component in much of your work, in whatever medium. Where does that come from?

SM: I suppose it's corny to say, but if caring about people is political, then I'm political. I am not interested in politics per se, I'm interested in people. Politicians make situations but I'm interested in how people respond to their situations. That's what it's all about really. I don't think *Hunger* is a political film, it's a human film.

C: Well, it's a political subject but you don't bring a partisan political position to it.

SM: One could say that Shakespeare is political, and absolutely he is. One could say that van Gogh is political, and absolutely he is. As an artist it's all about looking around you, at what's going on around you, trying to make some sense of it, and putting it in one or another shape or form.

Sex Addiction and the City: Steve McQueen on *Shame*

Jamie Dunn / 2012

> From *The Skinny*, January 6, 2012. Reprinted by permission.

It's never a good sign when your interviewee keeps their outdoor clothes on during the interview, especially when it takes place in a cozy bar, but I wasn't about to tell Steve McQueen, the burly Turner Prize–winning artist and filmmaker that he won't get the benefit of his tartan scarf/bomber jacket combo when he's back in the windy Glasgow night. McQueen is in town to present his extraordinary new feature *Shame* to a BAFTA Scotland audience at the Grosvenor cinema on Ashton Lane, and the forty-two-year-old Londoner is not in the mood for a long, drawn-out chat. His answers are short, sharp, and never sugar-coated.

Set in New York, which McQueen captures with the same seedy brilliance that Kubrick faked in his Big Apple-set, London-filmed *Eyes Wide Shut*, *Shame* follows Michael Fassbender's Brandon, a well-put-together young professional who seems to be living the high life in his flash bachelor pad in the clouds. Not only is he impressing his sleazy boss with his performance at work, he also demonstrates impressive skirt-chasing skills outside of the office. Brandon isn't a player making the most of single life, however: he's an addict, and the blonde he flirts with at the end of the bar or eyes up on the subway is his next hit. If she's not available, there are always call girls, webcam sex, and a masturbation schedule that even a fourteen-year-old with a lock on his bedroom door and a high-speed broadband connection would think was overkill.

"I'm interested in human compulsion," McQueen tells me when I ask about his choice of sex addiction as subject matter. "It's funny how we are being sold things all the time: told what to wear, how to wear it, what to do and see. It's kind of weird, isn't it? We don't have control over our lives. Similarly with addiction, the addiction dictates to you rather than you dictating to it, and sexual addiction was one of those things which I found fascinating because everyone has some relationship to sex—everyone."

Brandon hides his problems behind a veneer of order and routine, and McQueen opens the film by immersing us in this routine. "He gets out of bed, wipes sleep from his eye, goes to the sink, gets a glass of water, puts the cappuccino machine on, pees, masturbates. It's a rhythm, like tai chi," explains McQueen, "and within that journey, the first eight-and-a-half minutes of the movie, there's only one sentence being said. Slowly. One word. You get an idea who Brandon is through those actions, we don't need to give more information, any words."

Indeed, I would argue that McQueen's films are purer examples of visual storytelling than, say, *The Artist*, Michel Hazanavicius's much-feted silent movie pastiche that's currently a frontrunner in the upcoming awards season pantomime. Not only are large stretches of *Shame* sans dialogue, the first act of McQueen's debut feature *Hunger*, which re-creates the campaign by Republican inmates of Northern Ireland's Maze Prison to be classed as political prisoners, plays out with barely a word being uttered, leaving the camera to lead us through the brutal world of dirty protests and hunger strikes. McQueen also explored the notion of silent cinema as a video artist, from his wordless short film *Bear*, where two naked men (one played by the director) exchange ambiguous glances, to *Deadpan*, his 1997 film installation inspired by Buster Keaton.

When *Shame*'s dialogue does come, it's mundane, everyday. "When we talk, we talk a lot of shit," says McQueen, who himself rarely minces his words. "It's just to get through a situation or to make the person you're with feel comfortable. What we really say is not what we really mean or feel, and often in movies, the first twenty-five minutes, everything is about character—how they feel, where they've come from, their worst fears—but in reality that doesn't happen. What I wanted to do in this film is through the present reveal the past."

This description might suggest some British social realist approach, but McQueen—whose two feature films are characterized by extremely long takes, audacious tracking shots, and unconventional film grammar—belongs, rather, to our nation's lineage of baroque filmmakers such as Michael Powell, Nicolas Roeg, Peter Greenaway, and contemporaries Lynne Ramsey and Andrea Arnold. McQueen, however, doesn't appreciate being categorized as a visual stylist. "I don't put my stencil onto a subject matter." For him, it's the emotions to be communicated or the architecture of the surroundings that drives the aesthetic: "[the scene] has to inform me what it wants and I have to serve the subject, the idea."

The idea, however, is the least interesting aspect of *Shame*—the film's treatment of addiction and its protagonist's arc while battling his demons don't tread any ground that hasn't been explored elsewhere, from *The Lost Weekend* to *Trainspotting*. The film's strengths lie in McQueen's bold visuals and the ferocious performance from his go-to leading man, Fassbender—a working relationship that McQueen describes as "close, tight, and very intense."

There's also a third element that makes *Shame* fizz: Carey Mulligan, who plays Brandon's needy sister, Sissy. With a Marilyn Monroe–esque effervescence, Sissy sashays into her sibling's closed existence and wreaks havoc. According to McQueen, Mulligan also caused her fair share of chaos on set. "People think of Carey as a sort of English rose, but she's a tiger with teeth and claws—argumentative, disruptive, but all for the right reasons." Why Sissy so majorly messes with Brandon's mojo is unclear. Perhaps her presence unbalances the serial shagger's equilibrium because she gives him something to care about beyond his own sexual gratification? From their first scene together, which sees Brandon burst in on his uninvited houseguest having a shower, there also seems to be a heavy charge of incestuous attraction between the pair. Brandon says at one point "they're not bad people, they just come from a bad place," and another of the film's strengths is that what this "bad place" might be is left open for the audience to interpret.

"[Brandon] could have given you some long yarn about what could have possibly happened to them, but that wasn't interesting to me within the narrative form." What is interesting is that these siblings are dealing with whatever they are dealing with in two completely different ways. "Brandon is imploding and Sissy is exploding, she's the extrovert. That's why I made her a singer—she wants to let it out."

Let it out she does. In the film's most tender scene, we see Brandon listen to Sissy sing a mesmerizing version of "New York, New York" in a swanky cocktail bar. "Life is rather strange, isn't it? Sometimes the only way you want to connect with someone else is not through the obvious channels," says McQueen. "I like the idea that verse was the only way that Sissy can connect with her brother, Brandon, in the whole film; it's the only time that he actually listens." Mulligan croons the Sinatra classic with an exquisite breathless vulnerability but at an excruciatingly slow pace, with McQueen holding the heartbreaking performance in close-up for several minutes. "She's doing three things there: she's singing to the audience in the cinema, she's singing to the audience in her immediate surroundings, but also she's singing about her past and her hopeful present to Brandon."

As well as the song, the city of New York is also clearly significant to McQueen's film. "Your existence is framed by this huge city, whether it's Brandon's office, his apartment, a nightclub or whatever. It makes you feel quite small sometimes, insignificant, because you're faced with this huge mess of a city and your perspective becomes, who are you within this metropolis?"

Is *Shame* McQueen's commentary on our modern way of life, then?

"I don't know. It's just these windows [a recurring image in the film is of Brandon seeing his reflection when looking out of various high-rise windows] seem to frame who we are, frame the person within the city. They have this huge space, but they feel trapped. That's what this film's really about: freedom."

Interview: Director Steve McQueen on 12 *Years a Slave*

Matthew Toomey / 2014

From *The Film Pie*, January 22, 2014. Reprinted by permission.

Matthew Toomey: The Academy Award nominations were revealed less than twelve hours ago. Congratulations, I should say—firstly for your film and also for your nomination for best director.
Steve McQueen: Thank you very much. We were pleased with the nine nominations, and I'm very happy for my crew and the cast.
MT: Did you watch the nominations or did you wait for the phone calls and messages to start coming in?
SM: I did watch it live, and it was kind of surreal to be watching television and seeing your name called and your film called. It was one of those "once in a lifetime" situations.
MT: You've made two terrific features—*Hunger* and then *Shame*, my favorite film of 2011. They picked up their fair share of awards, but with *12 Years a Slave*, you've been thrown full-on into the madness that is the Hollywood award season. What's the experience been like so far?
SM: What's been great about it is the conversation and dialogue. Every Q&A I've been to for this film has felt like a town hall meeting. People are very passionate about the subject matter and there's been a huge amount of discussion.
MT: I heard your speech at the Golden Globes. The last person you thanked was Brad Pitt and you said this film would never have been made without him. Can you tell us about the extent of his involvement in the project?
SM: He's a producer who also acted in the film. To be honest, without Brad's clout I don't think the film would have got made. He's definitely someone that people listen to and respond to. He has a stature in Hollywood where if he says something then people listen. He was a huge part in this film's success.

MT: Did he approach you or did you approach him? How did you guys get together on this?

SM: It was his company. Plan B and Brad approached me, and we'd been having discussions since I made *Hunger*. They were very supportive and they asked me what I wanted to do.

MT: To talk quickly about the cast: you've got Michael Fassbender, Chiwetel Ejiofor, Benedict Cumberbatch ... but the performance that seems to be sticking with everyone is that of Lupita Nyong'o. I'd never even heard of her name three months ago. Where did you find her?

SM: She was a Yale Drama School student who auditioned before she even graduated. I saw a tape of her and then I asked her to come over. She was amazing. She's an incredible actress, and I was just very pleased to hear that she'd received an Oscar nomination.

MT: When you set out with a role like that, are you trying to discover a new actress?

SM: I don't really mind. I was very fortunate to find Michael Fassbender and Lupita Nyong'o. I'll work with anyone. It was just one of those things.

MT: With both *Shame* and *Hunger*, there was a noticeable lack of dialogue. It felt like that again here with *12 Years a Slave*. Yes, there are conversations, but it feels like no one says anything unless they absolutely have to. Am I right in saying that?

SM: Yeah. Most of the time when we speak to each other, we say a lot of rubbish. We never really know how we feel verbally. We never tell each other how we feel. We often use our mouths to get out of situations or to just get by.

I'm more interested in how we feel and how we act as human beings. Therefore, what we say isn't all that crucial. It's what we do that provides the evidence.

MT: So much of the story, so much of the content in *12 Years a Slave* was new to me. Watching it, looking back at this piece of history, I was just shaking my head and wondering how it happened. Was it new to you when you came across Solomon Northup's book?

SM: Not really. I'd done a lot of research into slavery before. What's been interesting for me is how many people didn't know about kidnapping and didn't know that African Americans lived free in the north. The fact they didn't know tells me a lot about the education of slavery in schools.

MT: Our perspective of events can change over time with the benefit of the hindsight and so it's remarkable that this book exists—written by Solomon back in 1853 just after he'd escaped—particularly as well because so few of those who were kidnapped could read and write. Aside from Solomon's words, is there a lot of other material written in that era that you could draw on to help create the film?

SM: Yes, and that's what we did. There were a lot of academics who had studied Solomon's work for a long time. We also went to a few museums and looked at artifacts and whatnot. It was pretty amazing.

MT: It's easy to look back at a piece of history like this and say, "Thank goodness things have changed for the better." But then I wonder if people in one hundred years' time are going to back at us today and shake their heads. Are wars, oppression, and discrimination something that we're never going to be able to truly defeat?

SM: I don't know and it's a sad thing. Will people look back one hundred years from now and shake their heads at the fact our clothes were made in sweatshops all over the world? I don't really know.

MT: And I have to ask, I'm a huge fan of film scores and I was curious about your choice to use Hans Zimmer as the film's composer. I always associate him with big, loud, epic action-type scores, but here he's a lot softer, a lot subtler.

SM: Hans is a talented artist, and I was very lucky to meet him and I was very lucky for him to accept. He wanted to be involved with this project, and I was very pleased.

MT: You've certainly got a fan in me, so I'd love to finish up by asking what's next? Do you have any projects in the works?

SM: I want to do a musical.

MT: Really? Have you got a particular one in mind?

SM: I'm still looking and trying to figure things out.

MT: I'll finish up by looping back to the Academy Awards, which will be held on March 2. I always like to have a punt on the Academy Awards every year so I have to ask—what do you think of your chances for the film and yourself?

SM: Not bad, but then I'd say that about everyone else too. One can never predict what will happen at the Oscars. Anyone that says they know later end up not knowing so I won't even try to predict anything . . . but please go ahead, have a flutter!

Steve McQueen and Donna De Salvo in Conversation

Donna De Salvo / 2016

Steve McQueen and Donna De Salvo in conversation for *Open Plan: Steve McQueen*, April 29, 2016, courtesy of the Whitney Museum of American Art, New York. Reprinted by permission.

Donna De Salvo: Welcome, and Steve, thank you so much for agreeing to engage in this conversation.

Steve McQueen: A pleasure.

DDS: I actually thought we would start kind of where we are, in a way, by just launching into a discussion about *End Credits* since that's the most current thing, and then talk perhaps about some of you earlier work, some of the different kind of—oh, don't, you look worried—some of the different sort of cinematic techniques that evolved in your work over time, how the crossovers happened with the feature films, and go through some of the points that I find especially compelling and so deeply original in your work. I don't know where this installation actually took place. Was this at the Schaulager or was the first time—

SM: That's the Schaulager, yeah, that was 2013. Well, the project started—it was just interesting, of course, what was interesting, Paul Robeson. The first time I heard about Paul Robeson was [from] my neighbor, Milton. He was a guy who always used to put newspaper cuttings in my door of whatever. I mean, he was a very interesting guy. I think he was just very interested in me, and one day I got this booklet through the door, and I opened it, and it's this Black guy, American, this Black guy on the front cover, and Welsh miners celebrate Paul Robeson's birthday, anniversary. I was like, who's this, a Black American in Wales? Miners? So I didn't know who this guy was, and through just sort of researching and finding out who he was, and Milton told me who this guy was. It was becoming very fascinating, and that was when I was about fourteen. And, of course, finding out more about him, and who he was, was interesting. It was just fascinating to me that no one—I didn't know who he was, even at fourteen. I thought, you know, he's such a major figure. And I just wanted to sort of find out a little bit more about him, and obviously I discovered these FBI files.

DDS: Yeah, I'm curious about how you got to the files. My understanding is they actually were online.

SM: Yeah, they were online, and classified documents [were] online. And, as you do, you sort of have these documents, and I got them enlarged like that, and of course I was scrolling up, as you do, next document, and somehow it scared me because sometimes you've got these things which were very blacked out, you know, dedacted [redacted], and there was just, they emerged from the screen almost like a whale sort of from the sea. It was very scary at night, and this thing emerging, and I was scrolling up. It obviously just fascinated me, this sort of process of viewing a document. Because no one here is going to read all the documents on Paul Robeson. But what you do, the whole idea of scroll, and the end credits in a movie, is you glimpse one or two things, you catch one or two things, there's time to catch things as they pass. And the whole idea of movement and catching things, it was fascinating, as well as obviously as the audio.

DDS: It's interesting, his is a great photograph actually of Robeson that's in the collection and on view in the galleries. Robeson was such an extraordinary figure in American culture. I'm not certain a lot of people now know who Robeson is frankly, or know about the government's torture of him. I don't know what else to call it really. Even two years after his death, the FBI was still compiling files, why I don't know, but that continued, and on his wife as well.

SM: Yeah, again, I think it's obviously the influence, how his legacy will spread, containing it, sort of finding out who has been influenced by what's going out. I think that obviously they were scared, they were very scared of his presence. I mean, until 1978, two years after he died. It's, yeah, it's odd to say the least.

DDS: It's interesting because I remember a few years ago meeting you in Amsterdam, and talking about doing something at the Whitney, and we talked. Actually one of the things you brought up was *End Credits*. I think it was in the context of another project that I was interested in doing that had to do with systems and structures, so that's a few years ago. It's quite interesting that it's come full circle in this way. And you could you talk a little bit about it, because for this installation, as opposed to the one at the Art Institute, you decided to also expand the files. You added more content here for the Whitney.

SM: Yeah, what I had before was eleven hours of audio, and there's five sort of voices. I think there's two male and two female. And we had eleven hours when I sort of showed it in 2013. We added ten now, so there's twenty-one hours. I mean, when we finally finish it, hopefully this year, there will be seventy-two hours of audio. That will be the whole compiled—

DDS: That would be the totality of the files?

SM: Yeah, exactly, the size of the files, the whole compilation.

DDS: And you've always used the same people who are reciting?

SM: Yes, always use the same people, so we obviously were running to fix that this year. I mean, it just costs a lot of money, I didn't realize how much it cost, so we had to stop, we ran out of money, and that was the idea, we didn't do it all in one go. And, of course, time, I mean it's a [real] labor situation. And just one of those things where the documents were just so horrid, and when you listen to things they talk about his wife and who she is, her skin color, who they have contact with. You know, it's a fascinating document of what was going on, and of course there were documents in the thirties as well, but we only got one from, this starts from '41 to '78, but it starts very early. There's this whole idea of conspiracy, letters, people being friends giving like postcards. It's incredible, it's all surveillance.

DDS: And some of it's quite banal, too. I mean, literally coming to this certain place, there's actually no reason to be following them when you read some of the material.

SM: Yeah, I think one of the things I love the best is the banality of [it], even this sort of dedacted [redacted] and certain sort of scribbles we talk about, and it's given equal power. As a document, as a piece of evidence, one describes the paper, the crossed-out confidential, you know, Roman numeral, blah, blah, blah. That for me was very important in a way to sort of address the whole document.

DDS: It's interesting because I remember a filmmaker once saying—it was Emile de Antonio—in a film he made where he talks about the Freedom of Information Act, yes, there's freedom but there's not always information. Because the redacted portions of it obviously are— one will never know what was in all of those. I'm curious when, given that this is in the context of *Open Plan*, and then we'll move on to talking a little bit about some of the earlier [work], but the thoughts that you had when you saw this huge space—because I remember something very distinct that you said, which I was so delighted to hear. You said, this is a cinematic space, the framing of the windows, and just to see this extraordinary eighteen-thousand-square-foot space without columns.

SM: Well, I think the space is about people in the space, definitely. It reminds me of an Antonioni movie in a way. It has a situation where the space and the people, and the whole idea of this vista, just this panoramic sort of window. And, for me, growing up in Europe, it's very weird when you live in the United States, in New York rather, and you've living on the fifteenth floor or twenty-first floor, you're looking out, it's very strange, because what happens is that you become—it's almost like a magnifying glass or a telescope being turned the other way. You become the one that's being sort of examined or looked at, or spied on in a way because your perspective from the world, and you are given this, how can I say, this sort of perspective. You are in the context of what you're looking at, and you become so small. It's kind of weird, it's very—it gets in your head. So just to see that happening in that space with the people, it's very—it has a very interesting sort of feel to it.

DDS: New York is increasingly filled with buildings where people are basically on view. That's a whole other issue, that's a whole other conversation I think in a way. Let's maybe go a little bit back now in history, if you're okay with that. Of course, this is *Bear*, which is a very, very early film—video—of yours, and I think one of the ones that you did when you were actually still in college, no?

SM: Yeah, last year. *Bear*, my God, that's a while back, 1993. What's the question?

DDS: Well, I'm curious in terms of the—

SM: I just don't want to bore anyone.

DDS: Well, we can jump over that one, but I mean these sort of early beginnings of a certain point of view that comes about in terms of the camera itself as an eye, if you will, as something that inserts itself into the space, and a power behind it as well.

SM: I mean, the questioning—a lot of questioning. Again, it was a situation where I wanted to have a situation of two equals, and it couldn't be the physicality of those two equals. So the sort of whole idea of, how can I say, it's almost like having two [*inaudible*] situation, but also seeing the physicality of it. There was no sound, so I wanted to have the whole sort of emotional journey as such from aggression to intimacy to whatever. And, again, you know, as a young man, you're moving the camera around, you're sort of investigating or experimenting, and just wanting to to come down to this sort of bare bones of things really, and that was it.

DDS: Was that a sort of natural thing for you in terms of using—I know you came out of art school, and so you also made paintings at one point.

SM: Yeah, again, I think that's more of a sort of evolution from the crayon to the paintbrush to the camera. I mean, always doing what was obviously with a perspective, but that was evolution, yeah. And, again, dealing with that those perspectives. I ended up with a camera because for me it was the sort of the thing—I think what it was is I couldn't be in a bloody studio on my own. I could never, the whole idea of [*inaudible*] and this canvas and paint on my own, it would just drive me bloody nuts. I think it's to do with that sort of communication with people, that conversation, that sort of being involved physically in a band, if you will, was very much important to me.

DDS: Well, these early films, though, it's interesting because you appear in many of these early films as well. So was that just because you were an available actor?

SM: I was cheap. Well, I'll be honest, I'll tell you a funny story. I wasn't meant to be in *Bear*. I got this guy to come; he didn't turn up. That was the truth, and then I got my kit off, and said, you know, let's roll the camera, let's go for it, so sometimes it happens, yeah.

DDS: And this one, of course, *Deadpan*, which is the one that, you know, has that reference to Keaton but also, and this idea that you talk about, about the expressivity of the face, which is so interesting. I've thought a lot about your talking about that idea of the face, and the expression of the face, and also the idea of, because many of the early films are silent films, and so much in Keaton's work the silent, everything has to be told. And I think we'll come to that—there's a clip from *Shame*, which just has a soundtrack but has absolutely no dialogue, everything is told.

SM: Is it the threesome?

DDS: No, I don't think I went—I might have gone with a "G" rating. I mean, I'm sorry about that.

SM: Okay, I'm sorry, I apologize. I really thought it was that because last time we did, movie on stripping. I want to go deadpan, I cannot.

DDS: So, I was going to go back to this—you're appearing here, but this is from the Schaulager, and I think one of the things I find so fascinating with *End Credits* is this kind of sculptural construct that you've made, and the way these works [move] into the space in that sort of way for you. The conventional filmmaker idea [is] the screen as being the only way to go. How did it come about, this idea of even making a sculptural space in a sense that is this totality—sound, the body—in the context of all of this?

SM: Well, I think film is sculpture. I always thought of myself as a sculptor just because you're dealing with three-dimensionality. You're dealing with weight, you're dealing with scale, and perspective. And I always thought of myself as a sculptor.

DDS: And the viewer's relationship to it?

SM: Oh, for sure—again, the great example is obviously upstairs, where you are as a viewer in comparison obviously to the work. It's very, very important.

DDS: It's interesting to watch people now, up in the space.

SM: I mean, it's all about the people. Of course, it's for the images we see, but it's just for the perspective. You see them sort of cut through the image in a silhouette and so forth, you're present with other people. Again, that's why cinema is so interesting because that's why I don't think it will ever die because you always have to be involved, you go to cinema to see a movie with other people. This is communion—commune experience. It's very important.

DDS: I was thinking a lot about also how works that you've made—this is *Drumroll*, which is an early piece that you made I think in Lower Manhattan?

SM: Yes, yes, yes, yes.

DDS: So New York and, I mean it's interesting: *Shame* was filmed in New York, and the whole interest in—

SM: America.

DDS: America in general or New York in particular? I'm not certain New York is like the rest of America, but that's a whole other—

SM: The question is what specifically, please? I just could go so many ways.

DDS: I think it's an observation, so we don't have to make it a question. But I was just sort of curious about this idea of situating your space because, for *Drumroll*, you are the one walking through space and creating this work. So, again, it's this sort of exploration of situating yourself in the world in this kind of way.

SM: Yeah, and what I wanted to do was I wanted to be totally—have a situation where I didn't have to think, all I want to do is roll this thing. How I rolled it—I mean, it's a situation often I talk to actors about in a certain sense of how as actors I want them to some point in time become almost like a sphere. So whatever they do, however they roll, it's perfect. Whatever they do, they can't make a mistake.

DDS: Is that about a sort of sense of embodiment and a—

SM: Yeah, I still call them [*inaudible*] acting and artwork, but it's a sense of being in a state where—I mean, again, I can only talk about it in this way, for example, if you're a bandleader or you're a musician like Miles Davis, and you write "So What." So within "So What" there's harmony and melody. So Cannonball Adderley or whoever can improvise within the harmony and the melody. They can't go out of it, they have to stay within it. They can do whatever they want within that, and that is a situation where you could roll, you could do whatever you want. There's freedom, but within the structure of the harmony and the melody. And I think what I was interested in *Drumroll* was a situation of being in the city of New York at the same time as having the situation where I didn't—I wasn't having a camera, and I wasn't being so studied, or having to focus. I wanted to be part of the city, to roll, to travel, to maneuver through the city.

DDS: So is it a dissolution in a sense of the lens and a kind of melding in some way?

SM: To some extent. Also the whole idea of just traveling, to move. It's a drum, it's an oil drum. It's sort of the economy, the whole idea of a price of a barrel of oil. It's just the whole idea of this motion, what makes this—I don't know, I wouldn't even say the world go around.

DDS: So there's a symbolic, well, no, it is: it's the lubricant that makes the world go around.

SM: Yeah, I suppose, it's a dangerous one. It can ignite at any time I suppose.

DDS: Well, that's very true, that's very true. I was curious, some of the influences you've talked about along those lines is someone like Bruce Nauman. I think you've talked about Nauman and Yvonne Rainer, and I wonder if you could just [talk about] how you came to their work and how you saw the dialogue between what they were doing and what you brought from that into your work.

SM: I think with Yvonne Rainer and Nauman [there] was this whole idea of versatility—you know, I think more than anything it was just about possibility.

DDS: Or that you could what you want to do.

SM: Yes, absolutely, and I just love the whole idea of with Nauman—it's just so much about sort of just this and recognizing it.

DDS: The psychological part of it, too—physical and psychological.

SM: Yeah, but the versatility, the possibility, and what's possible. And, again, for me [*inaudible*] I was a kid obviously imaging one's gone through. It's like you have to pass through so many things in life to sort of come out and be yourself. You know, Nauman as well as, Jimi Hendrix was one of them—you know what I mean, it's a passage. And it was very interesting to me because with the possibility of objects and material and what you could do with to get a specific kind of result.

DDS: It's so interesting because I think that in so much of your work there's the movement, but then there's also this incredible sustained close-up that takes place. I think of *Empire*—since I'm a Warhol person I'll throw it in there. And I think the way that plays in then in so much of your work—

SM: Well, *Empire* isn't close-up, is it—it's not close-up?

DDS: Well, it's not close-up, but it's a sustained view, that kind of single point perspective. I don't know how this one was filmed, if it was a single, just a single camera or—

SM: No, this one wasn't. It was a single camera, but it wasn't sustained, there were cuts in it. But your reference of *Empire*, of course, is a very monumental one in more ways than one. It's just, what I love about this is that it's so much about the double take, meaning that, okay, we all know the Empire State Building, we all know it. But then you look at it, you look at it, you look at it, and you go, oh, it's slightly—you really study it, you know, no one looks at it for that long, no one looks at it for that long, but you, again, we're looking at, it's film, it's not the actual building, so it's doing something else. So it's light, it's sculpture, it's reflecting, it's illuminating the audience, similar to upstairs, you know—the image is illuminating the audience, making them present, making them visible. Interesting, yeah, could go on forever.

DDS: You know, I'm curious [about] your decision to include *Moonlit*, the sculpture, of the French granite covered in silver leaf. We never got to really talk about that. So now I'm going to ask you to talk about that, since they're up there.

SM: Well, again, I was just thinking about weight, weight was very important. Weight. And to look at something and have the idea of weight. And, okay, it's granite, it's from somewhere in France, it's granite, and at the same time I wanted to, I don't know, there's a tactile nature of it I wanted to have, get on it. And at first I painted it in silver paint, and I did this and this; all of a sudden, oh, silver leaf, you can get this silver leaf and you could cover it, you could actually—it's very tactile, very sort of. . . . I just love the whole idea of working and molding the paper leaf around the rock. And then I was thinking, again, I don't know, sometimes you come, you get a tail before you get the head, and then I was like, okay, it's almost like film for me, because it's almost like black-and-white film, the three-dimensionality of it. You know, black-and-white film and silver elements to it. So there was this situation where I wanted it to have not two-dimension but a three-dimension[al] situation, and to have that sort of heft as such. And I wanted it to be something other out of—I wanted it to be presented with something because these rocks were presented to me, but also I wanted to sort of interact with it.

DDS: What do you mean when you say the rocks were presented to you?

SM: Well, I never made them, they occurred as such.

DDS: And you chose them, specifically?

SM: Yeah, you choose this one, this one, of course, but yes. I chose them, but they were there already and such.

DDS: I mean, they do have weight, and they're also an image. It's a very interesting combination of the—when you talk about the sort of detail, if you really study those and really look, and the fact that it's not, it's only lit by natural light. There's a kind of sense of something almost, somewhat romantic, I have to say.

SM: Again, yes, of course, but also moonlit and of course the light projected onto the—it's like a projection. I mean, I don't know if you've experienced—I've been to the West Indies. I remember my grandmother, there [were no] streetlights, and it was all moonlight, but it was so beautiful. This projection of light, this casting of shadows, this light which makes form, and somehow those elements were sort of embodied in what I was trying to do.

DDS: I'm very happy that they're part of it. I mean, to me, also the two screens—

SM: But then again, everything is projection, everything is sculpture, because everything is filmed to some extent because it's how we're visible right now is through these lights, we're being projected, we're made visible into the space. I remember, I did this piece called *Illuminer*, and it was me in a French Parisian hotel room. And I remember it was a nightmare. I had to do this work for Marian Goodman in Paris, and I had no bloody idea. I don't know what to do, what's this going on, it's a couple of days. And I don't know what came over me, but I put the TV on, and it was this documentary on I think the first Iraq War, and it was about the Navy Seals, and their procedure, how they sort of are chosen, selected. It was a very kind of violent American documentary but translated in French. You've got the American and the French translation. I was in a hotel room, as you do, you're naked, hello, hello, and I put the camera on top of the television, and

I just took the camera and I just point it at myself on the bed. So it's interesting because it's sort of this violence projected me, because then again what happens is it was a very early video camera, so the pixilation was struggling to sort of catch me, struggling to identify me, mold me, and shape me, make an image of me. So what was projected onto me were these images of violence on this bed. So it's almost like a Monet sort of nude, and on the bed I'm sort of black on this white sheet. It's almost like, you know—but it's color. So it's kind of interesting. It was just really kind of interesting that at the time, that these images, and now of course you get the sound and the audio and the machine gun going and whatnot, the horror or whatever. But my existence has, and all of our existence, in fact, has been sort of—how we are sitting here today, how we're having this conversation is because of the past, and a lot of the past is wars and so forth and whatnot. You know, a lot of unfortunate situations have occurred for us to be sitting here now.

DDS: Yes, yes. I mean, it's the irony of kind of a beautiful light on some level, lighting you in this room, but also absolutely horrific in what it's about. It's like this inherent contradiction on some fundamental level. It's interesting to think of *Moonlit* and the dialogue between those two. It would be kind of a great two-room installation for another time. So, again, these very close-up images to me are—this is one of Charlotte Rampling where you are basically putting your hand, your finger on her eye. I think there's an install, one of that.

SM: I think it's wrong to say that a lot of them are a close-up because unfortunately, sorry—

DDS: This is a still image, though, of your cousin, correct?

SM: Okay, yes, this is a still of my cousin Marcus. It's a piece called *7th Nov.*, and again it's about—he unfortunately shot and killed his brother, and it's just about what happened to him and so forth and whatnot. And, yeah, the thing with the scar on his head, as he said, that's another story. So that's that. But I want to say, [to] go back to close-up, because not all of them are close-up as such. I'm not interested in images—you know, in fact they bore me. What I'm interested in is what things can actually do, how they can actually translate more than anything else.

DDS: Talk more about this notion, though, of how the image bores you.

SM: I mean, of course they excite me, too.

DDS: You mean, the aesthetic, just the—

SM: Yeah, this sort of idea of, you know, it's about finding things which are—how can I say this—which tell you something more than what you see, obviously, and how it's about the stone that you throw into the pond. It's not about the stone—the ripples, how it affects. And those images can be the most banal images in the world, but it does something which is quite powerful.

DDS: Then all of the things in a sense are telling stories in one way or another.

SM: I think everything's a story. This bottle of water's a story—I mean, everything's a story.

DDS: I mean, because as things—I mean this *Western Deep*, which is a truly, and *Caribs' Leap*, truly extraordinary film in terms of the way you use the images. And the reason I showed some of those earlier images is particularly for people who aren't as familiar here with those—but that sense of embodiment, of the body—and I don't want to fetishize the body as an abstract concept because I think that can become very problematic, or at least I see it in that if it's just theorized in some way, because you're talking about specific bodies, specific people, who are engaged in activities—in this case, the miners doing these exercises to be deemed fit then, whether or not they can be, go back in the mine, and—

SM: It's what people want to focus on. That's not my debate, that's other people's debate or some people's debate, it's not all people's debate, thank God. But it's about, my situation's location. This is only a tool to do something, you know, it's not of itself.

DDS: But the sort of choice of narratives, choice of subjects, let's get onto that. I mean, the specifics of something like this, or in *Gravesend*, you know, now we're getting even to like back to *Drumroll* in a sense, that the subject here is also something that makes the world run, but that takes a human capital, if you will, in order to get it out into the world. And so those subjects throughout your work are, I think, deeply meaningful to you.

SM: I mean, just to give a little bit of context to these images is that I was interested in working in the Congo, and I was interested in this material called coltan. If you don't know what coltan is, it's in most of your bags or pockets. It's a conductor, it doesn't overheat, it's in every mobile phone, every digital, electronical piece of equipment. And the majority of that mineral is found in the Congo. And it was for me very similar to the rubber situation with King Leopold II, the king of Belgium who basically owned the Congo and went into the Congo and started sort of harvesting all this rubber. And if you didn't get enough rubber, as a native person, you didn't gather enough rubber, you got a hand cut off. So, for me, it was this rush, it was also the parallel situation of technology, the whole idea of the motorcar, the bicycle, the conveyor belt, those things which needed rubber, and now these things which need coltan, if it's a mobile phone or PlayStation, whatever. I mean, it's crazy. There was this time where—what was it, the price of coltan went up to a certain amount of time, so doctors and lawyers were leaving hats and canes behind and going in the bush to shallow mine the stuff because PlayStation 2 was coming out, and they stockpiled. It was crazy. So the parallel for me with coltan was very sort of fascinating in the same way of the Industrial Revolution and now the Digital Revolution. So I went into the Congo and, as you do, during not the safest period of time and sort of just was interested in the mining and how this thing goes, you know, the raw mining with hands and shovels to it was in your pocket right now. So that's narrative.

DDS: When you went into those situations—in terms of, I mean just the pragmatics actually of access to these places, and—

SM: Oh, it was crazy.

DDS: Yeah, I mean what—

SM: Oh, you want a story, okay. There was this guy who was, he was—what was he like—he was like the guy, he was like Dennis Hopper in *Apocalypse Now*. He was a guy who was sort of into, he was protecting gorillas, but he knew how to get us to these mines. And we were not prepared properly, we had tents that leaked, we had about a seventeen-guy convoy of men carrying our stuff and whatnot, and we fly into the place called Walikale—look at it on Google, it's kind of in the middle of nowhere—and we walk for three days to get to this mine. And then we get there, and things happen and we start filming and whatever. And when the guys get scared because, you know, some of the gorillas were hurt, some gorillas were there and they were hurt, there were white men there so they're coming. So we had to, next day, we shot for like five hours and we had to get it out of there. Again, for me, it was like walking in Kew Gardens. You're always oblivious to things until shit happens, you know what I mean? And the guy was scared, he was crying, and then, but you know we just walked out, we got everyone, we walked out, and it was weird, it was really kind of cliché logs over rivers. It just, it was bizarre. I wouldn't do it now.

DDS: Really.

SM: No, I was—you know, you're young, you don't think of things like that. And then we got to this space near the border of Rwanda, and this guy says, "Oh, you were there, we cleared that area last week." I thought, "You cleared that area last week." Obviously he wasn't using his Hoover, but it was rough, it was rough, it was awful in fact.

DDS: I have a slide of the Venice project, can we talk about that?

SM: Which one [in] Venice?

DDS: This one.

SM: Oh, *Gravesend*. No, that's, what is that—

DDS: No, *Giardini*.

SM: *Giardini*, excuse me.

DDS: I remember so distinctly this project because in a way it was a surprise that you chose to film the gardens, the Giardini in the Venice Biennale grounds off season when no, essentially it's the complete opposite of when the art world descends, and there's a lot of Prada dresses and various other things floating around. I mean, it's a completely different place. And I was so deeply moved by the sense of desolation but also that there is a complete life that goes on there. I took it almost as a commentary on the art world. I don't know if that's how you meant it, but that's how I kind of came to it.

SM: Well, for me, I was interested in parks [*inaudible*] wangers on it. I was interested in parks.

DDS: Well, you did do a park in Amsterdam.

SM: I'm boring myself. No, but no, I was interested in these public spaces, in parks, because what I loved about parks in certain periods, of course, certain places, you know, people playing and the kids and having picnics and stuff like that, and it was beautiful. And at night it turns into something completely different. I did that on purpose. It becomes this sort of place of pursuit and to be pursued, and, you know, people—it's the whole idea of the cruising and other things going on there. You know, the homeless possibly move in there when everyone moves out. It becomes this different nocturnal, another kind of playground, another kind park.

DDS: A lot of feral dogs there, too.

SM: Yeah, yeah, again it's a home day and night, and I loved the idea of going back to, again, the obvious in some ways. Again, the obvious, okay, maybe that's why it's interesting for me because it's so obvious, no one does it, so I want to do it.

DDS: That's what was so extraordinary. I was privileged, I was fortunate to have been in the Giardini off season and have this completely different experience of it. And you focused even on bugs crawling on trees.

SM: To stray cats and this woman, there's a woman in *Giardini*, she has a shopping trolley, [an] old woman. I don't know if she's alive anymore, but she's been there forever, and she's there to feed the cats, for example. And why I sort of added these dogs—these are all greyhounds that were meant to be dead, always the rescued greyhounds. They were all sort of the racing greyhounds where often what they do is they hang them, kill them after. So I interested in also that whole idea of these saved—you know, they sort of, they're meant to be dead, poor animals. But also these dogs were very much, very Venetian because they were very hunting dogs for the well to do.

DDS: Oh, for the Doge.

SM: But I just love—they're like skeletons, these dogs, and their limbs are obviously like the trees. So we got a lot of these dogs together, these salvaged dogs, rescue dogs, rather.

So that was interesting, to be going there, and going to Venice at that time and to see people sleeping rough and whatnot, and to sort of, wanting to sort of curate some of that. So I was just interested in that sort of, that nocturnal-ness and also that off-season, that sort of, you know, discarded environment. And then, of course, come whenever—was it May, June—it's painted up, it's spruced up, it's all done up, and whatnot.

DDS: And no one has any idea that it has a whole other life.

SM: No one really cares.

DDS: Well, is that true? Yes.

SM: Moving on and—

DDS: I think it would be good—oh, well, before we move into, I thought it would be great to show a few film clips, but this, of course, was in your most recent [work]. Well, this was in Venice, the last Venice, *Ashes*, and such a deeply moving story about someone who you came to know, and—

SM: So young.

DDS: How old was he when he—

SM: He was twenty-four, I think, twenty-four when he died, and I, so what it was, I was doing this piece called *Western Deep/Caribs' Leap* for Okwui Enwezor's Documenta. And what happened was that I had this footage from the stuff I did with *Caribs' Leap*. I basically went to Grenada to film—Grenada is a western island where my parents come from. What happened in Grenada, first of all there was the Arawaks who lived in Grenada, and then there was the Caribs that came over from Central America, South America, ate, killed all the Arawaks, then after that the French came. And what happened in the specific area where my parents come from, where this was filmed, called Sauteurs, was that instead of surrendering to the French, the Caribs leapt to their death. So where the cemetery is, and where this obviously was—Ashes, this is called Sauteurs—and, of course, when they jumped to their death they put a Catholic Church there, not to commemorate them. Anyway, but of course what happened then was they brought in the Africans, the French, and then there was like a twenty-year war with the British, and the British came in. So what's interesting about these islands, they kind of repopulated like three or four times, and it's just interesting, the whole idea of flux. That was interesting in shooting in Grenada at that time, as well as what I was doing with the miners in South Africa. So this gentleman here, Ashes, was just this beautiful, just such a stunning man, extraordinarily stunning man. He was a fisherman, and he was deep-sea fisherman, he swam, dived for lobsters. His father—I remember his father very early on when I, because my parents still live in a village—had the bends, and of course they didn't have any decompression chambers in Grenada, and he died. I remember him very well. So Ashes was this guy who was a very beautiful man, very black, jet black, beautiful black, and he had these very fine features, he was stunning, you saw him with his blond dreadlocks. He was just amazing, like, you know, this person would walk past. And every time we—Robby Müller, who was my cameraman on this one.

Robby, he shot with Wim Wenders, and Jim Jarmusch, and Lars von Trier, and Robby is sort of a neighbor of mine in the Netherlands. So Robby would shoot on Super 8, he loved it, he came along. So this guy would always almost like walk through our frame. Well, we would always be over here, and then we'd see Ashes over there. I thought, interesting. We'd be doing other things, but anyway, I said to Robby, "Robby, let's take him out on a boat and let's shoot him, let's shoot him. I don't know why, but we'll take him out on a boat and then shoot him." So we did, we shot him, we shot him, we shot him, we shot him. And I didn't use any other footage, of course, for *Caribs' Leap* in the end. I just forgot about it. So I went back to Grenada, five years later, they found out that he, Ashes, had died. We shot this, this footage was shot in 2002, I went back in 2007, I found out that he had died. He had been killed by these—I mean, what's going on in Grenada, in the West Indies, is that there's island called Saint Lucia. And in Saint Lucia, you know, the economy's very, very bad, in agriculture, it's terrible, [*inaudible*] trade in Central America with Americans, it's cheaper, bananas cheaper, produce whatever. So these small farmers don't have anything to grow, so basically they grow weed now, a lot of them, and it's kind of semilegal there. And what happened was that these guys had this weed, and there's an island called Isle [*inaudible*], this little deserted island, where they stash some of the drugs. And, of course, Ashes, he's a fisherman, he goes out to these places, and there's a beautiful island. It's like classic *Robinson Crusoe*, it's a classic story. The young boy finds his treasure, finds his gold, which is bags of weed. He makes five trips to take all the drugs, the bad guys come and find who took their stuff, and you'll hopefully get your chance to see the piece, and yeah, he was killed quite brutally. So I found out he died, and I remember I shot the footage. I went back to look for the footage, and it was just shocking because it was very, and here was a guy—don't forget, okay, when we shot this footage, he was killed two months after we shot this, obviously I didn't know that. And what you have is this beautiful man, virile, beautiful, you know, naked to a certain extent, freedom, the idea of freedom, of moving towards this endless horizon of possibilities. So I did a piece where I showed like all the footage, they cut it, but it wasn't finished for me. I showed it in London just as, just on this side, and it wasn't finished for me. So I went back to Grenada, and I found his grave, and he was buried in a pauper's grave, you know—it was just a pile of dirt, and some other people. This is the cemetery. So this cemetery is, if you're not affiliated to a church in Grenada, this is often where you, in Sauteurs, this is where you're buried. So you see some mounds there, and it was a pauper's grave; it was a mound, no marking, nothing, there's a lot of them there. So his aunt, who I found, put a stone on the grave. I thought, "Okay, I'm going to make, I want to make him a grave." And that was it. So we shot that. So basically what happens when this piece, is you have one side of Ashes, and the other side of these two guys, people he knew, making his tomb, and that was it. And also what was interesting for me—I mean, you've got to see the piece, and me going on, I'm just telling you a story, and it's not the piece, of course, so it's completely different from what I'm talking about, but I just wanted to give the structure. And, of course, on that boat, you know Robby's not well anymore—Robby, he can't talk, he can't walk, he's kind of, he's not well, Robby's not well at all. So on that boat are these three guys, and the person who is front of the lens is gone, and the person who was behind the lens is not the person who he was anymore. So it's very interesting for me as a piece in a way, so I'm giving you some strings.

DDS: Let's talk about the difference also, I mean, I think obviously the feature films that you have done—

SM: I'll say one thing about this piece. So what's interesting about this piece, of course, you go from one side of the screen to this beautiful guy smiling and there's everything, and you get to the other side of the screen where his death is, his future, his—I don't know what you want to call it, whatever—

DDS: It's truly blue skies one side.

SM: Yeah, it's very disorientating in a way because it's finality and possibility. Anyway, sorry.

DDS: No, not at all. I mean, you're alive, you're dead. It's the most profound thing.

SM: It's life.

DDS: It's life. But let's just talk a bit about these feature films. So I have a few clips—I don't know which one we're going to look at—

SM: Oh, stay for the clips. Oh, you're going, yeah, go on. I'll stay for the movie [*laughter*].

DDS: I have one from *Shame*, one from *Hunger*, and one from *12 Years a Slave*. So, let's look at the one from *Shame*. They have to key it up there for a minute.

SM: I don't even know what—

DDS: It's the subway scene.

SM: Oh, okay.

[*Film clip from* Shame *plays.*]

DDS: That's just such an extraordinary film. That's when they first meet, and that whole thing of being done completely without any dialogue. The dialogue is in their expression. But, you know, could you talk a bit about basically working in this context as opposed to the way we've worked upstairs, let's say. I mean, now you're working with a crew of people, you're always collaborative, but this is a whole other kind of level of collaboration and control.

SM: Well, I don't see the difference so much. I mean, of course it's different if one is narrative and one is abstract, to a certain extent, fractured, whatever. It's just, as I said before, I've said it a thousand times, it's like writing a novel and writing poetry—you know, using the same tools to do different things, that's all. I like people, so it's easy.

DDS: You make it sound so effortless, Steve.

SM: I don't really want to sort of go into that. It's not that, I mean it's not that compli[cated]. I don't want it make [*inaudible*] easy, I don't want to make it that, you know, I can make it very mysterious as most other people do, but it's not that, it's not that way at all.

DDS: No, I mean, I can see from working with you, and one of the great joys of working with you on this project has been this kind of way in which you sort of process things, and you're incredibly open to listening, and then you sort of come to the decision. And it's been, as a curator, wonderful to work with someone who works in that way, who sees, and like you're in it in this incredible way, but you're processing like, this is all these things are going through. And then you come to this place which seems like resolution—I mean, I don't know, maybe beyond it, maybe you're not expressing any anxiety you have and you've controlled that very well, but there does seem to be a decision that gets made, and you've come to it in some way.

SM: Well, yeah, you edit a lot. You talk, you get everything and cram it all in one room and all such in your head and you edit, you take it out, no, no, no, yes, no, yeah, okay, maybe, okay, no, no, not anymore. And then what's left is what's right. I mean, you know, there's a lot [of] information, but you just take it what's—you know, it's working very quickly. Again, I've been doing it for a while, so you know it's maybe quicker than it would have been when I was a kid struggling. Again, when you're in an art school for the first time, I've been told what to do for eighteen years as a child, and all of a sudden you've got your studio. I remember breaking down for two months, telling, asking people to tell me what to do, because you're being processed all through your life, you know, what to do and when to do it.

DDS: And film school didn't teach very much.

SM: Oh—

DDS: I know you've said—

SM: Well, film school, film school, film school was, film school. I mean, it teaches a trade, and I get it, but not everyone does things the same. Not every butcher cuts meat the same, and we were being taught the same. And, again, I was spoiled, I came from art school where you can experiment, you try to find your language, you experiment, you made mistakes. Making mistakes was the best thing about being in art school because you could experiment, and you can't make a mistake with things that cost—you know, stock and footage and so forth. We told you to put it in this way, not backwards. You can't throw the camera in the air, you know, this is, you can't cross the line. It's like, oh my God, and you feel like you're in a straitjacket, so I left.

DDS: I'd like to show, and then we'll start to wrap up, but the scene in *12 Years a Slave*, and talk a bit-I know, maybe you're tired of talking about *12 Years a Slave*; we're not tired of hearing of you talk about it. It's such an extraordinary movie, so profound in its portrayal, I mean none of—I can speak for many people—none of us had ever seen a film that portrayed slavery in the US in the way that *12 Years a Slave* did. And there's one scene, it's the scene of Northup hanging on the tree. It's very hard to watch, but to me it sums up so much about what you have brought, or I think you brought from your work as an artist into this kind of feature film. Do you mind, can we show it?

SM: Sure, and we can talk about it, yeah, sure.

DDS: Okay, can we show the clip from *12 Years a Slave*, please?

[*Film clip from* 12 Years a Slave *plays.*]

DDS: Real time, cinematic time in that, you know, I've never seen anything like that before.

SM: I don't know what to say really. Well, I knew before I did it, I wanted to do something which was sort of—you know, yeah I wanted to sort of put it on screen as it were. I wanted that to be some kind of image that would be in people's heads of all the people that were lynched. It was very important to have it on the screen for that, not often you have a situation where you have a movie where the [*inaudible*] appears and it cuts away, or it will be on for two seconds. Oh, it's so horrible, oh my God. No, let's deal with this, let's sit with this, let's look at this, you know, and it was for me a symbol of all the people in some ways who had been lynched. It was important to have people sit and look, and not look away, and not turn away, and having to deal with it. It was very, very important for me, yeah, very, very important.

DDS: It's an image that's hard to say things about because it just—and yet it speaks sadly to a condition that is not historic anymore, sadly, as it moved into history.

SM: It continues in different ways, doesn't it?

DDS: Yeah, yeah. I mean, I think so many of the things about your perspective on the US—I don't want to fetishize that because I think that can become a whole, I don't know any more about what constitutes the—

SM: Well, I think, you know, and regardless of where you are—and we're all Americans in that way. Again, I don't—

DDS: What do you mean?

SM: Well, you know, when I was growing up everything on television, everything I ate, everything I was thinking—so I don't feel a foreigner in any sense, shape, or form of the word at all. I mean, just as I'm part of Europe, you know, I'm a part of this world I live in. So, yeah, I mean, if you will, I've been coming here since I was seven years old—

DDS: What, to the US?

SM: The majority of my family live here in the United States, not in England, but some of them stayed in England. So it's not, you know, again this whole idea, I remember said, "Well, you as a Brit, you know, you're making this film." I mean, you know, it's nonsense, absolutely hogwash.

DDS: [*Inaudible*]

SM: No, I won't do it. What's up on that movie? No, what I mean by that, you know, my mother and my sister, for example, were taken to Brazil possibly or taken to the West Indies, and some of them were taken to North America. I mean, you know, they cut and dice people up like that, and Brit, no, I won't buy that nationalism, I won't buy it at all.

DDS: Well, to me, I think one of the great things about talking about things through the vehicle of art and artists is this exchange of ideas, and in a sense how things actually work in, not just in a network global way, but in a human way, in a deeply, deeply human way. So—

SM: We're done.

DDS: Done.

SM: Do we have one more clip—do we?

DDS: Yeah, you want to show *Hunger*?

SM: *Hunger*, yeah, I want to see the piss, excuse me.

DDS: You want to see the piss. Okay, take the piss—

SM: Please.

DDS: Let's show the final clip, from *Hunger*.

[*Film clip from* Hunger *plays.*]

DDS: Wow, again, that's such an extraordinary duration, and Margaret Thatcher's voice coming in at the end, and the reality of what it all is.

SM: Oh, yeah, I wanted that burden, I wanted that weight, I wanted it very much, I wanted it, very much. And I can't tell you why, but I wanted that weight, I wanted that burden. And it was something I remember as a kid, like I said, on TV—there was this image of this guy and a number underneath his name, excuse me, and a number underneath his image. And I asked my mother, "Why does that guy have his number underneath his image, was it his age"? No, it was how many days this person had been on a hunger strike. And I remember thinking about it and thinking that's kind of interesting in a way, of in order to be heard one doesn't eat, so it was very oral. And of course, it always stuck in my head, and years later [I did] research on this, and I remember Pauline Kael did an interview with Godard two days after Bobby Sands died, in fact, it was at MoMA.

And Godard said, the reason why the Baader-Meinhof and Bobby Sands are important is because they're childish. Of course, and Godard [*inaudible*], what the hell are you talking about, what is this shite? And somehow I sort of equated that to—and I imagine everyone here has had that experience—where you're sitting at a table, and your mother and father says to you, as a child, you're not leaving this table until you finish your food, you're not leaving this table. And the only power you have as a child is to refuse to eat. What time you go to bed, what clothes you wear, et cetera, et cetera, is sort of dictated to you by your parents, but the only power one has is to refrain from eating. And after a certain time, of course, your mom or your dad says to you, "Okay, leave the table, go upstairs, go to bed now," whatever they say, but that's the only power you have, in a way. You know, everything has been dictated to you, the clothes you wear, the food you eat, school, what to do, how to do it, et cetera, et cetera. So it was kind of interesting for me to think that way, and I think that was the seed and such of why I was fascinated with this subject matter. I wanted to go there, I really wanted to go there. So when I was in Belfast with myself and Enda, I was interested in asking the questions which were the questions in between the history books. The words, the space in between the words in the history book. Was it raining that day, okay, what kind of rain? Was it spitting, was it hard, you know? When do you get used to the smell? When do you stop noticing it? When do you get used to the blue bottles in the summer? When you're on dirty protest for five years, you want to bring that person back you're interviewing back to those sensual moments, you know, the sound of the clanging of the door, obviously the smell, the taste, all those things that actually bring you are the strongest senses about our memory. So those were the things I was very interested in investigating, for some reason I wanted the burden of that. And I remember when we came up from Cannes, we went to Belfast, we had bodyguards and shit, and a lot of people were hiding under, death threats, hiding under chairs and sofas and the tables thinking shit's going to happen. The funny thing was nothing happened. The movie started a dialogue, it did; actually art can actually be a tool to sort of start a dialogue or be a catalyst for something, and that was the first time the British acknowledged what was going on in those H-Blocks, and it started a conversation. So I was very pleased about that, not knowing what the end result was going to be. And, again, it was mad, you know, how the movie was made and how it was financed. You know, there was a very brave young woman called Jan Younghusband who gave me money to make it, and I think she'd be given the sack, so had the movie not been a success she would have been sacked. Had the movie not been made in 2007, if it was in 2008, I always tell Michael, he would have been doing daytime soap, the economy, and after that no money. The film would not have been made in 2008, in 2009.

DDS: Well, I think that idea [of] starting the conversation, and what is the power of putting things out there is something that is deeply, deeply valued, and I know we're going to open it up to questions, but before we just wrap that up, I just want to say once again how thrilled, honored, all that kind of stuff, how deeply meaningful it's been to work with you and to have your work here at the Whitney and as part, not only just part of this project but part of this institution, this city, and a country that you feel very at home at and are part of. So, shall we open it up to some questions?

SM: Yeah, I'm just happy about the gig, you know, I'm serious. Okay, thanks.

DDS: You're so good, Steve.

[*Applause*]

Steve McQueen and Dr. Cornel West on Paul Robeson, Art, and Politics

Cornel West / 2016

Steve McQueen and Dr. Cornel West on Paul Robeson, Art, and Politics for *Open Plan: Steve McQueen*, May 1, 2016, courtesy of the Whitney Museum of American Art, New York. Reprinted by permission.

Steve McQueen: Well, thank you for coming. I just want to pass on the fact that Harry [Belafonte] is not here today and we are all thinking of him. And I just wanted to start the discussion. I'm very happy to have Mr. Cornel West, Dr. Cornel West, and the whole idea of May Day, the first of May, Workers' Day—I remember as a kid my father, who worked for London Transport, he was a builder—that was a very big day in our house. Because the political aspects of Workers' Day, and, of course, we had a national holiday on that day, but Mrs. Margaret Thatcher moved that day. She could actually do that. She could move the holiday so that there wasn't a Workers' Day, there was no May Day anymore.

Cornel West: [*Laughs*]

SM: That's another story. So, I suppose what I want to start off with—can we get the first image, please, of Mr. Paul Robeson up? So, I first found out—and I want to ask you after how you first found out about Paul. Because I first found out about Paul Robeson through a neighbor of mine called Milton. And in my area in London, West London, I was living in Shepherd's Bush, which was inner city, and then we moved out into the suburbs. And I think that was a big reason why I'm sitting here now. The suburb was called Ealing, and in this day there was a lot of West Indian people living [there]. And Milton came from Grenada, which is obviously where my parents came from. So there was a few of us sat there round. And he used to [put] things in my mailbox. You know, articles about whatever political aspects of the world was going on. He always used to [put] it in my letterbox. And one day he mailed me a pamphlet on Paul Robeson. And it was: "Miners Celebrate Paul Robeson's Birthday and Anniversary." And I thought, Welsh miners celebrate this Black American guy? Who is that?

CW: [*Laughs*]

SM: And I had no idea. And that was my introduction to Paul Robeson through these Welsh miners. I just wondered, how you did you first have that connection yourself?

CW: Well, I first want to say it is just a blessing to be on this stage with such a towering artist, Steve McQueen. Now I stay true, I stay true, and I want to thank my dear sister Donna [De Salvo], one of the finest curators in the country, for facilitating this. And we do want to access the spirit of our dear Brother Harry Belafonte, because Brother Steve McQueen stands in a tradition of free artists who were willing to tell the truth, and the condition of truth is not only to allow suffering to speak, but to stay in contact with the humanity of those that you are depicting. And that's a challenge not just for Hollywood but for hosts of artists across the board. So when I actually had the chance to become acquainted with Paul Robeson it was in the [Free] Breakfast program of the Black Panther Party [that] I was teaching in Jamaica Plain, I was then a student in Cambridge, [Massachusetts], and we had educational time for young people. And in 1950, we charged genocide. William Patterson, going to the United Nations, putting the United States on trial for the violation of the human rights of Black people. And that's very important, because it would be just fourteen years later when Martin Luther King Jr. would call Malcolm X, and Malcolm X called for the same thing. And Martin Luther King Jr. said, "I will join you, Malcolm." That is June '64. "I will join you, Malcolm, and do exactly the same thing that Paul Robeson, Du Bois, William Patterson, and others attempted to do." So, I said to myself, I got to know about Paul. Then I discovered I had actually seen him in films. But I didn't know as a young teenager that he was such a great, powerful, and courageous artist. So he blew my mind.

SM: [*Laughs*]

CW: He blew my mind! And then after that, of course, I just went to the library. I read *Here I Stand*—woah. Paul Robeson. Yes, indeed, indeed. And I read some biographical material. And I wanted to know, where did he come from? Who was this Paul Leroy Robeson? Baby son of William Drew Robeson and Maria Louisa Robeson. His father [was] pastor of Witherspoon Presbyterian Church in Princeton. He was born in Princeton, 70 Witherspoon Street. He had been pushed out by Princeton University and other elites because he was too free a Black preacher, . . . having been the major Black spokesman in Princeton. But he later on joined the AME Zion Church and [that] tradition, and went on to become a Black, magnificent pastor. His mother died when he was six years old, so he didn't know her that well. And his father would die when he was seventeen.

But his brother would end up the pastor of Mother Bethel AME Zion Church in Harlem at 135th Street, a little bit of a back street, near City College. And so it turns out that that there was this rich tradition in his family. His father went to Lincoln University. Born a slave, *twelve years* a slave. Born a slave but he ends up at Lincoln University. A powerful pastor.

SM: On that note, this image behind us is of Paul Robeson, fifty-six years ago today.

CW: Yes.

SM: It's a pretty powerful image, as these things go. I mean, Queen's Park, I've been there. Thousands of people. I think what for me was so important about Paul when I was growing up, learning about him, was the fact that it was all about travel, when you're an African American man who goes outside of America. And then he finds out, he discovers a bigger world and a perspective on himself. It's almost like the telescope has turned and now he is the thing which is being looked at—in perspective of the world—when it was the other way around when he was in the United States. Malcolm did the same. James Baldwin did the same. Jazz musicians did the same. And it was about having a world perspective in order to find out what was going on back in their yard but also what was going on in the world, and how they changed, how that really sort of impacted them. And you know, we have authors now going off [and] living in other countries because they want to have a bigger perspective. I was always surprised, I was always shocked, in a way, [by] how many people don't have passports in this country. And how many people do not travel to have more of a global aspect to who you are in your position in the world. Because it is not—it's like looking at your feet when you could actually be looking around you. And I don't know if you have any ideas about that?

CW: No, that's a powerful point. So very much so. It's very interesting, in certain sense, that Jack Johnson is one of the great symbols. We were just talking about Prince, I was just on Sunset Boulevard—they had a tribute to Prince with all the musicians from the Revolution, New Power Generation, all of those who worked with him. And Prince, for all his talk about Jack Johnson, that was his favorite figure.

SM: Wow, I did not know that.

CW: Oh yeah. Ralph Ellison. *Trading Twelves* with Albert Murray. Jack Johnson's hero. And of course, Miles Davis made an album in tribute to Jack Johnson. What was it about Jack Johnson globally on the international stage? The only space of fairness in white supremacist America was a boxing ring where you had fair rules, and under those fair rules, he's knocking vanilla brothers out. So what does that mean? It's an acknowledgment of Black humanity. It's an acknowledgment of Black excellence. It's an acknowledgment of Black mastery of craft and art. And when [he] first knocked a white brother out, there were riots all across the nation, including right here in New York City on the subway. Front page: "Black Man Knocks out White Man under Conditions of Fairness." That's subversive just on a symbolic level. So, it's Paul Robeson who becomes the most famous Negro in the whole world in the thirties and forties.

SM: I would say there was a moment when he was the most famous person in the world.

CW: The most famous person in the world?

SM: Well, because—let me explain.

CW: That's interesting. That's interesting, my brother. That's interesting.

SM: Let me pull that back in.

CW: [*Laughs*] Yeah.

SM: Allow me, allow me. No! What I mean, you know—

CW: Yeah?

SM: Paul sung, I mean, the language he actually spoke, but he [also] sung in eleven languages. He was in China, he was in Russia, he was on the front in Spain, you know, and in Paris. I mean, to be *intimate*, to be intimate, and what I mean by intimate is I mean you're singing a population's language and you're breaking their heart with your voice. You have to. And people knew him. I'm just saying [that] at a certain point, but maybe [it's] a bit of a boast. But not too much of a boast, I don't think. At a certain point he was ... *one of the* most famous people in the world.

CW: In the world!

SM: Fact. Kill me. It's a fact.

CW: No, you've got a strong case. You make a strong case. I mean, but given the fact that most of the people in the world were Chinese, whoever was the leading Chinese singer ... [*laughs*] could have been *the most* famous—

SM: Bingo. Bingo.

CW: Think of the numbers, you know?

SM: I told you, I told you.

CW: But it's true—I was thinking of FDR—usually the heads of the empire, those elites that are at the top, become highly visible all around the world for a variety of different reasons. But when it comes to that *intimate* connection, I love that you talk about that. It's true, because when he's singing both the language that he grew up [speaking] and then singing the twenty-some other languages he knew, he's making soul connection with people that FDR was not making.

SM: No, exactly. You know, when you think of Black America, when you think of translation, you think of reach, ... you think of musicians. And that pierces any barrier, any kind of moat, any kind of armor. It pierces it. And that humanity, that love, that versatility, the ability to do that is so far reaching. But now you have to bring your body there.

CW: Absolutely.

SM: As well as your voice. That's what I mean by Paul and Malcolm and so forth. Because when you're outside—you know, there was a famous quote about Paul Robeson: "Paul became African when he went to London." Because he was meeting so many international people there that he put himself into that sort of position, as an African, not necessarily as a Negro.

CW: That's exactly [it], meeting the African leaders who would move into powerful positions on the continent.

SM: Yeah, there was a score there.

CW: No, I think that you make a powerful point. And there's a sense in which the art and the music had already gone international and he was actually going as one of the representatives of it. Because the blues had already gone, the spirituals had already gone, the Jubilee Singers had gone to Europe and created the economic foundations for Fisk University way back in the 1860s and 1870s. And Mr. Europe himself taking his band all around Europe itself. Europe was, James Europe, he was a Black—

SM: I was about to ask you who James Europe is, was—

CW: He was a Black band conductor. He got there before—did I get that right? James Europe? I get that right? I want to make sure I got that right, though. I just got off the plane. So you can't—

SM: [*To an audience member*] Hey, is [there] in your arms, guy, holding that camera phone? In your arms? We will give you the tape, we'll give you the tape. You can [just] watch us, right? Okay? Good.

CW: What if he was taking a picture or whatever? You can get stuck on that thing.

SM: We'll give you the tape. We'll give them a tape.

CW: Ah, I see. I got you, I see.

SM: [*To the audience member*] Relax.

CW: But James Europe had already traveled with Black musicians all over Europe.

SM: Yeah, yeah, yeah.

CW: That's before Fletcher Henderson and the others—Duke [Ellington], Count [Basie], and Billy Eckstine. And the other great ones.

SM: So this quote—

[*On the screen is a photograph of Robeson's gravestone. The epitaph reads: "The artist must elect to fight for freedom or slavery. I have made my choice. I had no alternative."*]

CW: Oh, yeah. Look at that.

SM: It's on Paul Robeson's grave. And I think that this is such a powerful thing to have on your tombstone. I think it's pretty amazing. And in relationship to, again, I think we have to bring the [past] into the now, as always. In relation to unfortunate Prince's death, I think it's interesting [what] we were talking about beforehand. It's a very, very powerful statement, I think. You know, for the last twenty or more years, that's what Prince was talking about, that autonomy, writing "SLAVE" on his own face. I was wondering if you could talk a little bit about that, as far as freedom is concerned in so far as art, and what Paul represented in a way.... How do you use your art as a way to start a debate, in order to create?

CW: Absolutely. I mean, in some ways it goes back to Plato excluding most of the poets from the republic. That's one of the greatest tributes to art in the history of Western literature. Because anytime you're excluding poets that means they have tremendous power. If you dismiss them, they're just trivial entities. But if you exclude them, that's powerful. Well, Black music—Black art—has always been something that the powers that be had to keep close control over. Because it provides a foretaste of freedom for an unfree people. The artists, in that sense, are the vanguard of the species. I mean, Shelley himself says in the great revolutionary pamphlet "A Defense of Poetry" [that] poets are the unacknowledged legislators of the world. He's not talking about versifiers, he's talking about all those who [have] had the courage to use their imagination and empathy to conceive of an alternative world vis-à-vis the world in place. So, art has that utopian possibility and [the] power of allowing us to imagine alternatives to the present. Every status quo does not want people to imagine alternatives to the present. *12 Years a Slave* was about what? The humanity of a Black people whose humanity had been thoroughly called into question. And if you're living in dehumanized condition [and] then you conceive yourself as human, you have an alternative vision. You could make your life a work of art. You could produce an artifact. You could produce some art object. And in that sense, then, I think that the great musicians who not only create beautiful, beautiful sounds and beautiful portraits, and so forth, but then take a stand politically—that's a difficult thing. Why? Because the cost that you are going to pay is going to hit you so hard.

SM: I mean—

CW: Prince put that "SLAVE" on in 1993 and took it off in 2000. Phew. Well, he's talking about the cost. Granted, he did that after he'd made some money, so that was a good move [*laughs*]. But the cost that he had to pay? Phew.

SM: I mean, I always thought, [as we were] speaking about before, [that] after [Hurricane] Katrina I was waiting for a situation like Live Aid to happen. We [could have had] all these Black artists and the like come together and do a concert for that cause. I think that would have been amazing. I mean, and everyone at that point in time, you know, Black artists, white artists, [could have] come to do a concert or some kind of presentation in that same way. To be visible and visual in the world and to bring back attention to that spot . . . would have been tremendous. People would have thought that, you know, that people [would] have felt seen.

CW: Absolutely.

SM: And respected, respected. It's like when you see a homeless person in the street and you ignore him. But when you actually do acknowledge him and give them money—like, "Hey man"—he [or she] realizes that he or she is alive. "I'm visible. I am here. I am present. I am alive." So when you ignore [something], I just thought that [a concert] could have been such a great [event]. And I don't understand, it's, like, mad to me, how come that didn't happen. It was incredible. We spoke about that.

CW: I think part of it is, of course, the last forty years have been such a shift from a "we" consciousness to an "I" consciousness. It's about "me, me, me." It's about careerism, it's about cronyism, it's about nepotism, it's about making money. So that you have to have a "we" consciousness to even conceive of coming together. Going against the grain of individual careers to empower a larger community, including the community of artists. And that's what a highly commodified, commercialized, marketized culture's all about. It reinforces rapacious individualism, narrow careerism. And that the essence of careerism is what? Conformity. This brother [Robeson] was a nonconformist. At the essence of careerism is what? Complacency. He was courageous. And in the end, [given] dominant forms of careerism, when it comes to having to make a serious choice, is cowardice. He was the opposite. He was not a coward. Du Bois wasn't either. Alice Childress wasn't either. Lorraine Hansberry wasn't either. Charles White wasn't either. Harry Belafonte wasn't either. That's why I say this brother [McQueen] represents that legacy today. But in a certain sense, it's hard for you because you're out there by yourself.

SM: I'm pretty vain.

CW: You know? What other artists [are] coming around, I mean—

SM: What I suppose what I'm saying is that if everyone came together—

CW: Yes.

SM: Then—

CW: You have some power. That's true.

SM: I mean, if everyone just comes together, then, you know, that's it. Those the rules. You know? There's no ifs, buts, or maybes. You've got to pass through us, and that's it. I think—

CW: But how many artists defended Prince?

SM: Yeah. *Aha.*

CW: It's about the number of Black people in the National Hockey [League].
SM: Yeah. No, he was out there—
CW: He was out there all by himself.
SM: He was out on his own and everyone said he was mad. "What is this? And slavery? Writing 'SLAVE' on your face? It's outrageous." And look what's happening now. He was twenty years ahead of his time. Yet everyone is like, "Oh, you know, we can't put it on Apple or whatever." Tidal, or whatever debate is going on. It's kind of . . . it's fascinating. Anyway, moving on swiftly.
CW: You know, but the mirror of this issue is fascinating. When I think, for example, the greatest entertainer in the American empire today is Beyoncé. She's got control of her body, she's got control of her money. But she's no Aretha.
SM: Tell us why.
CW: Why? And the reason is because—and this is connected to Robeson, you see—the reason is because Aretha is a soul stirrer as opposed to a body stimulator. That she comes from the depths of her soul and the dark corners of her heart. The genius that she has of mastering her craft is there, but each performance she brings her big soul and heart and puts it on the table for us to partake and constitute a commune and a community. Whereas these days, in a culture of superficial spectacle, you have titillation and stimulation with bodily gyration. And I ain't got nothing against that, you know. I mean, I'm looking like everybody else. You know what I mean? I'm a Christian but not a Puritan, you know. But I also come to have my soul stirred—the way Sam Cooke and Johnnie Taylor and Lou Rawls come out of soul stirrers, the way Luther [Vandross] did.
SM: But can't you have both? I mean, Prince, I mean, talk about titillation and sex and God and everything, gyration and—
CW: Totally.
SM: Pumping and humping and—
CW: Absolutely.
SM: Funking, I mean, I mean like, you know, I quite like that. I quite like both. I mean *Lovesexy*—
CW: *Lovesexy* goin' on to something else—
SM: I love Aretha. But I like both.
CW: And it's true, but at the same time, though, Prince was singing "The Cross."
SM: Yes. Yes, true.
CW: Prince would sing "Mother's Child."
SM: [*Sings "The Cross"*] "Black day, stormy night." Come on. "No love, no hope, in sight." Okay.
CW: [*Laughs*]
SM: Because "He is . . ." [*laughs*]. Oh, Prince, we love you. We love you.

CW: No, that's real. I mean, Prince, he's like Marvin Gaye in that sense, you see. He's got sexuality, he's got spirituality, so intertwined together. So it's "Let's Get It On" *and* "What's Going On." . . . They're being true to themselves. When you are a free person, let alone a free Black man or a free Black woman, then you have got to do things that cut so radically against the grain, including your own community. Including your own community. Now that's what Paul Robeson had to do. You see, when you read the vicious attacks on this brother [led by] Roy Wilkins, Carl Rowan, and others, [the] vilifying, demonizing: "Since when has he made any contributions to the struggle? He's been only concerned about his career." And you say, "Quit lying, you petty, bourgeois Negros. You all are so maladjusted to a status quo and to Cold War liberalism." They were critical of Cold War liberalism, they were concerned about a critique of the empire. And they're concerned about critiques of poverty. And Martin Luther King Jr. would [receive] the same kind of response when he made the shift in '65, '66, '67, and that's why, when he died, 72 percent of Americans disapproved of him [and] 55 percent of Black people disapproved of him. He couldn't go to churches, he couldn't go to certain Black contexts because he was an "extension of Hanoi" given his critique of the American imperial subjugation and war in Vietnam, you see. That's the same tradition, same tradition in that. Yet now, of course, now that the worms have got him, everybody's in love with him. That's how it is, that's how it is.

SM: I mean, what's—

CW: We lack courage.

SM: [What] I'm also interested [in] about Paul was his fearlessness. I mean, my goodness, you know, the surveillance that he knew was being undertaken by the FBI.

CW: That floor [upstairs] is powerful. We saw that, we saw that.

SM: And it's just the fact that he, I mean, there was that time, I think it was '59, where, you know, he was in Russia, and [he] attempted suicide because of all of the pressure.

CW: That's right. Moscow, yeah.

SM: Absolutely, and one wonders why. No one knows what actually occurred at that moment. They [had him under] surveillance, putting false things in the press, et cetera. And that kind of hounding, you know, drove him to ill health. And I suppose I understand if an artist doesn't want to go there or just wants a simple life. I get it, I understand it. And I appreciate it.

CW: Yeah.

SM: You know? It's just, what are you willing to give up? What are you willing to do? It's a tricky thing, it's a tricky thing. I mean, I'm too [*inaudible*] like the next guy. And it's like, how do you pursue a certain kind of way of working or thinking in order to create [and] sustain your place as a human being? That's what I want to be, a human being. How do you do that? I've asked myself that question. I sometimes [want to] throw myself off [a] cliff because . . . and I don't even want to look at how I'm going to land. Because it, for me, it's a point where I have to, I have to. And I've told myself to throw myself off, [but] I don't know where I'm going to land. I think it's important, in some ways, to do that, to do [it] just because it might hurt, and all that kind of stuff. And you have to maintain yourself as a human being as well as an artist.

CW: Yes, yes. That's great.

SM: It's imperative.

CW: That's very, very true.

SM: So I leave my shoes behind. I love my shoes, they're—

CW: That's for sure. That's where family and friends and community play a crucial role.

SM: Yeah, yeah.

CW: You see, there is no Paul Robeson without Essie, his wife.

SM: No, she's amazing.

CW: My God. Unbelievable. Heroic, sacrificial. And of course, [their] relationship wasn't a pure and pristine one because no relationship is pure and pristine. They got through it with all kinds of mess and joy. . . . And at the same time, [she was a] truth-teller. But without her, I don't think Paul could have made it. Same is true without Ben, his brother, same is true without Helen and Sam Rosen.

SM: Yeah. I think Paul—

CW: Close partners.

SM: I think he was extraordinarily lucky because, I mean—

CW: Harry Belafonte too, [for] support.

SM: Yes, he was extremely lucky.

CW: Yes.

SM: And you know it was a situation, again, it was not a perfect relationship. It was, you know, it was an open relationship to some extent.

CW: Right.

SM: And I think also the fact that [*laughs*] . . . I think that's another conversation, I felt, because it gets to a point where, you know, it's desire, it's sex, it's all kinds of things, but at the same time, there's a certain sense of union, of partnership, [and] I think he [was] obviously extraordinary lucky to have his wife.

CW: But I do think that anybody who has the audacity to be an artist has to be on intimate terms with the despair, you know. Goethe himself, a great artist, he believed to know despair was to have lived. And Goethe knew what he was talking about, because he had suicidal tendencies up until *The Sorrows of the Young Werther* [before he] moved into his own, you know, classical Weimar stage. Meaning what? Anybody who looks candidly, honestly, unflinchingly, at the world in which we live has good grounds for suicidal proclivities if you have a sensitivity to suffering. The question is, can you fortify yourself in such a way that you can transform your sensitivity into a truth-telling? In which the despair is an integral element but it doesn't have the last word. So that hope and despair, that's different from optimism, [it's] not American optimism, that's Disneyland talk. But hope and despair. So when the blues itself—no optimism in the blues, no pessimism in the blues, they're prisoners of hope. Because they're wrestling with catastrophe. They're wrestling with despair. And I think this is true for any artist who wants to make that kind of move, I mean, in my own Black church tradition, we call it "steppin' out on nothing and landing on something." Meaning that you have to push yourself to the edge of life's abyss and the abyss is there staring you in the face. What you gonna do about it? Here comes the tradition. Here comes courage. Here comes community. Here comes struggle. Lo and behold, something comes forth. A sound, a story, a narrative, a poem. Or a life tied to a movement. And you get change and transformation. And of course, three steps forward, two steps back. Back and forth, back and forth. I mean, the last ten years of Brother Paul Robeson's life, '49, '51, [living at] Walnut Street at his sister Marian's in Philadelphia, he's going to 31 Grace Court in Brooklyn Heights, visiting Du Bois, both of them under FBI surveillance, and Paul's under house arrest. That's serious. The two greatest—at least Black male—freedom fighters in their own ways with their own blind spots and limitations. Under house arrest. Malcolm, Martin, same thing. Fannie Lou, same thing. That is the cost. And I'd say, I think it is a worthy cost, but very few people are willing actually to take it up, especially these days.

SM: Can we press fast-forward on the tape here?
CW: Absolutely.
SM: A bit of time travel? No, no. Back from what you just talked about to now. To Baltimore.
CW: Oh, yes.
SM: To, you know, President Obama, you know, the [current] situation. I mean, this has been amazing. His presidency has been amazing in a way. And what has happened in that time. And I have been just—I mean, again, take Obama's administration as far as others are concerned. I feel [that] at a certain time, I think, a certain artist, I had felt that they had the authority to make the work they wanted to make because there was this Black person, I really do believe that. I think, I mean—right, [in terms of] myself, absolutely, there was an authority that I could do this. And I think the reason why, the only reason, some reasons, why this film was made was because Obama was in office. I don't think it would have been made very easily outside of his office [sic]. And, of course, many sort of artistic endeavors done in the last sort of, in this administration. But also the

whole impact of Baltimore, the sort of, the ripple effect, and so forth, and in [terms of] what you're talking about. Could you talk a little about that?

CW: Yeah, I think that there's no doubt that there was going to be a number of consequences, both positive and negative, of something as historically unprecedented as a Black man and Black family in a White House built primarily by enslaved Africans. And so one of the positive effects certainly is a certain kind of straightening of one's back up, a certain kind of self-confidence, a certain opening in white power structures so that they're much more sensitive to peoples of color, but especially of Black folk given the fact that they're seeing a brilliant, charismatic Black man almost every day on television. So on that symbolic level that can never be denied. I think in many ways it's going to be one of his grand contributions. Now when it comes to substance, that's something else. When it comes to substance, that's something else. I mean, you got every twenty-eight hours a Black or brown person shot by a policeman or security guard for nine years and not one policeman [is] going to jail as a result of federal pressure. You see . . . something just ain't right.

SM: Well, it's interesting—

CW: There's no translation of that Black power into protecting these vulnerable ones in the way in which the White House protected Wall Street executives, you see when Brother Barack met with Wall Street execs in March of 2009, he said, "I stand between you and the pitchforks. I am with you, I will protect you." He's been true to his word. Not one of them [is] going to jail. All kind of crimes committed on Wall Street across the board. All they gotta do is just pay money and never acknowledge that they did anything. Well, that to me is criminal. Given in addition to the crimes they committed, you see. But if Jamal and Letitia get caught, gone. Gone. Police shot. Or we're gonna have a federal investigation. What kind of results flow from federal investigations? Hardly anything because our media is so market-driven that the cycles are so quick, it's over. It's over. Onto the next thing. Onto the next Trump, Twitter, or whatever it is. How to respond? So in that sense, you got the symbolic power [with] the president at the head of the empire. But substantially? Black child poverty rate up. Wealth inequality up. Black wealth 58 percent of what it was. So that's suffering on the ground but it's hidden and concealed in the culture of spectacle and image. It's all about what kind of image you project. What kind of spectacle you can have a person be distracted by. As opposed to focusing on the things that matter. I can imagine if Paul Robeson came back today—Lord, have mercy—and looked around, what would he see? He would see all of these highly skilled, polished professionals who are gaining access to unprecedented opportunities but tend to not raise their voices given the fact that one out of two Black children under six are living in extreme poverty in the richest nation in the history of the world.

That's a crime against humanity. But where's the voices? No, they're well-adjusted to the injustice. They're concerned with their material toys and success. Paul Robeson said, "Take your success. I want to be great." And to be a great man is to focus on the weak and vulnerable, even if you had to pay a cost. To give up your popularity for integrity. That's Robeson, that's Du Bois. That's Alice Childress, that's Lorraine Hansberry.

SM: Can you keep both? [*Laughs*]

CW: I think that you can keep both, absolutely. Because Paul Robeson still had money. Even when they took his passport and deprived him of his livelihood.

SM: Yeah.

CW: But that probably had a lot to do with Essie too, though.

SM: Okay.

CW: They worked that out together.

SM: So, I mean—

CW: They worked that out together. But I want you to be both successful and continue to do what you do. You use your success [for] truth-telling and witness bear[ing]. And that's very important. But success itself is fetishized in our market-driven society.

SM: So what do you see as success as such? As any artist or [in] any kind of situation or [as] someone in the public eye, what do you see as success as such? It's a strange word. It's very odd.

CW: No, success is material toys, trophy spouse, living large in some vanilla suburbs, high visibility, and think[ing] that your sheer success is a substantial contribution to the struggle for freedom. So that's the confusion of the gravy train with the freedom train. You can have all the Black faces in high places. And just as I know we got a Black president and a Black attorney general and you got a Black Homeland Security cabinet member, and yet folks still catchin' hell. Decrepit schools, jobs with a living wage not available, indecent housing, and then trigger-happy policing. And it continues on and on and on. And Paul Robeson would say, "Wait a minute. We need to have a critique of capitalism, a critique of empire, a critique of patriarchy, a critique of homophobia, a critique of anti-Arab, anti-Jewish, anti-Palestinian sensibility, and try to use our success to put a spotlight on it." And he did that in Spain. He did that in the 1960s—

SM: Absolutely.

CW: He was there with Martin in 1957, as you know. It isn't that very well-known, this was the first March on Washington, the earlier March on Washington. Paul showed up there on his own. Showed up there on his own, wasn't asked at all. It's like Curtis Mayfield showing up [at] the civil rights rallies with his guitar and his agent said, "That's the last thing you want to do, Curtis, your career is over. You know you wrote 'We're a Winner'? That's never gonna be played on the radio." It wasn't. Curtis didn't care. He showed up anyway. John Coltrane sat in the second row when Malcolm X spoke at the minister's Socialist Forum. They said, "Trane, you are losing your mind. You're associating with Malcolm X? *My Favorite Things* is going to be your last record." Trane said, "Hey, I'm a free Black man. I'm just showin' up with my horn. I want to see what Malcolm [has] got to say." And they put their microphone up to his face. And what did Trane say? "What did you think about Malcolm?" "Very impressive. Very impressive." See? Something like that takes courage. Because they'll cut you off in a second, in a minute. But he went on to be true to himself. And he's not the only one. Mary Lou Williams and other great artists were doing that.

SM: It's interesting, you know, I had it in my head [about Marvin Gaye's] *What's Going On* before you said Curtis Mayfield, before you were talking about musicians. I mean, I think that album, was it '71? Please, I'm—

CW: April 1971.

SM: [It] was such a tremendous—I mean, of course, I was only three. In fact, no, I was two. I remember it very well.

CW: [*Laughs*] I think you were just two.

SM: Yeah. Maybe, yeah. Of course—

CW: You were born in '69, right?

SM: '69. Two, even.

CW: [*Laughs*] Just two years old.

SM: I'm not doing myself any good here [*laughs*]. Anyway, I look younger than I [am]. Moving on. I mean—no, that album. I mean, it can't, it's interesting how one goes back in time to sort of get references to what [kinds of] things were happening. But I remember listening to that album for the first time, in fact I listened to it for the first time when I was sixteen, and it was such an impactful album even then.

CW: Oh, yes.

SM: So how was it then, as someone who was almost like a Paul Robeson, you know, breaking free of the shackles of Motown and doing what he wanted to do? Because I think "What's Going On" was the first tune—he didn't have the album yet—and then Barry Gordy was very much against it.

CW: Very much against, very much. But Barry Gordy did cave in . . . in the end. That's very true.

SM: I mean, [with] that kind of resistance at first, and of course, lacking in encouragement, he wanted to sort of go forth. I wonder if you could talk a little bit about that album, because for me, you're such a wonderful speaker about that kind of aural path.

CW: I think, sort of like Paul Robeson, they were sensitive to the emerging forces of resistance in their particular historical moment. I mean, there's no

Robeson without the Black Freedom Movement escalating in the thirties. In the forties, for example, when he called for the crusade against lynching, within thirteen months you had fifty-six Black people who were killed.

SM: Wow.

CW: You had a lynching in Monroe, Georgia. You had major, major attacks on Black folk in Tennessee and so forth, and Du Bois told. . . . They were sensitive to what was going on in the larger community. Same is true with Marvin Gaye. By '71, what's happening? 1971? Good God, since 1965 you get sixteen years of intense social motion and social movement. And Malcolm? Malcolm's dead in '65, Lorraine's dead in '65, Martin's dead in '68. He's writing it in the seventies and then, of course, his brother's just coming back from Vietnam. That's the second song on the album: "What's Happening, Brother."

SM: Yes.

CW: He's sensitive to what's going on. And he's being true to himself. By being true to himself means he's just not reflecting. A great artist is always a thermostat, not a thermometer.

SM: It's true, it's true.

CW: A great artist has got to shape the climate of opinion, not just register the way a thermometer does. Most artists these days are not just thermometers, but they're copying copies, a simulacra. Whereas Paul, he's original. Marvin's original. Aretha's original.

SM: I mean, what's interesting to me about what you just said, I mean, it always gives me goose pimples when I think of Paul, you know, these paths [that] were being taken away.

CW: Yes.

SM: And him singing in front of ten thousand or more people on the border of the United States and Canada. And in front of the workers, you know?

CW: Exactly.

SM: He couldn't be defeated. And what the art, you know, that's what I mean about piercing the armor and breaching barriers in order—

CW: That's right.

SM: Because the intimacy of that music brought [listeners] much closer to him. And you know, for example, he's singing on the Spanish front, the Spanish Civil War. The most amazing thing for me about Paul was when they took his passport and he [was still] singing to people. There was a concert hall in London, I think it was.[1] When was it? It was, I think, after the war, it was just after the war. Could be '46, '47, and there was a concert for Paul, [called] "Let Paul Sing." Okay? I can't remember the exact date. "Let Paul Sing." But it was the . . . weirdest concert in the world because Paul wasn't present. It was sold out, a thousand people in the auditorium, [yet] he was singing in the United States. But it was one of the first times there was, you know, the cable that they sort of trailed [across] the Atlantic?

CW: Yes.

SM: It was coming down the microphone. And it was sold out.

CW: Wow, wow.

SM: And there was this microphone on the stage. Empty stage. And, of course, they didn't know what it was going to sound like. It was like, oh my goodness, it was going to be terrible, whatever, and then there was this [*taps the microphone*]. "Oh my! Hello? Is Paul there?" [*taps the microphone*]. And it was crystal clear. And everyone was clapping when they heard him. And he was singing in, I think, I imagine—I don't know where in the States he was singing, in his house, to this packed audience in London [*sic*]. And it was called "Let Paul Sing." And it was amazing.

CW: Woah.

SM: Can you imagine? I mean, it gives me goose pimples *now*.

CW: That's true.

SM: That art can actually pierce armor, you know, there's no barrier to . . . of course they're going to stop artists or try to stop artists. And it's just one of those things where I just thought that, what's necessary now, I feel, is, and of course, what Prince made, [he] wrote this song about Baltimore or whatever. But the possibilities of what can actually happen through a visual order or work, in any kind of work, it's just amazing. Sorry, but that always gives me goose pimples.

CW: That's a powerful, powerful—

SM: And that connection to Europe, the connection to the outside, is very important. I mean, I'm British, you know, I'm [from] Ealing, West London, and I've been coming here, most of my family are from the United States. But this [is a] situation where one has to travel, one has to see the world, one has to understand what's going on in Paris, what's going on in Belgium, what's going on in London, Amsterdam, et cetera, to understand what you are in the context of the world—not just those places, but everywhere else. Middle East and so forth and whatnot. It's very important.

CW: Absolutely, and our dear friend Paul Gilroy talks about this in terms of the interplay between "R-O-O-T-S" and "R-O-U-T-E-S," so that the roots that you have allow you to dig deep in your particularity to get in contact with both your humanity and the humanity of others, so that the routes that you take have substance and have real content. Because you can end up with a homogeneous universalism way at the top that is not rooted in anything. And you end up with just a market-driven culture which is oftentimes just noise rather than song. But at the same time, [if] you dig deep enough—because he was deep into his roots. He's singing the spirituals, he's singing Black music, and then he's connecting it with other people's roots so that that human connection is made. But it's a human connection that is empowering so that other people can take seriously what's [written] on his grave, you see. Who is willing to stand? His book: *Here I Stand*. And not in a self-righteous way. I think Paul Robeson was wrong on "Uncle Joe" when he talked about Stalin. Stalin's a gangster. He's a thug. I know them, I grew up with gangsters and thugs. I got gangster proclivities myself. He's a gangster. But he saw Stalin as an option that was supporting decolonization in Africa and other parts of the world. So he ended up having these allegiances that oftentimes in his public language we know privately he was saying something else. So then in that sense you say, "Wait a minute, what is this Uncle Joe business?" You see? I want to be consistent across the board; you tie it to the wretched of the earth, they got the wretched of the earth in Russia, in the Soviet empire too. And the same is true across the board, but most importantly, he was willing to do something that was so unpopular that he got vilified. And then you have to really then defend him given the vicious vilification [by] J. Edgar Hoover who had done the same thing to Marcus Garvey, same thing to Malcolm, same thing to Martin.

SM: Well, the thing about gangsters or such, you know, I've met my fair share of dodgy people—

CW: Yes, yes.

SM: —is that they are so seductive. They're great, they just, oh, they just seduce you, they say, "Oh, and of course that's what happened with Paul."

CW: Yeah, yeah.

SM: But at some point, he found out what was actually going on. But there was a very strange situation [in which] you find out what exactly is going on, but to go back to the United States and say that means that, of course, you're wrong. But also it takes—it cuts, it cuts the foundation from your feet.

CW: Yes.

SM: So what you do? And it was a very unfortunate peril for him.

CW: Absolutely.

SM: And you know, all that work he was doing, because there was something that was very righteous [about] what he was doing. But promoting [it] as such, or supporting the situation, which was very difficult, how do you do that? I mean, I get [it], I sympathize. I mean, in hindsight—yeah, he should have done this, should have [done that]. But you know, at that time—

CW: Yes.

SM: At the height of Jim Crow, it was very difficult. And you know, what do you say? I mean, [take] what he said in Paris, and like—

CW: Oh, yeah. 1949.

SM: Can we get the '49 image on next? Maybe it's the next one after? We can go back to look at these. Yeah. I mean, this is—

[*A photograph, captioned "Robeson addressing the Paris Peace Conference, Library of Congress, 1949," is now projected.*]

CW: Look at that fire—look at that fire in his eyes. My God, my God.

SM: Could you talk a little bit about that?

CW: Yes, this is one of the turning points, because he was there in Paris where he engaged in a critique of the American empire and especially at that time you are not supposed to in any way engage in a critique of the US government outside, especially, the territory of the US government. Then he was lied on. Because there was a reference to Hitler and they said somehow—he didn't say that, but every major newspaper put that out—that he was comparing the United States to Hitler and Nazism and so forth. And so after that, my God, the cancelations, the vilification, and of course the State Department and the Department of Justice targeted him in very, very vicious ways. Not just taking his passport but ensuring that he could not economically survive based on any kind of access to a job here.

SM: I think also in that statement there was, I think [in terms of] how it was reported, but there was a situation, I think what was reported [was] that Paul was taking, you know, the United States [to] the International Criminal Court for the crimes of [what was] happening in the South and . . . the Jim Crow situation. And it's kind of interesting because that was a peril that was kind of similar to, say, [the] situation what happened with Malcolm, he stated the same thing. That that's what he wanted to do, he wanted to take the United States [to court]. I think that that was [a] huge turning point, when things get international, same thing—

CW: Oh, yes.

SM: —same thing with Martin Luther King. When it's local, it's okay. But when it gets to situations of global questioning of the United States [by] these people, that's when things got serious. That's [what happened with] Vietnam, against the Vietnam War.

CW: That's right.

SM: And Martin Luther King. That's when it gets serious. That's when things start, people's hair starts breaking up. It's not just a local affair, it's a global affair. And I think that's serious. I mean, that's pretty problematic.

CW: Absolutely. But Paul Robeson, I think, early in life, was taught that to be a force for good in a consistent way might result in you dying. And he was willing to die. He experienced it with his father already, you see. Early in his life, he experiences it at Rutgers [University]. He was the only Black student and only the third Black student in the history of Rutgers, valedictorian, was [playing] about thirteen different sports. He got his letters, Phi Beta Kappa, his junior year, you see. Then he goes to Columbia Law, goes to Wall Street for a while, but a white secretary refuses to take dictation from a Negro so he leaves and moves to

Provincetown and meets an Irish genius named Eugene O'Neill, who embraces him. Eugene O'Neill was a serious antiracist Irish brother. He brought him into the plays *All God's Chillun Got Wings* and—what are some of the others? *The Hairy Ape, The Emperor Jones*.

SM: How [do] you think that Paul's father was an influence? Because, of course, he was a preacher. I mean, I wanted to ask about religion in all three of these [figures]. You think about Malcolm, you think about Martin Luther King, you think about Paul, I mean, you know, and all [those] in between. I mean, religion is such . . . I mean, of course when Paul said he was an atheist . . . he [was under the] influence of socialism and whatnot, whatever. But how do you think that played a part in who he was and [in terms of the] others?

CW: It was fundamental. I mean, he used to give sermons in place of his father at the AME Zion Church. After he was kicked out of the Witherspoon Street Presbyterian Church in Princeton, he went down to Summerville in New Jersey. He lived with his father, one on one, because his brothers and sisters had left, his mother had died. He was one on one, you see. And they had conversations. He would give speeches and sermons to his father with his father as the audience. It's that kind of intimacy and that kind of equipping himself, preparing himself. And his father was profoundly religious. Now, in the end, he would certainly become agnostic and atheistic as a result of his own excursions in secular thought, in Marx and Freud and so forth. But the spirituality, [that goes] back to the roots because these roots [are] not just a matter of having cognitive commitments to religious claims, you see. You can be thoroughly agnostic and in love with Aretha, but ain't no Aretha without the Black church. All she does is just pick up a microphone and start singing and you're going to hear the tradition of the Black church music. James Baldwin was like that, agnostic. He said, "I can't write without Bessie Smith." Now, of course, Baldwin comes out of the Black church. He said he had to leave the church in order to speak to God and preach the gospel, which is often the case given the narrowness of the churches. But those roots are there, those deep spiritual, cultural roots. And they remain there for Paul Robeson. And of course, during his time in which he was under house arrest, one of the few places that would allow him to speak publicly was his brother's church, Mother Zion Church up in Harlem, you see. It was one of the few places he's an alpha brother, I'm an alpha brother, Martin Luther King, Donny Hathaway is an alpha, Du Bois is an alpha, all kinds of alpha brothers at times [get pushed] away—too controversial. And his best friend, W. E. B. Du Bois, kicked out in 1948 [from] the NAACP—he's a cofounder of the NAACP! Same thing: pushed back, isolated, marginalized. But sustained by spirit and sustained by cultural expression [despite] both of them [being] agnostics in terms of their religion.

SM: So, we've got a situation also now with a movement, a groundswell, an organic movement which I think is really beautiful: Black Lives Matter.

CW: Yes.

SM: It's such a beautiful thing. It came about through people wanting to get together to do something, and anytime something like that happens, it's not just—it is organized in [a] way that it happens through the ground, through the soil, up to people in the way that people are coming together and talking and discussing and organizing themselves. And I mean, do you have any contact with the people involved in that, and can you discuss them in relation to Paul?

CW: Oh, absolutely. In fact, we're having a big meeting in Chicago with all the major young leaders, not just the Black Lives Matter hashtag, there's a difference [between] the hashtag of Black Lives Matter and the motion on the ground. Anytime you become a movement, the corporate media likes to appropriate certain individuals at the hashtag level and incorporate them quickly. But on the ground, the ones who went to jail, the ones who still organize and sacrifice and so forth, that is very important. But keep this in mind, because it's not solely political. It's very much like [a] slave insurrection, like Gabriel Prosser's slave insurrection that began with the funeral of a slave child. And Gabriel said, "You know, I can't take this no more." That wasn't just political. There's a level of disrespect that certain folk reach, a point they can no longer tolerate. Michael Brown Jr.'s body was on that tree for four and a half hours with the dogs urinating on it and the mother and father standing there and couldn't gain access to it. It wasn't political in resistance. You can only disrespect us so much. We got to do something. That's what was happening. That's deeply spiritual. And cultural. And you got folk with a variety of different ideologies who know you ain't going to put up with this. This is too much. And you got folks straightening their backs up and standing based on those words, it's a great sight. Especially the younger generation, because the younger generation has been told over and over again, "Be like the successful ones at the top. The system works, all you gotta do is work hard." And they said, "That's a lie. We refuse to believe that."

SM: We got to do something. We go to do something. We got to do something. We got to do something.

CW: We got to do something, we can't just do it by voting for the next Black mayor and governor. What did [*inaudible*] say? "I voted for a Black president twice and still got shot."

SM: [*Laughs*]

CW: And that's just symbolic. It's structures here, it's systems here, that need to be contested. And of course, that's just the beginning of the conversation, more and more young folk. And not just Black folk, because you have a lot of white brothers and sisters, brown brothers and sisters, red and yellow, but younger ones. I mean, it's the Bernie Sanders crowd. It's the young ones on fire.

[*A film poster is projected with the caption* "Lobby card for Emperor Jones, 1933."]

SM: Oh, okay. *Emperor Jones. Emperor Jones.*

CW: That's Eugene O'Neill. There he is.

SM: Yeah, yeah. It's the example. We got to do something. We got to do something. I mean, sometimes it's difficult to do something in the situation of not having the power or the resources or the facility to actually bring something about in a sphere, we should, people, [but] we don't have the power, you don't have the infrastructure to do that. Or you are denied that. Because of your ideas or because of what you want to do. And that is a huge issue, how one can get ownership and control in order to sort of produce what they want to produce. Because often things are shut down because of certain ideas that people want to do are not seen or deemed [to be] political or deemed and perceived as something which is not, say, wanted, to be quite direct.

CW: Yes, yes.

SM: And I feel that control is the key, but one has to have that. But it is very difficult. Look at the studios, look at the cable companies, the television companies, the record companies.

CW: How did you work that out with your magnificent, artistic film? I mean, you got Hollywood with you. There's not a Black person in Hollywood who can greenlight a film.

SM: No.

CW: You got one in Atlanta who can greenlight it. But he's into *Madea* and things, we pray for him. And he's talented, he's a talented brother. But he's not part of the Hollywood system, right? And he's not known for telling political truths. He's talented. And I give him his talent, I love Brother Tyler Perry in many ways. He's come from a very difficult situation, and so on, but we have to be very honest and candid. Very honest and candid. You know, he's no Steve McQueen—and I said that, and not you. I don't want to get you in trouble. Because we love Tyler. But we got to tell the truth about that Negro, too. He's gonna be doing *Medea* when he's seventy years old. He's going to have to grow up sooner rather than later and deal with some of the other issues and so on, you see. But how did you pull it off?

SM: Good question. There was a dose of naivete, which goes a long way, and also a large spoonful of "Well, I'm gonna get it made. I'm gonna do this." Oh yeah, I never thought for a second it wouldn't get made. It didn't, I didn't, and a lot of people say, "Oh really, I don't know." Saying, "Oh, I don't think this film is going to get made." I was like, really, I've done everything. Up until now in my life, I did everything I've wanted to do. Up until now, I've done everything I've wanted to do other than *Codes of Conduct*, which was shut down [by] HBO. I've done everything, and that was a realization for me in a way of "Oh, people can stop me doing what I want to do." I was surprised. So I've been spoiled, in a way, but that's the norm. I *haven't* been spoiled, I've been living a normal life. So I've just realized that people can stop you from doing what you want to do. They can shut it down. And that is kind of, that's kind of—

CW: You've had some powerful voices saying no right in front of your face.

SM: Yeah, yeah. Absolutely.

CW: Oh, yes.

SM: It was interesting, it's interesting. It's interesting, that, because, you know, it would be great to work with a Black studio head. It would be great to work with someone who has the money or who can facilitate things, which actually can bring in revenue and actually get produced and made, because sometimes you're dealing with people who don't really understand what you're trying to do because they're not living what I live. And therefore it's difficult for them, but you can explain it and you could translate it. But at the end of the day, you know, they want a certain thing from you as, possibly, a Black artist, they have a certain understanding of what Black is. And that's a kind of Black they want to see. And you know, I—listen, I made a movie about a hunger strike in Northern Ireland. And you know, no one had made that movie. I made a movie about a sex addict, no one had made that movie. I made a movie about slavery, trust me, no one had made that movie. So when I wanted to do *Codes of Conduct*, it was for me the same thing, you know. "Oh, you know, it would be looked at in a certain way, but let's get it made. Let's see what happens." And it sort of stopped. So it's interesting how that can happen. I don't want that ever to happen to me again. It's [like], how dare they? But that's what happens. But it's their money, they can do what they want.

CW: But that means you got self-respect and self-confidence. Where does that self-confidence and self-respect come from?

SM: It's the norm, innit?

CW: No, no. Not at all.

SM: I don't know.

CW: Self-respecting folk? Self-confidence?

SM: Uh, I've never, I don't know, big pressure—

CW: That's a grand spiritual achievement. That belief in yourself in the face of the most powerful forces in your industry saying this film will never be made and you not only make the film but won an Academy Award? You think that's normal?

SM: I don't want to think about it. No, I do think it's normal. And it should be. No, no, I do think it's normal, and I don't want to make people think, "Oh my goodness, it's such a mountain, it's such a Mount Everest. How I could ever pass?" You could do it. Just basically get on with it. Write your story, you know. No!

CW: [*Laughs*]

SM: You have to think like that, otherwise you're going to scare yourself from doing it. It's that simple. If you have a good story, if you have a great story, and you can get stuff together, write a great script, or try to get it done, and actually make a great film, then that's it. It's as simple as—I'm sorry—it's simple as that. It has to be as simple as that. Otherwise, you'll be looking [around] all the time scaring yourself. No, it's simple. It has to be. I'm sorry. I know it sounds very naïve in that way, but that's how I got it made. So take from it. It's that simple. You got it, do it, end of story. Do it, you know? What do you say before? What do you say before? We got to do something.

CW: You got to—

SM: What was the mantra? What was it? I can't remember. Help me, people. Listen, what did he say?

CW: [*Laughs*]

SM: We got to do something, yeah? That was it. Yeah. We got to do something? Do it. Don't think of it as something which is unreachable or, "Oh my goodness," just do it. I'm sorry, but it's that simple. I mean, yes, you might not get there or you might get there, but if you put things in your path, [just] thinking about it is so difficult. It's like going to the gym. "Oh, I don't want to go, oh my God, I don't want to go." But when you're doing it, you're doing it. Do it. That's why I might get sponsored by Nike or something like that.

CW: [*Laughs*] I don't know that gym analogy works for winning Academy Awards. But I do hear what—

SM: I'm sorry, I don't want to sound so trivial. But it is that way.

CW: In your own skin, it's a matter of just doing it.

SM: Come on, now.

CW: Because you got this tremendous self-confidence, skill, vision, determination, fortitude, the wind at your back from your parents, your tradition, your historical consciousness—a lot of people don't have that.

SM: Yes, but I can't allow that to cripple me.

CW: Yes, I agree. I agree.

SM: If you think like that it will only cripple you.

CW: I—well, okay.

SM: And you have to have this situation [where you can] clear the page, clear the desk, and just do it. You know it's great material, you know you got something going on, and you have to just at the end of the day physically get things together to do it. Don't think about it, because if you think about it . . . but do it. Fortunately, I just feel it's that simple, not that you'll get it done, but don't make it into some kind of, you know, Mount Everest. Just bloody do it.

CW: No, that's real, that's real. Can we have voices from the audience? Absolutely, absolutely. You have all been so kind to allow us to go on like this. . . . Should we have a—okay.

Question: I just wanted to share some thoughts I had about your speaking. You mentioned that moment when you can make a change and immediately [what] came to mind [was] that moment when Jay-Z had that boondoggle with Barneys [department store]. And you said there's a lot of voices saying, "Conform, conform here. We need you to conform." And he kind of did at that moment, I thought. I mean, we all lived that together pretty much. But the other thing was early on you said that this media wants us to be alone. And the whole community of "we" doesn't exist anymore. And recently, there's a show that kind of makes people want to be together. And it's called *Game of Thrones*, and I know it's a [mainstream] media show, but HBO shut down the possibility of that. It is kind of striking, they made [their] lawyers issue letters to bars that were letting people gather just to watch a TV show. And I thought, wow, that's so amazing, they want us to be alone so desperately so they can market to us individually and control us that they won't even let us gather when there's—and it's so rare that there's a show that people actually want to watch together, and it's like a real moment for everybody join up in a communal way. And, boom, they shut it down. It was shocking to me. What do you think about that?

CW: Nah, I mean, I'm unacquainted with that, but it makes a lot of sense. I mean, marketers want constituencies and they want consumers, whereas freedom fighters want citizens and they want communities. There's a qualitative difference. Freedom fighters want organizing and mobilizing—that's not the same as internet connections. [The] internet can be used for community. But it can be used for a whole lot of other things too. But we do live in a moment in which the atomistic individualism and careerism is so dominant and so pervasive that you have to cut radically against the grain . . . communities require integrity, honesty, and decency. Markets are about cupidity, mendacity, oftentimes false advertising. Not all of the time, but often the case. And in the end, trying to get us to conform to the next new and novel product produced for profit. For profit. Very different ways of being in the world. We live the tension.

Q: Cornel, I was just wondering if you could talk a little bit about your thoughts on the work upstairs [McQueen's installation *End Credits*], because I was very interested in the fact that specifically that piece is about the file that the FBI put together on Robeson because of his association with communism or what people, like, [how] people assumed he was a Communist [given] the time he spent in the Soviet Union. So could you talk a little bit about your response to that specifically in Robeson's history?

CW: Yeah, one is that any person who musters the courage to tell the truth about America in regard to white supremacy will be subject to targeting by the repressive apparatus—FBI here, CIA outside. Especially if you're trying to organize and mobilize. So what I saw upstairs was not just the fact that they were trying to connect him to the Soviet Union but that he was trying to awaken Black, white, red, yellow, all colors together, to bring a critique and a movement that would fundamentally transform the States. And the fact that they could try and link him to the Soviet Union and the Communist Party and so forth was for them motivation to squelching him. Because they did the same to Martin Luther King Jr. And they had signs of Martin Luther King Jr. all throughout the South: "Martin Luther King Jr., Communist Coon." Now, Martin Luther King Jr.'s relation to communism was about the same as my relation to, you know, Eskimo feudalism. And I ain't got nothing against the Eskimos, you know, but that's not something I think about, you see. So these lies, that's where mendacity comes in, to hide and conceal their own criminality. And yet it was very real, because, again, as I say, we never want to view any one of these figures as isolated individuals. They are part of a tradition of struggle. There's Claudia Jones, very close to Paul Robeson. She died within the same six weeks as Malcolm X, as Lorraine Hansberry, as Nat King Cole. We lost all four of them within six weeks. Robeson gave one of the eulogies for Lorraine Hansberry. It's a powerful eulogy. Malcolm and Paul Robeson at the same funeral! Malcolm asked to be introduced to Paul Robeson. Robeson said, "I love Malcolm X even though I'm an atheist, so I'm not too much into the Islamic sensibilities." But he said, "No, this is not the moment, I'm too overcome." Malcolm was, of course, assassinated within a matter of weeks. So they never got a chance to meet. So that was repression is very, very real. And it will always be the case. But the crucial thing to keep in mind is there is no such thing as white supremacy without resistance of some form.... No such thing as capitalism without resistance to something. It's that resistance that keeps—

SM: Can we talk about fear?

CW: Yes, yes.

SM: I mean, are you ever afraid? I mean, I think that's the thing, there's this word, this reality of fear. Fear of what? I don't know. There's people afraid, afraid of, I don't know. Obviously, I don't know, of the powers that be, losing money, popularity, fear of attacks. Fear. I think that's huge in this room and this situation.

CW: Absolutely, absolutely. I mean, Paul Robeson is one of the great examples of a de-n----rized Black person. Because every Black person in America is n----rized. Totally less beautiful, less intelligent, less moral, and told you ought to be intimidated and scared and fearful if you speak the truth because you'll be crushed like a cockroach. Symbolically or literally. So you just keep these people full of fear [and] you don't have to worry about a transformation of the status quo. And it is the Gabriel Prossers and Nat Turners, the Marcus Garveys, the all—we can go on—and the musicians, that say, "Now we need to de-n----rize this n----rized people." This is different than Larry Wilmore calling the president the N-word, which happened last night at the White House Correspondents' [Association Dinner]. You heard about that?

SM: No. No, what happened?

CW: Yeah, Larry Wilmore at the very end. He dropped, "Mr. President, I want you to know that you're *my* n---a." Right on national TV and all around the world. They got a big controversy about [that], blah, blah, blah. Now, now, now, that's a distraction. A n----rized person is somebody who's afraid to talk about how the vicious legacy of white supremacy is wounding people. It's not some kind of frivolous dialogue for mainstream media. He [Robeson] was de-n----rized because he had fear, he worked through the fear, and it made him courageous and fearless and brave to tell the truth knowing he could die. Malcolm was a de-n----rized Muslim. Martin was a de-n----rized Christian. Donny Hathaway was a de-n----rized—well, I don't know what he believed, but he could sing [*laughs*]. But you have to have that freedom. But you got to work through the fear. And this [is] part of the problem, I mean, part of the problem these days [is] in terms of our professional class. We've got a lot of Black people who got a lot of money, a lot of status, and some of them got a lot of power. But they still scared. So they're just n----rized professionals. They still scared. They won't tell the truth on the job, they won't be in solidarity when it's time to struggle. Look at all the hip-hop artists that talk bad in the studio. But when it comes to Ferguson, how many of them are down there?

SM: Yeah, exactly. It's what I said right at the beginning about the anger and a situation like Katrina.

CW: Katrina was the same way. Absolutely.

SM: And again, I mean, you know—

CW: We got to go up to a lot of these artists. "I thought you're one of the baddest motherhuckers [*sic*] comin' down to the plate? Man, you're scared to go in the street." [*Imitating*] "Well I had a talk with my agent, and my agent [asked] me *please*." Then you tell them about Curtis, then you tell about Nina Simone, then you tell them about other artists whose agent told them to do so and so, and they stood up, [and] not in the spirit of self-righteousness. So of course we're wrestling with fear. People talk about death threats, who are living under death threats, talking about [how] they're going to mess with your momma, that's serious stuff. That's very serious stuff. But then the question is, what is the one thing that breaks the back of fear? It's love. It's love, the reason why everybody in this room would take a bullet for they momma—just being normative at this point to generalize in a way. The reason why everybody would take a bullet for your mom is because you love her. Now you ain't gonna take a bullet for me and Steve, y'all don't know us well enough. We appreciate it, we understand that. Even though for this brother, I'd take a bullet at least in my arm, maybe not the heart yet.

SM: [*Laughs*]

CW: Oh, yeah. Because he represents the younger generation of my tradition. That's a tradition I've been willing to die for—passing it on to him and the others who come along. Because it was passed on to me. And they were willing to inject me with a love that breaks the back of fear. Paul Robeson had that kind of love in him.

Q: Listen, I want to thank you so much for talking about fear and what it can do to you. And my question is that today I learned more about Paul Robeson and what he did and how he stood up than I did the display in which surveillance and what the government is doing, has done, to innocent people. That is front and center. So my question for you, Steve, is you show on both screens the surveillance and you hear the redacted passages and that sort of thing. But did you consider having the other screen show some of the miraculous, courageous things in the year, you know, 1920, and so on, when Paul Robeson was living?

SM: No, I didn't. What I was interested in, in those documents, what they were for me, these documents were like sheets of music. And I wanted to play the music like we have, you know, sometimes we get things obviously on the paper which is, you know, numbers, roman numeral, crossed out, redacted, to every description which was on that piece of paper. That musical, that sheet of music, as well as the fact which is written, I wanted to have that sort of analytical description of what was going on. It was very important for me, very important to sort of have it as it is. There was a load of facts—that's what happened, that that was being looked at. It's almost like braille, every bump, every fold, every crease, every word. I wanted it to be vocalized. It was very important. And [to] hear the music of the piece. So you know, one could— you know, I'm interested in what happens in the room with this piece. And how it translates, how it gets into one's veins. Because when you first get in there, you know, maybe there are people milling around and then you sit down, and then there is a shooting in your ear, some sort of radio dial, and then you're hooked in, and then you're in this flow of sound, all the audio of what happened, as well as seeing things; parts you're reading, sentences, and maybe a phrase, the whole idea of end credits. Because if I gave you *the* Paul Robeson . . . I mean, the audio, what we have right now, when I first presented it, it was eleven hours of audio, what we have now is twenty hours of audio. When we finish it, it will be seventy-two hours of audio. That's how lengthy the documents are. And the whole idea of having this sort of audio, I mean, you're never gonna catch all of it. But to have an impression of verbally and visually was what I was about, to show you the magnitude, the weight, and the scary size of [the] crime which was committed against him. It's important.

CW: It's also true, though, that he's in the process of making a powerful, powerful film about the brother. He's one of the few in the world who could do that. Once that hits, it's like BC/AD in terms of Robeson being known around the world. Now if we jump back to the thirties and forties, he's the most famous—

SM: In the world.

CW: In the world [*laughs*]. Exactly, I'm learning a lot of things up here. But in terms of answering your question, that fully fleshifized [*sic*] courage, vision, being victimized but refusing to be solely a victim, resisting but still, in the end, having to deal with some really powerful forces . . . because, again, the last ten years of his life, you know, cannot be overlooked. People reach a point where they can only take so much. And when his wife died, when his friends died, he's betrayed by his close partners, the Black middle class pulls the rug [out] from under him, the government is trying to crush him, and so forth. He's still standing with dignity, but he's not as strong as he was in the thirties and the forties. He's got some white Jewish Communists standing with him, he's got some Black Communists, he's got some artists. Who was on that list when they had his birthday [celebration]? It must have been about 1963. Very few. How many scholars went with him? Very few. Coltrane's on there. . . . Serious, courageous ones are on there, you know. So that the abandonment is very real, but he's still standing tall with grace and dignity till the end. But when we get that full-fledged filmic representation. Phew. We got *12 Years a Slave*.

SM: He sacrificed, he spoke to Martin Luther King, and he said, "Dr. Martin Luther King," he said, "listen. I'm, you know, you don't need to [do] anything, I'll take the heat for you." He took a bullet for him. "I'll take the heat. I'll drive them off this way while you go that way."

CW: That's exactly right. Absolutely.

SM: Anyway, I think that we should wrap up. Also, I just wanted to say that this [is] the first time that I've met Cornel. Mr. Cornel, Dr. Cornel West—

CW: Brother West, Brother West, Brother West, Brother West [*laughs*]. We're brothers, we're cousins.

SM: I apologize. I'm honored to have you onstage. And thank you, you are a true artist, sir. You are a true artist. Thank you so, so, so much. Thank you very much.

CW: Thank you, thank you. Steve McQueen! Steve McQueen! That was wonderful, brother. Magnificent. Steve McQueen.

Note

1. "Let Paul Sing," billed as a "public meeting," was held on Sunday, March 11, 1956, at the Lesser Free Trade Hall in Manchester. Working Class Movement Library, "Paul Robeson," accessed July 19, 2024, https://www.wcml.org.uk/wcml/en/our-collections/creativity-and-culture/music/paul-robeson/.

Steve McQueen on *Widows*, Viola Davis, the Politics of Chicago, and More

Gregory Ellwood / 2018

From *The Playlist*, November 16, 2018. Reprinted by permission.

Steve McQueen continues to surprise. After the Oscar-winning *12 Years a Slave*, you might have thought the London-born filmmaker would attempt another thought-provoking epic, and he has, in a way. *Widows* is a genre movie with quite a bit to say about the environment that fosters criminals at every level of society. Basically, everyone is out to get money. Whether through political power, intimidation, or as simply a means for survival.

The film is based on a popular ITV series of the same title that aired in the UK beginning in 1983. As McQueen notes in our interview, the series left a profound impression on him as a youngster, and he always thought of tackling a new version. Like the original, this current *Widows* centers on four women whose husband or boyfriend has been killed in the middle of a major bank heist. They are then charged with pulling off another heist to make up for their loved one's mistake.

This quartet of talented actresses including Viola Davis, Michelle Rodriguez, Elizabeth Debicki, and Cynthia Erivo who—the two former in particular—give riveting performances. Brian Tyree Henry is an up-and-coming Chicago politician who has his own criminal enterprise while Daniel Kaluuya plays his second-in-command who becomes increasingly dangerous as the movie plays on. Mixed up in this showdown is Colin Farrell as a politician trying to forge his own identity far from the shadow of his corrupt father, played by Robert Duvall.

During a phone interview earlier this month, McQueen passionately talked about the film and how it's more than just a typical studio thriller.

The Playlist: Where did your passion to make this come from, to turn what was a miniseries into a feature-length movie?

Steve McQueen: It has been thirty-five years, searching your soul. [I was] watching TV, and this program came on, called *Widows*, written by Lynda La Plante. I just sort of identified with the women. Them being judged by their appearance, and deemed not capable, and that somehow being judged as a hard child in London and hated. Also, seeing them sort of put [it on] its head and circumnavigate the stereotype is wonderful. This thrill of how they accomplished what they did.

TP: Did you go to New Regency to get it off the ground?

SM: Yes, they knew I wanted to make it. It's funny. I met Lynda back in Paris. There was an occasion, and there was a side room where there was a private audience with the Queen. The ten of us, and Ms. La Plante, was in the line, with the Queen. I actually just spoke to her. What happened to *Widows*? She told me it went to Disney. I spoke to New Regency about that, and how I wanted this project for the next one. They were very supportive of me, and they got it for me.

TP: Where did the idea come from to set it in Chicago?

SM: It came from me. I think all those contexts I wanted to deal with, for me, were evident in Chicago. I wanted to basically place this narrative in a heightened, in a Western, [but] contemporary setting. That for me was really was Chicago, to begin with. Dealing with race. Dealing with politics, corruption, policing, religion, economics, poverty, et cetera, et cetera. There are all these aspects of life that I found in this microcosm of Chicago, but also that in the localism of Chicago was also about the globalism we all find ourselves in at this moment in time.

TP: Where did you find the nuances of the city? It feels like you and Gillian have written something that someone would really need to know about the intricacies of the city to make it feel this authentic.

SM: I have been visiting Chicago for twenty-two years. I came here, and I was invited to show up at the Museum of Contemporary Arts in Chicago. At the same time, my girlfriend, who is now my longtime partner, went to the Democratic Convention when Bill Clinton was president. My journey from my starting point twenty years ago with my first introduction to Chicago until now has always been about art and politics.

TP: How did Gillian Flynn come on board as your coscreenwriter? How did you guys work together to fashion the script?

SM: Gillian came on board after I put the rights in place in Chicago. We were both very lucky that we both wanted to collaborate on this project. It was one of those things where you talk and talk and talk, and go back and forth with scripts. My version. Her version. We would meet up and talk through things. We went to FBI headquarters here and spoke to private detectives. We spoke to religious leaders and congressmen—all off [the] record. It was like being private investigators in a way. It got to the point where when we were writing, it was like two guitarists. You couldn't tell who was playing which note. It was amazing.

TP: You mentioned your love of the original miniseries. Were there certain beats that you were like, "Listen, I don't care what else we do, but we have to put A, B, C, and D in because that's the genesis of this story that needs to be there?"

SM: Well, the main genesis of the story was these men, husbands basically, come to this heist and they died in tragic circumstances and the women had to pull off their last job. That's the basis. Everything else was up for grabs, really.

TP: While you were writing, were you thinking of actors and actresses you wanted to play these roles?

SM: No. I never do that because I always want the freedom to do what the hell I want. See, if I put a name in mind for a part, it limits you. I never want that. So after, I start to think, "Okay, who can be the best for this?" And you start to audition or talk to people, and what not.

TP: Just one last question about the screenplay. I think you really started working on it in 2015? Is that correct?

SM: Oh God, no. Way before that. I mean, I started thinking about it and sort of priming it in 2013. At the same time as *12 Years*. Again, at the same time, when you start really putting pen to paper was actually like the end of 2014, something like that, yeah.

TP: Did the election in 2016, did Brexit, did that whole year sort of change anything that you had put in thematically? Did that affect where the script went? Robert Duvall's character, in particular, has some things to say that tie into recent political events.

SM: No. We had the politics already, but what did happen was that I wanted it to be this sort of this hanging on of the baton. At the same time, that was very evident in the history of Chicago, that kind of nepotism. So, we added in this element of the changing of the old guard into the new somehow or way. The reason why I did that because I thought, "Okay, we have to understand where this comes from." Again, it's like the whole idea of this whole film is about understanding the context of this heist, and [in order] to do so, one has to understand this city. I didn't want to put blinkers on just for the heist. I wanted the supporters to understand the context of where this was happening.

TP: So you finished the script, and you've got these incredible roles, and for a number of great actresses, primarily, and some actors as well.

SM: And actors as well.

TP: How did Viola become your Veronica? Was that a harder pitch than you thought it would be or was she on board right away?

SM: It was Zen. She was offered a role where she could be a great woman. Where she has a lover, a husband. She had a vagina, and all her decisions were made from love. I think she was very excited about that. I think she's an amazing actor.

TP: The other great performers that blew me away was Elizabeth's. Had you seen her in something before? Was it just meeting with her that you knew that she had this great performance in her?

SM: She was in a Jean Genet play called *The Maids*, which I loved. She was great in it, so I called her in for an audition, and that was it. I met her firstly at some kind movie premiere which I didn't want to be at, but I didn't know her. But then I heard of this Jean Genet play she was in, and I thought, let's try an audition. She just hit the ball out of the park, and that was it.

TP: Another thing I love about this movie is you give Michelle Rodriguez a chance to really show her dramatic chops, which I feel like few filmmakers or directors have allowed her to do before, just based on the material she's been offered. How did that casting come about?

SM: As a person, she's kind of neat. Again, her first movie, *Girlfight*. I think I just trusted in my instincts on it, really. I didn't really know, but I trusted my instinct. I offered her the role, but she said no. And I went to meet her and then I just knew this was a very sensitive sort of retrospective [*sic*] woman and she [needed to] overcome things in her mind about the character. And she did. The character reminded her of her mother. Therefore, she was too close to her at one point; I think that was why she said no. Then she went to find her way and was just tremendous in this picture. Tremendous.

TP: In this film, there are explosions, and there are gun battles, there are chases and stuff. Was that fun for you to go in . . .

SM: Once again, it never negated the weight or the seriousness of this. It never negated the weight or the seriousness of the film.

TP: Right.

SM: I've done a movie about a hunger strike. I've done a movie about a sex addict, slave rape. This is a film about the state in which we find ourselves, and corruption, race, poverty, sexism. This is a fine line of where we are right now, where we find ourselves; this is as serious as any film I've ever made. The fact that there is a heist-sort of [story] running through this project doesn't take away the weight of it at all. If anything, it is about these women mobilizing themselves in order to make space, this sort of do something that we can keep our heads above the water. Yes. It is a little bit of a fictional stretch, but isn't every movie like that?

TP: Sure.

SM: Again, that's what it is. I mean, if it had men in it, it wouldn't matter. It's all about what metaphors one uses to talk about the world that we live in today. That's why again it's just because it has this idea of a heist running through it; it doesn't lessen the point of what I'm talking about. If anyone thinks it's less than this sexism, racism, and corruption, and everything else I talk about in this picture has less test than anything I've done before, I will ask them to look again.

TP: I think it's an incredible film. I really appreciate you taking the time.

SM: Can I just add the whole idea of this picture to me is to bring it "in." Basically, I want the people that I'm making this film about, I want the people that I'm making fun about, I want them to come to the cinema, as well as the people that I've been very fortunate to have to support my pictures before. Yes. It's about aiming it at a large audience, because that's my responsibility as a filmmaker, especially in these times. We can't put ourselves in bubbles. One has to zero-in on and at the same time not lower the standards of what one is talking about because you get that from [films like] *The Godfather*. You get that from films like *Chinatown*. These films had broad mass appeal, but [also] had this serious sort of story to tell.

Interview: Steve McQueen Q&A

Simon Grant / 2019

From *Tate, Etc.*, June 25, 2019. Copyright © Tate 2019. Reprinted by permission of the Tate Trustees.

Simon Grant: There were several events in your childhood that left a distinct impression—Tottenham winning the FA Cup, the Brixton riots, and Bobby Sands. What interested you about Bobby Sands and the IRA prisoners' late 1970s blanket protests?

Steve McQueen: I remember as an eleven-year-old seeing Bobby Sands on BBC news every night. There was a number underneath his image, and I thought that that was his age, but I noticed that each night the number increased, and I realized that wasn't his age, it was the number of days he had gone without food. To an eleven-year-old, the idea of someone who in order to be heard was not eating left an impression on me. I don't know why this image stayed with me, but it is a very strong memory.

SG: So when it came to doing the research for the film in Northern Ireland with previous inmates of cell block H of the Maze Prison, as well as some of the prison officers, what was that experience like?

SM: I felt privileged to hear their story. They were extraordinarily articulate—pushing language to its limits, just as there were times when they pushed the body to its limits.

SG: What kind of questions were you asking them?

SM: Everything. It is a case of wanting to know not just the big questions, but also the details, such as the daily rituals, and how people survived in the situations and the arguments and the dialogue. I wanted to have a very rounded picture of their experience.

SG: Did you do that by focusing on the sensory experience—touch, taste, smell—which play a prominent part of *Hunger*?

SM: These things are there in order to help the bigger questions of the film. For example, in one scene, when the first prisoner is put into the cells, he finds a fly and focuses on that fly. A couple of days before him going into prison I don't think he will have even looked at a fly twice. These sort of scenes are there in order to bring to the fore the environment or situation that they are in. It's not just for decoration, it's actually to enhance the situation that these people find themselves in—be it prison officers or prisoners.

SG: How did you manage to film the violent scenes of beatings in the prison, as in a way you are reviving the experience in some way?

SM: To a certain extent, yes. It was very hard, but we had to shoot it. It's one of those situations that was very unfamiliar to me. It's one of those situations where you know you're going to use all your skills to do something and sometimes it affects you and you've got to get over it and get on with it. And it was one of those. The architecture of the place dictated the camera also.

SG: The detail in the lingering shots of the camera, for example the slow panning shot across the shit-smeared walls of the prison cells and the maggot-infested food on the floor, is remarkable. Was it really like this for the prisoners?

SM: Yes. And the people who dressed that set were ex-prisoners.

SG: When I saw that imagery I was reminded me of Richard Hamilton's painting *The Citizen* that depicts Bobby Sands in his blanket. The painting seems incredibly aesthetic and clean by comparison to your gritty portrayal of the filth and degradation.

SM: Well, the situation was that there was no image of what was going on in the prison, except ninety seconds of TV footage. So Richard Hamilton had the license to do that, and the painting is still a strong image . . .

SG: The structure of the film is divided into three distinct sections, with the twenty-minute, single-shot dialogue between Bobby Sands and the priest at the center. Was there a deliberate structure set out in your mind from the beginning?

SM: Yes, I had this idea of the structure as like a river that turns into a rapid which turns into a waterfall. This analogy of narrative, of a route, is what I wanted to bring the audience along to a situation that he can or she can identify with her surroundings. Then there is a fracture, a disturbance. The reality that ensues is distorted, of course. The waterfall is the suspense of reality—death. In some ways the situation in this film's narrative is that it goes against nature of course, because as human beings we do anything to survive. So, that someone would decide to die is very profound.

SG: Then I was very taken by the scene at the beginning of the film where the prison officer is at home having his breakfast. You cut to underneath the table where we see the napkin on his lap. Some crumbs falls onto the napkin from his toast. . . . Why did you do it like that?

SM: For the detail. These things which are singularly insignificant in the film such as the snowflake that falls on prison officer's knuckle—could be very significant in the context of this. What does it mean? It's an incredibly crucial element to the character in some way. I'm not forcing the action at all; I'm presenting it. It is the same consideration when thinking about where to put the camera. It's these kinds of decisions you make in order to how best to translate an environment. And often as the case with the filming the prison scenes at least, the architecture dictated to me where to put the camera. But often it's the case you have to find it.

SG: Did you get a different sense of Bobby Sands, not just the political situation, but after having made *Hunger*?

SM: At eleven years old, it's totally abstract. You have no real concept when you're thinking about it, but the seed that has been planted is very strong. And as you grow up as an adult it is still strong, even if you know the context of it. So when I got over there, of course it changed again. My approach to it was how people make these extraordinary situations ordinary. For example, prison officers are going back home to their families from a workplace that is horrific, and prisoners are having to live in that situation for four and a half years. So I am interested in how people deal with those decisions that politicians make, and the environments which are created from those decisions, which they have to survive in.

SG: So is that why you have the disembodied voice of Thatcher that appears at various stages in the film?

SM: The voice is so powerful, so you didn't need to show her face. I wanted to remain in the prison and I didn't want the situation where there were punctures in that concentrated situation. To have her voice—the voice is almost like vapor—is very strong.

SG: Michael Fassbender who plays Bobby Sands prepared himself for the role of Sands going through his hunger strike by undergoing ten weeks of supervised fasting. How did you work with that?

SM: When we were shooting that period no one would normally speak to him apart from me. From twelve weeks he would be taken back to his room, and I would go back and have a conversation with him. (There were too many people asking, "Are you okay, are you alright," so he needed to focus on his role.) I understand now why fasting is so important in those situations. It focuses you. Often it's the case it that it's the first time you are actually aware of yourself, because you've reduced yourself, everything has been taken away from you as far as food is concerned—sex drive, et cetera. You get to a state where it is very inward looking, and I think it just helped the role, in a way, and obviously him personally in order to direct his own emotion.

SG: The central scene with Sands and the priest is an extraordinary part of the film, not just because of its length . . .

SM: It was what was necessary for the role for the conversation. Up until that point, it is a cascade of words. Everything else was pushed to its limit. Every question, everything was looked at from inside out. It was a conversation that actually didn't happen in real life, but it was a situation I thought was necessary for the film, because in some ways you have to understand what were the reasons to live and what were the reasons to die.

SG: And now the assimilation of this history into mainstream politics has changed the political landscape . . .

SM: Well, it's interesting. The Bobby Sands story is one of the most historical events in the last twenty-seven years, but it has been swept under the carpet.

Every Story Has Already Been Told: Steve McQueen Interview and Portfolio

William J. Simmons / 2020

From *Framework: The Journal of Cinema and Media* 61, no. 1 (2020): 55–67. Reprinted by permission of Wayne State University Press.

Many years after queer and queer-of-color theories made such a binary indefensible, art history and film studies remain committed to a distinction between criticality and pleasure. The former remains a desirable activist strategy and the latter is deemed banal, complicit, and expendable. Many have troubled these reductive categories. Eve Kosofsky Sedgwick, for instance, proposes reparative reading and the ongoing necessity for marginalized subjects to connect meaningfully and perhaps unexpectedly with problematic cultural phenomena. In a similar vein, C. Namwali Serpell has suggested the numerous (and pleasurable) critical possibilities in something as debased and thrilling as the cliché.[1]

Yet we often continue to relate to culture with a paranoid expectation that there must be more than pleasure, indeed a space that refutes the pleasurable as a mere superficial layer to be peeled back for a truer cross-section of the film's deconstructive musculature. The excision performed by criticality has deep psychic and material ramifications for minoritarian subjects, especially artists of color, whose cultural output is frequently aligned with a documentary status, that is, some sort of truth about the community allegedly represented by the individual or a truth about that community's oppositional struggle.

Steve McQueen's work has been lauded for its realism, criticality, and transcendence of the caricatures of genre, but, as I wonder in a recent essay in *Jump Cut: A Review of Contemporary Media*, how then might we locate works like *Widows* (2018) whose relationship to "truth" is entirely different?[2] The truth of *Widows* and other McQueen films seems to lie in a pleasurable space. With *Widows*, the pleasure manifests in McQueen's enjoyment of the original ITV series as a young person, and certainly the pleasure of being able to remake that youthful attachment into something else, something his own. A TV show that in retrospect might seem overwrought and problematic is for McQueen the source of fascination, which, following Sedgwick, could be a deeply queer form of attachment. In works like *Shame* (2011), it could be the sheer pleasure of bodies, voyeurism, and spectacle, as is also manifest in McQueen's video works like *Illuminer* (2001) and *Bear* (1993).

Then there are the pleasures and tragedies of repetition, reformulation, rehearsal, and permutation (to use McQueen's term suggested below). The protagonist of *Shame* gets off again and again and hates himself for it again and again, and we watch it—judgmentally, empathetically, and/or pornographically—again and again, just as we self-consciously love watching his beautiful sister sing a song we have all heard before. *Widows* similarly recuperates and alters the past when McQueen repeats and modifies his enjoyment of the original franchise. Or is it enjoyment that elicits fear or discomfort by looping, cycling, rebuilding, and rehearsing, as with the homage to Buster Keaton in *Deadpan* (1997), the sarcastic preciousness of *Queen and Country* (2007–2009), the simultaneously tragic and matter-of-fact *Ashes* (1997), or the discomfiting loop of *Static* (2009)? *12 Years a Slave* (2013) is likewise part of a discomfiting history of adaptations, each deeply painful in their own way, which tragically mirror the endless permutations of racial violence since the writing of Solomon Northup's memoir.

A normative art historical analysis would look to precedents for McQueen's work—a process that is itself less a generative repetition than a clichéd one in its insistence that critique is the only path history can follow in order to move forward. As Ronald E. Gregg reminded me when reading a draft of this introduction, there is indeed a pleasure in the voyeurism of history, of gazing upon the "long take" of history (for which McQueen, it so happens, has been renowned, especially in *12 Years a Slave*). It follows that I initially wanted to see McQueen's *Illuminer* as an homage to Warhol's *Sleep* (1963), but with Gregg's comments in mind, it occurs to me now that *Illuminer* has less to say about referentiality and more to do with evoking the fashioning of history itself. We see McQueen's body in the process of becoming, consuming, and making discourse, and we derive some form of pleasure from engaging with that process, if only or necessarily at a distance. So, we might consider how and why art exists at the behest of history over affective attachment, since history is itself a series of affective rehearsals of loved and repugnant events, or even boredom. Equally important is thinking through how emotion can be historicized and how history can be emotionalized, especially when considering how the work of artists of color are read differently in these contexts than those of white artists. What I am interested in modeling for this short introduction is the importance of attachment, and often reattachment, as a process that springs from both love and critique, hope and fear, deconstruction and enjoyment. I see McQueen as operating in between these spaces at times, when at others he wishes to remain something other than in-between. I argue for this especially in the context of artists of color, whose capacity to enjoy has often been circumscribed by white critics and historians. At the same time, this is not yet another tired rallying cry for the radicality of pleasure, which has often been mobilized in the whitest of feminisms and queer theories. I simply hope to foreground the importance of desire, love, and attachment, as McQueen has, and suggest that we consider how and why things appear to us as critical or complicit, liminal, or fixed, in any given historical moment, and to whom we afford the opportunity to be both and neither.

William J. Simmons: In many readings of your work, there is an insistence on your being critical or deconstructive. There was much discussion with *Widows*, for instance, about how you are critiquing or deconstructing film noir or the action film. However, you clearly also loved the original ITV series. I'm interested in the tension between deconstruction and love or appreciation in your films, something beyond critique.

Steve McQueen: What I loved about *Widows* was the idea—these women who were trying to make their way in a world where they were on their own and vulnerable. The only way they could actually exist in their case was to come together. I pushed it a little bit from the original, which was three white women and one Black woman. It became two Black women, a Latina woman, and a white woman. That was just because of the makeup of Chicago. It was about the fact that regardless of their background or where they're from, there was a kind of equality, and the heist needed all of them. They have to come together to survive and to thrive in that environment, being that they were targeted not only by the powers that be but also by an underworld. I love the fact that these women, and I use the word love, come together—different backgrounds, different classes—and achieved what they had to achieve in order to survive.

WJS: So, when you were thinking about your relationship to the source material, were you looking to expose its racial and gendered inequities or failings?

SM: It's about taking it further. If the idea is great and you can take it further, that's interesting. Remaking it has no point. Where do you go with it? I wanted to take it to the relationship with Chicago, to race, class, gender, and politics, and not push away what I would have liked to have seen. Using Chicago as a metaphor for what I wanted to do with this film was very rewarding. Gillian Flynn and I did a lot of research, of course, and that was the goal—to push the narrative forward from the original idea, since it was such a great premise.

WJS: I wanted to connect this conversation to *12 Years a Slave* as well since it, like *Widows*, is based on something that came before. The original book by

Solomon Northup also existed as a lecture tour, a stage play, and an adaptation by Gordon Parks. It follows that Henry Louis Gates Jr. wrote: "No story tells itself on its own: even 'true' stories have to be re-created within the confines and various formal possibilities for expression offered by a given medium."[3] Where do you locate yourself within that series of translations?

SM: Solomon wrote the book in 1853, and each version of the story is told differently. It's a whole tradition, and it's been passed from generation to generation to generation. Of course, everyone will add their five pence to the story, and it will become different from how it was told originally, but the source of it will remain. Other than academics, a lot of people didn't even know about it, even with Gordon Parks's picture. Again: What could I add to the story? By bringing that story from the past into the present, what would it lose? Of course, it was also translated differently from the book to the stage play as well, because it was directed at abolitionists. You have to look at that story and change it into something else. You can look at that story and detect what was being exploited, look at it in a different way, and interpret it in 2013. Every story has already been told. How we present it is the important thing.

WJS: In this process of translation . . .

SM: Permutation.

WJS: Right, permutation. In this process of permutation, the specter of truth hovers over all of this. Some writers and historians of color, for instance, noted how your depiction of slavery did not have the usual melodramatic edge.[4] Your relationship to truth and documentary, however, is different in *12 Years* than it is in your artworks or *Hunger* [2008], for instance. How do you relate to documentary as a genre?

SM: Every film is a documentary. That's the only way I can answer that question.

WJS: Maybe that brings us back to race and gender. One could argue that artists of color are tied to documentary in a very different way than white artists are. There is a different expectation for truth, or a problematic notion that one person can speak to the truth of the collective. This process disallows a minoritarian imaginary.

SM: We need more people of color with cameras and more financial means for them to make films. There needs to be balance, another view. We have one side, and we need the other side. If two people are looking at an apple, there will be two different stories. More people of color and LGBTQ people need to make films and to make the films they want to make. One of the biggest influences on me was queer cinema, because I grew up in a time where there was an explosion of it. To see that, to be immersed in that way of looking at things and how things were seen with a different gaze was very important to my development, both as an artist and as a human being.

Notes

1. See C. Namwali Serpell, "A Heap of Cliché," in *Critique and Postcritique*, edited by Elizabeth S. Anker and Rita Felski (Durham, NC: Duke University Press, 2017), 153–82.
2. William J. Simmons, "On Affect and Criticality in Steve McQueen's *Widows*," *Jump Cut: A Review of Contemporary Media* 58 (2019), https://www.ejumpcut.org/currentissue/Simmons-Widows/index.html.
3. Henry Louis Gates Jr., "*12 Years a Slave*: Trek from Slave to Screen," in *Twelve Years a Slave*, edited by Gates and Kevin M. Burke (New York: W. W. Norton and Company, 2017), 355.
4. See, for example, Erica L. Ball, "The Unbearable Liminality of Blackness: Reconsidering Violence in Steve McQueen's *12 Years a Slave*," *Transition* 119 (2016): 175–86.

Transcript: In Conversation with Steve McQueen

Paul Gilroy / 2020

Reprinted by permission. Copyright © Steve McQueen. Courtesy of the artist, Thomas Dane Gallery, and the University College London Sarah Parker Remond Centre for the Study of Racism and Racialisation.

Paul Gilroy: Good morning, everybody. It's Paul Gilroy here, director of the Sarah Parker Remond Centre for the Study of Racism and Racialisation at UCL. My guest this morning needs no introduction, so I won't try and introduce him. It is Steve McQueen, award-winning artist, film director, household name, and general catalyst for the positive. Steve, thank you so much. I know you really are incredibly busy, and it's just a joy to be able to talk to you about what's going on around us and about the new work that you've got in process, particularly this amazing medley of films, *Small Axe*, which is beginning in a week or so. I thought one place to begin would be just to say I've always thought racism doesn't let Black people have a history, it keeps us in the present always; we're always in the present. So, we're denied a history, and we're not allowed to think with reference to a future. So, it just seems to me that to make this amazing collection of historical material, and to pitch it into the situation that we're in, is a way of not just restoring the history but of orienting people towards a possible future. So, I just wondered what you thought about that history.

Steve McQueen: Thanks for the introduction, Paul, first of all. For me it was always about planting myself in a situation where I had an idea of who I was, where I was and where I wanted to go—and I say "I," meaning we." It was very difficult sometimes growing up in the UK as a Black child—as a Black, male, young child—and how I am now, to get some kind of bearings of what the future holds. But also, everything was always unstable because no one thought that you had any roots here or any stability here—I mean, roots as far as stability. So, you could be pushed and you could be toppled over. So, for me, *Small Axe* was about shoring up the foundations of who we are and where we came from and what we contributed to this country on so many levels and influenced it on so many levels. So, that's what *Small Axe* for me was about.

PG: Yeah, I feel that, and I think that—I haven't seen all of the five films, but the ones I've seen certainly do that but they go beyond saying simply in some sense we belong to this place, in some sense you have to recognize that this place has no future without recognizing our belonging here . . .

SM: Absolutely.

PG: It pushed through to something even further than that, which is about saying actually you don't have to fear that belonging; that in admitting us into, if you like, the nation's official portrait of itself, you're not going to lose anything. You don't have to fear that admission, you don't have to fear the entry ticket. It's belated, and it's been so much connected to all the cruel, horrible things that are in the background with Windrush and all of that, but you really do not have to fear letting us into that portrait.

SM: Yeah. It's been a long time in the making; this has been eleven years. So, immediately after *Hunger* I knew this was what I want to do. There was sort of a rough plan, but at the end of the day it was one of those situations of having to get the platform to do it, and I knew always it would have to be the BBC, for example, because for me these weren't local stories, these were national stories. And at the same time, I knew these were movies, feature films, because these stories needed this plinth, they needed that sort of canvas that only cinema could do. And the fact of having that platform and having that canvas is also allowing us to talk about what you say about the portrait or the picture that we're in, that we are part of this story and we've changed things in a way that can never be reversed. And it's amazing. And I think in some ways, for me it wasn't just about acknowledging it, it was about celebrating it; and that's it.

PG: It's interesting you put it like that because I think the first film, *Mangrove*, is very much a film of protest, but it's also a film about the nature of justice; and as it comes first before the others it makes justice absolutely fundamental. And our movement in this country—which has been in part a movement to belong and to be seen to belong—is also movement for justice. And so I think it's very interesting that you made that one first, and in a way it's a recognizable political story that speaks very directly to the context of Black Lives Matter, speaks very directly to the context of the Windrush scandal and the horrors that continue. I know we all know the Windrush things been going on for twenty to thirty years, and we all know people who've been victims of it over that time. And it's not just about what Theresa May did, although what she did was awful, it's not just about that because Labour and Conservative—all of them, they've all been doing it, and they've all been doing it for the longest time. But now when some of that starts to come to light, it creates a new setting for that demand for justice. And I think that's really fundamental that justice is absolutely nailed on in the biggest, biggest letters and the loudest voice from the beginning of the whole medley of films.

SM: Justice. Morality. Consciousness. I mean, it's in order to put one foot in front of the other when you go out on the road, exit your house, how are you going to survive? Any and everybody. So the fact that the first film's about the Mangrove Nine, and the whole idea of what happened to them and how they triumphed with their own voices, taking on the establishment with their own voices, using the tools of the establishment but with their own voices, was beautiful. That's what happens with music, that's what happens in every kind of aspect of creative life. And I think the whole idea of something which is Black, and the whole idea of something which is beautiful as far as talking about justice and freedom, can reverberate throughout the land, it can influence any and everybody. It's a case of that sort of moral stance, that justice as you talk about, and how it can be reverberated throughout the land, and every level—education, employment, everything—can be affected by that. But not just for a few, but for all. That's what it's about. And how much that we affected that, and we've changed that. We're not just making noise about a small part of the situation, our noise is reverberating throughout the land, throughout the bloodstream of the country and beyond, and beyond, and beyond.

PG: I wonder about that because of course a number of the people—the families of the Mangrove people—are still around, are still alive. And that must give you a very difficult, complicated task. All of the films in a way seem to have a relationship to reality, to real people, to real places, to real elements in a longer history of life in Britain, in Europe. I wonder what that's like, particularly in the case of *Mangrove* because you had to present the material, I'm sure, to the people who were part of it. How did they react to watching a film of it?

SM: Well, interestingly, my father was a friend of one of the Mangrove Nine, and he was a very close friend of his, and he used to come around my house all the time. I just used to be lying on the floor watching TV while these two guys would be chatting, because you couldn't join the conversation because it's adults talking or whatever. But I didn't know who he was; I didn't know about the Mangrove Nine until maybe fifteen years ago. My father used to go to the Backayard, my father used to go to the Mangrove. My relatives are from Grenada and Trinidad, so it was integrated within, we were living in Shepherd's Bush before my family moved out into the suburbs into Ealing. So, I kind of knew people that I didn't even know were involved. And that sort of negotiation, of course, it's been difficult at certain points because you're dealing with people who were dealing with post-traumatic stress disorder for years, for decades, and had no sort of help, and the children of those people going through that. So, there was a lot of trauma, absolutely still is. And you're never going to get it 100 percent right for anyone, but for the majority it's been an amazing experience. And I think those conversations with some of the relatives now are still happening, because I think to put it on the big screen as we did and giving these stories a victory that in some ways they never really had because it was some parts of the community who saw them as champions and heroes but not all [of the] community. And these aren't just local heroes, these are national heroes. And that's what I wanted to do, and I think for the majority of relatives and the next of kin it's been a great experience. And now there's the conversation we're having to have, just because we're dealing with trauma, and we're dealing with the children of—and it's heavy, it's heavy. It's not an easy, easy thing at all.

PG: No, absolutely. How that passes from one generation to another is really a strong undercurrent in all the material that I've seen—that sense of intergenerational responsibility, intergenerational conversation. And, of course, that's very much gendered actually, certainly in *Red, White and Blue*. It's a curiously intimate and interesting study of how a Black father and a Black son speak to one another and acquire the capacity to communicate across some of the difficult things and anxieties and pressure—the pressure that they're under in that life at that time. So, I think it's really important for people to appreciate how much the generational responsibilities cut into all of these films. And you now yourself, I imagine, also feel this, that there are things we have to do to speak to people who are younger than ourselves. You say you didn't know about it till fifteen years ago. They won't know about it until they see what you've put in front of them. So, there's that aspect too. I know it's really important to what you've done, otherwise you wouldn't have done it that way, because I know how focused on details you are. So, I think the idea that all of those details, all of those minutiae, the recovery of that history, of that experience, so carefully so that every little detail corresponds to how people lived and what they saw and what they thought. And all of that is very, very powerful in the material too. All of the details—I don't mean the cars and all that, I'm talking about the details of interaction, the details of space, the space in which the family find themselves in *Red, White and Blue* is a beautiful reconstruction of a certain kind of West Indian life. That must have been done with love—it was done lovingly, because it comes off as lovingly.

SM: I think the details of even how you speak to your parents, where you sit at the table, grace, all kinds of stuff I remember, which was part of the form of communication. And again, it's kind of weird, I don't be analytical about it in a way because it's a part of me, but when you take yourself out of it and you look at it, and you look at it: "How? Why? Oh, this will be like this." And then, again, it's eating at the dinner table. That was the only time that you could actually have necessarily a conversation, a proper conversation, because everyone would be going to work, they were coming back from work, people would be tired, there wasn't a moment. The only time you could actually have facetime, at least that I remember with my parents, was at the dinner table or when we did a board game, or things like that. That was the only time. So, it was always about activity and possibly getting something in and having that dialogue. Little things like that. And food, of course, and it's kind of crazy, but everything throughout was about the food.

PG: And about the board game. I mean, I didn't think I would live to see an image of a Black family playing Scrabble, that's part of the recovery of the kind of cultural complexity of their life and formation. I love that sequence in the film, and I think lots of people will recognize that as an image that cuts against all the sort of—you say trauma—that idea that Black families are somehow diseased, that there's somehow something wrong with them, that their kinship's not right, that they have too much of this and too little of that, too much Victorian this, too much violent that, too much tension.

SM: I had so much love in my family, so much love, so much love. And that love always came out through protection. And that's the thing about *Red, White and Blue* with Leroy Logan's father—similar to mine, and others. And I imagine a lot of people identify with it, because my father would be my father because he didn't want to see me hurt, because he had been [bearing] the brunt of so much things. Imagine people going and coming at nine to five, and what they had to go through to come home with their wages to give to the children, and to be fearful of what could happen to them, because they were taking the brunt of it. So, I knew that my father was very much—when I said I wanted to go to art school, my father was like, "Art school? Um, okay." He always told me to get a trade, he wanted me to have something in my arsenal that no one could ever take away from me. Because he knew the white establishment could take that away from me to say, "Okay, you're not worthy of this, you're not deserving of this," and take it away from me. But if you had a trade, and you could do something, that couldn't be taken away from you. And that was his way of just trying to protect me.

PG: That dynamic of protection you handle in *Red, White and Blue*—I don't think this is a spoiler now, so I hope it's a safe thing to say: there's a moment obviously after Leroy's father has been brutally and cruelly assaulted by—after the assault, let's give the minimum away—after the assault, Leroy goes to see him in hospital and there's a kind of very poignant, very intense encounter between the two of them, where that dynamic of protection is reversed generationally. So, instead of the parent seeking to protect the child, you have the child erupting with the desire to protect the parent.

SM: That's the main thing, that's great the way you've picked up on that. And, of course, the father being quite embarrassed about it in a way. There's a certain way he looks at him with his face all swollen and distorted, and his son looking at him. And then what triggers the son is the reaction of his mother, not necessarily the father, because he has to hold up in front of the father. But when he looked at his mother, that's when he breaks down. And that's when things slightly shift as far as the weight is concerned, not the fact that he takes over but he realizes his responsibility, the son now knows what his responsibility is now [what] his father had before, that he has to take on the baton, he has to move on. He's the one that has to take on whatever the father was holding on before.

PG: Yeah, and just that sense of seeing your parent as a victim, seeing your parent as vulnerable. That's a shock, and that shock does a lot of work in the plumping of that beautiful film. Well, I won't say any more about that, but there are lots of things that struck me about it. The other thing I guess I want to mention—I know I said I wasn't going to—is how it shows (and there are elements of this in the first film too) that Black people can have ordinary lives. It's not sort of deviant, it's not only trauma. It's an ordinary life. And, to me, the power of seeing it in an ordinary way, in a house where people treat each other as well as they can, they work for each other to realize each other's possibilities to have an ordinary life and do ordinary things, and have joy and laughter and all of that, that comes across very strongly in the way that that interior life of that family is captured. Yeah, they have conflicts, but they sort them out, they work them out. There's a moment where you think it's going to tear, and we all know those moments happen. But there's also repair that goes on; there's care there, there's love there, there's joy there. It makes it kind of ordinary—people have problems, they work through their problems. That's not something that you see all that often in cinematic representation of Black family life.

SM: No, and it's sort of what happens to us on every single day of our lives. But yes, you're quite right, it's not projected or given that attention and other things are. What's interesting about that family is that it's all about trying to achieve more, it's all about achievement, it's all about, "Come on, we can do this. Come on, we can work through this. Come on, let's do this." It goes that way for the family, but it also goes well up to the Metropolitan Police when Leroy joins it, and he thinks he can progress in the same way—yes, I imagine there will be mistakes along the way, but he can actually proceed and progress. But it's not that kind of environment; it's unforgiving for him as a Black man. His development was stunted because of racism within the Metropolitan Police, and that's the thing about it, you see the trial and tribulations of the family and how it comes together and how wonderful they are at getting him to that point. And then he goes to another situation where that environment is not welcoming at all, and that's because of who he is as a person. And I think from '83 to '84, that's where we are right now. This is not where the series stops, actually—the last piece of the series of films is *Education*—but as far as I'm concerned, as progress is concerned in this country and the UK, this is where it stops as far as how one tries to integrate to make change. Not necessarily integrate, but to try and sort of change it within—that's exactly what Leroy says: he's trying to change the organization from within to make it better, and that's been stumped. I've got to add one thing because a very important element in this, in goodness, is John Boyega. And what happened to John during the Black Lives Matter demonstration in London was hugely integrated with *Red, White and Blue*, because while we were making this, this is what happened. And I know for a fact, and he's said it himself, that the process of making *Red, White and Blue* and what happened when he spoke at the demonstration, and afterwards when we did the pick-ups, was very im-pivotable [*sic*] in what was going on. So, art in some ways was imitating life for sure. I mean, we could talk about *Star Wars* and John, him being the golden boy as they say in *Red, White and Blue*, and him being the golden boy in *Star Wars*. But his development [was] being stunted within the process, within that series of films. And it was art imitating life, and therefore he was playing that.

PG: Yeah, I suppose the implicit suggestion that being a member of the Metropolitan Police is a bit like being a stormtrooper in the Evil Empire.

SM: Well, you said it!

PG: Can we just speak briefly now about the *Lovers Rock* film? It moved me greatly. It moved me greatly because I found its sensuous, loving appreciation of the work that music does, and has done, and goes on doing in the lives of people is a very rare thing. And actually, the sort of sensuous part of it wasn't just the sound, because the sound of the music seems to kind of saturate the visual presentation of the film in some very rare way. And I found myself being able to smell what was being cooked in that kitchen. It all came together into the body in that way—it's a very rare thing. I don't know how you managed to do that. Is that something you want to share?

SM: It's the sensual. The only way I can explain it is through music. Because what you do is you set the tempo, you write the harmony, the melody, or whatever it is, and people can improvise within that. Because these are amazing actors, first and foremost, so they know the limitations of what they could do within the sort of timeframe of 1980, and the language, how they move, and even how they speak to each other. And we had an amazing choreographer. So we had this situation going on, and I think when Black people were in the room with other young Black people, and seeing who was in charge, it definitely fueled something. And to feel comfortable and have some kind of plan of what we were going to do, where they can move within that frame, that was the starting point. And again, it's love. I know it's kind of weird to say that, but it's love that you can appreciate with partners. And how one used to dance, the tradition in some ways has not been deemed as important, but I remember when people used to touch the lady's elbow and then work their way down the forearm to the wrist, to the hand, and hoping that she would grasp, because if she didn't grasp, that would mean she's not into it. But it was about touching the elbow first, getting the attention, pulling the hand all the way down the forearm to the wrist and hoping she'll clasp. If she clasped, then there's a dance. And again, the sensuality of it and the movement and then the music. I love that tune "Turn Out the Light" by the Investigators— "Tell me what you think about me, baby," like some guy asking, "I hope you like me." It's just so vulnerable and beautiful, and it was where we were at making that picture. It was all about that kind of possibility, and it was beautiful, it was marvelous. Sometimes as an artist, as a filmmaker, you're invited; you get to a point where you are invited and you're just there. Because in that environment that I set up there, that would have happened without a camera anyway. That would have happened without a camera. At some point we were just invited, and the whole idea of what happened afterwards was the a cappella bit of the film when we were singing "Silly Games"—I mean, that just happened. And Dennis Bovell, who produced that picture, is in it. He plays someone who's in that picture, the old guy in that. It just occurred, emerged. Sometimes you've just got to hold on, and that's about it.

PG: Obviously, that genre of music is really important, but in that party they're also playing other music. The other magical part of it was when "Kunta Kinte" comes on, because that has got a very particular kind of sound for people who don't know dub music. It's got that very sort of insistent . . . it's almost like a kind of prototype of some sort of avant-garde electronic thing.

SM: Totally. For me, it's like a dog whistle going off. Working with Courttia Newland on the music and the script, I heard this tune and I was like, "This is it." Because I knew I wanted dub. Okay, look at the ritual: at the beginning of the blues we have the girls dancing to Chic or "Kung Fu Fighting," the guys leaning on the wall checking out the ladies—it's almost like a ritual, isn't it? And then, of course, turning into lovers, and then at the end, when the dub comes on, it just takes off. It's futuristic, there's nothing about the present and everything about the future and possibilities; it's about possibilities and the future and something else. These guys, these women, they work five days a week for the blues, the racism, the nonsense that they put up with in the week to get there on a Saturday night to let off. And it's all about the future; it's never about the present. It's never about the present, and it's never about the past—it's always about the future. So that's why I just let off, that's when I let off because it's all about not being present but being somewhere else. And like you said to me—and we talked about this before briefly—you used the word "church," and I think maybe church is the only time in the week where Black people come together on a Sunday as such, and basically elevate themselves to another place. And that's always about the future. They elevate themselves within church to somewhere else, and I think that's it.

PG: It's very powerful. I'm sure you're going to get a very big reaction to that—I mean, you will to all of it—but to that in particular, because there's never been anything remotely like that.

SM: My aunt was so emotional, because the story is about my aunt. Long ago, my uncle used to leave the back door open for her to go and come back on a Saturday night, because my grandmother wouldn't let her out. And my grandmother saw it at the NFT and she was so emotional about it, she was sobbing in tears. And it was about remembering that moment—I can't speak for her, I shouldn't. But I think it was that whole idea of . . . it's almost like the top of your head would lift off, it was something else.

PG: It's transcendent, but also it's interesting you say that her reaction was tears. I'd seen a rough version of the *Mangrove* film, and I found when I saw the final version I was weeping, and I hadn't expected to be hit so hard given that I was roughly familiar with what you'd done.

SM: And also what you know. But that's what art can do, that's what art can do. I mean, if anyone knows anything about Mangrove Nine it's you, but it's one of those things where art takes it to another situation. It's not the formal aspects in the book, maybe it's the emotional, it's the space, the smell, the real jeopardy that people are under, the threat. But also the fact that none of the Mangrove Nine men are alive today, not one of them. The only people left are Altheia Jones-LeCointe and Barbara Beese, and that's it. None of the men are alive to this day, and that's the thing. And I've said it before, they were not seen as national heroes, but with art, with film, we can make them that. Absolutely, we can make them that.

PG: It's interesting you mention Barbara Beese, because of course one of the other things you've done, and it's very interesting, is you've taken the photographs that were made at the time of the demonstrations and you've brought them to life in a way that is incredibly vivid and extraordinary. Because again, you think you know what happened and you've got an idea from looking at those old black-and-white photographs people like Horace Ové took of that demonstration where she has a pig's head. And here it is. I don't know how to account for—I don't have a vocabulary available for how you've brought it to life in a way that's so vivid. I suppose it's partly the actors, it's partly, as you said before, these are great actors who are given an opportunity to present the full repertoire of their skill.

SM: But also they were playing themselves. The actress who played Barbara Beese had a conversation with her about Darcus Jr. and the fact that she knew that—she was in care, Barbara—and the fact that if they lost the case that possibly her child, her son, would have to be in care. And that hit her, apparently, when that conversation happened. So, they were playing themselves, more than maybe ever before because they didn't often get the chance to play their roots. And I think that was very important. Alastair Siddons cowriting the script with me, and his commitment to the detail of the trial—at that point there were no transcripts of the trial. So Alastair found—I think it was the *Kensington Post* or *Kensington Gazette*—there was a journalist there every day who had transcribed the whole of the case in newspapers, so all of that was virtually verbatim. And of course, there's a transition from the first half to the second half when we get into the formal aspect. For me, *Mangrove*—this is interesting, one of the producers said this—he said, "It feels like a Western," and I thought, "Yeah, you're absolutely right, it is a Western!" Some guy just wanting to open a little saloon, maybe he was a bad guy before, was on the wrong side of the tracks before, and he just wants to go straight with his saloon. But, of course, that sheriff who knew him before is always hassling him, and then things just take off. So, it is a kind of fable.

PG: PC Pulley should get a mention here because that's a great performance from him. The actor, Sam Spruell, gives a great performance because he doesn't overplay it, and his bewilderment—he should get some sort of prize for his bewilderment. I don't want to give things away, but I loved his bewilderment in that moment of the film. And I think we might try at UCL to give some belated recognition to Altheia Jones-LeCointe, who was a UCL student. I'd like to think that when people have her history and memory restored to them that they will want to honor her for the role she played in bringing a better, deeper, richer conception of justice in the life of . . .

SM: . . . in the whole of the entire UK. She changed history, for sure. For sure, she changed history, Darcus Howe changed history, all of those guys changed history. There's not an if, but, or maybe about it. But the fact of the matter is that during people like Darcus's and other people's lives there wasn't that real recognition—it was some guy on TV possibly, or you saw him after the uprising in 2011 and you saw him on TV as an old guy. Again, a lot of people didn't actually know him and know what he did, and others like him did, and for me that's so important right now. And it's really strange, of course, making these films at the time of George Floyd and corona [the COVID-19 pandemic]—timing or whatever it is. You know, I'd rather George Floyd be alive today, but he didn't die in vain, that's for sure. So, the timing is a bit weird in a way, but we have to sort of take advantage of course, somehow.

PG: And we don't know what the effects of all this will be.

SM: And it could be worse, it could be worse, it could be worse.

PG: Steve, thank you very, very much. I really appreciate you making the time, I know you're under pressure.

SM: And I've got to say thank you to you. For all the listeners out there, I've known Paul since I was nineteen years old, when I first met him at Goldsmiths University. And I used to knock on his door, myself and a guy called Desmond used to knock on his door, and he was always welcoming, and he was always open to talking to me as a nineteen-year-old. Could you imagine? You imagine someone like that would just swat the person away and say, "Come back tomorrow." He opened his door, and I used to sit down and just talk to him. So, if there's ever a lesson in that, it's just to listen to young people, because actually I do think that was very important for me, Paul, that you opened that door to me when I was nineteen years old and I could have this conversation with you, because it was just very important to have someone listen. And not necessarily [because] I was making perfect sense at all, but the fact that I had someone like you listening to me is so important. I think if anyone out there is in the vicinity of younger people, and they're looking for something, just to give them a bit of time is going to help them tremendously. So, Paul, again—weird me turning the tables on you like this—but thank you sir, thank you so much, thank you. Take care. Thank you.

PG: Bye-bye, and thanks.

"These Are the Untold Stories that Make up Our Nation": Steve McQueen on *Small Axe*

David Olusoga / 2020

From *Sight and Sound*, November 13, 2020. Reprinted by permission. With thanks to *Sight and Sound* and David Olusaoga, courtesy of the British Film Institute.

Small Axe—five luminous and astonishingly powerful films from Steve McQueen—would have been well-received no matter when they had arrived. But the fact is that their moment of arrival is now: the dying months of 2020, with the embers of the political fires lit by Black Lives Matter still glowing. What that means is that these films themselves will, inevitably, become part of the historical moment we are all living through and trying to make sense of. That John Boyega was center stage at one of the most significant of the Black Lives Matter protests of the summer, in London's Hyde Park, and also plays the central role in *Red, White and Blue*, one of the *Small Axe* pentalogy, ties the two phenomena together even more firmly.

The five films—*Mangrove*; *Lovers Rock*; *Red, White and Blue*; *Alex Wheatle*; and *Education*—are all based on real events, ranging from the infamous Mangrove Nine trial of 1970 to McQueen's own memories of the tales of one of his relatives, a youth spent sneaking out to blues parties. Between them they span the years 1968 to 1984, and lovingly re-create lost epochs in the history of Black Britain.

Yet *Small Axe* is, in a way, just as much about 2020—the year Britain suddenly and unexpectedly became able to properly hear the voices and the protests of its Black population. Through *Small Axe*, audiences will encounter not just Black voices but Black stories, and aspects of the Black British experience that many will be unfamiliar with. *Small Axe* is so clearly destined to be remembered as a product and emblem of 2020 that the fact that McQueen and his writers had begun work on the project long before the murder of George Floyd in Minneapolis may well be conveniently forgotten. Even knowing that fact, it is difficult not to experience these five very different films through the prism of recent events.

Small Axe is an epic—Black Britain's *Heimat*. It's at times a celebration and at others an act of remembrance. But just as thrilling as the histories it breathes life into is the abundance of Black talent and creativity it puts on display. There is McQueen himself, unseen but pulling the artistic and emotional levers, and there is the astonishing array of Black British acting talent he deploys; putting young Black actors into roles in which they are able to be their authentic selves.

Above all, these films are personal—personal to the director whose experiences of racialized low expectations and failed schools flowed into *Education*; personal to Alex Wheatle, a member of the *Small Axe* writers' room whose early life became the subject of one of the more hard-hitting of the five films. They will also be highly personal, particularly in the heightened atmosphere of 2020, to many Black Britons, for whom these stories and characters will touch raw nerves and stir repressed memories—as they did for me.

But *Small Axe* raises difficult questions not just about the history of British racism. It also stands as an indictment of the UK film and television industry and its failure to value Black stories and harness Black talent. Watching Shaun Parkes play Frank Crichlow, the persecuted owner of the Mangrove restaurant, raises the question: why has Parkes not previously been given a lead role? Watching Malachi Kirby playing the young Darcus Howe, also in *Mangrove*, makes me wonder why it was that Kirby's big break came on an American production, the 2016 remake of *Roots*, in which he played the lead role of Kunta Kinte.

2020 has seen a shift in consciousness. The events of this summer might be remembered as the moment of transition between two phases in the history of Black Britain. McQueen's *Small Axe* can and should perform a similar function in the story of British film and television. After this there are no viable excuses for marginalizing Black stories and Black voices.

David Olusoga: Can I start by saying, I watched these films thinking I've got to take notes and ask you some sensible questions. And then they did that thing that good art does, they snapped me into a different place. I've been really emotional about them. I've thought about parts of my life I haven't thought about for years.

I've thought about my experiences, which are nowhere near as extreme as Alex Wheatle's or as Kingsley's in *Education*, but I have some crossover and some parallel. I've thought about people I haven't thought about for years, and what became of them. And I've thought about both the joys and the crushing pressure of living in a racialized society, so I want to say thank you.

I spend a lot of time hearing people say, "Thank you for telling us our history stories, you don't know what it means" and it's really good to be able to say that to somebody else. There's something unexpectedly profound in seeing your stories told back in a way that you can't intellectualize, in a way that's deeply emotional.

Steve McQueen: Thank you very much. I've had similar responses from others too. My sister, when she saw *Mangrove*, said she wanted to shout out at the screen, out of emotion, out of joy. And then my aunt—who I based the film on—saw *Lovers Rock*, and she also used the word "emotional."

Because, as you said, it's brought things back, things which never got looked at before on that scale, to reflect back on you that I am, I exist. This did happen. I am real.

DO: It's much more powerful than I think the people making it realize. My experience of making TV about Black British history, is: I thought I knew how important it was and what it meant to people, and actually I totally underestimated it.

SM: For me, these films should have been made thirty-five years ago, twenty-five years ago, but they weren't and I suppose in my mad head, I wanted to make as many films as I could to fix that. There's no way anyone would have given me—or anybody else—any money at that time to make a film about the Mangrove Nine. You were not welcome. Fifty years later, everyone is celebrating those particular people.

DO: And fifty years later also puts it on the edge of human memory. Was there a sort of a recovery process? Of, "We're going to lose these people and their stories unless we act"?

SM: Definitely. When I started doing *Small Axe*, people were dying, and I thought, "I have to do it now."

A lot of people said to me: "Why did you not do this at the beginning of your film career?" But I couldn't have because I didn't have the maturity then, I didn't have the distance, I didn't have the strength. I needed to do other things before I could come back to me.

DO: They're all true stories. *Mangrove* is a true story in terms of it's a public event, but even *Lovers Rock* is based on . . .

SM: . . . my aunt, yeah. My uncle used to leave the back door open for her to go to [blues parties in] Ladbroke Grove because my grandmother would definitely not allow her to go! And next morning, knocking on the door: "Get ready for church." [*Laughs*]

Education [the film] is a mixture of things, it's about the ESN schools—educationally subnormal schools—and my own unfortunate journey through education in London when I was growing up. All the films, in some ways, I've based on reality.

DO: If I can speak personally again: I left watching *Education* till last, and it's the one that's impacted me the most. You mentioned your education; I was diagnosed special educational needs. I was in a remedial class. There was myself and the kids who'd just come from Vietnam who couldn't speak English.

I remember being aware that this was the road to disaster—that I wasn't being educated; I was being warehoused. My mother was terrified for me, she was agitating and pushing, and I was being educated at home, because we knew that schools weren't happening. And only latterly realizing that that was a common phenomenon. There are a lot of people out there for whom *Education* is going to be a punch in the guts. You had similar experiences?

SM: Very much. My school was sectioned to houses. And at fourteen you're put into either 3C1, which is, say, the normal kids' education, or 3C2, which is the people who are going to be the laborers or bricklayers, you know, the manual workers. And above and below were 3X, which were the brightest kids; and 3Y, which were all the kids who weren't particularly bright. So I was cast aside really, and the journey of my life was drawn in the sand when I was fourteen years old.

I went back to my school in 2000, handing out achievement awards, and the headmaster [told me that] when I was there, the school was institutionally racist. But I knew that. Some of my friends had recently bumped into my old deputy head, and he said that he realized the school was failing Black children and said to the headmaster: "We need to do something." And the headmaster said: "You do know what this will mean? More Black children will go to the school because it will be successful." So, basically, the school was investing in Black failure.

DO: There's a lot of Black people for whom these films—like they have done for me—are going to remind them of their past in a way that's going to be challenging and uncomfortable. But for a lot of people watching, none of this stuff is known, all of this is new. But these stories were always there. What people often say to me is: "How do you discover all of these history stories?" And I say, "I haven't discovered anything, I read different books and I know different people from you, because I'm from a different community." But these stories wouldn't have been told if you hadn't made these films.

SM: Well, this is a bit upsetting, David. Sometimes . . . I want the burden. I hope that by doing it, one can inspire other people to do other things. It's like when you make a program. To push on the next generation. But when you say that, it scares me.

DO: You used the word that I was going to, which is "burden," the "burden of representation."

SM: Give it to me. I want that burden. You get a lot of white people saying, "Oh Steve, the burden of this." It's like, "The burden of what?" We have to talk about this. What would I do otherwise? Write love songs? These stories are so rich. I feel the opposite, I feel blessed.

DO: I often think that. I feel lucky in a way that those people have neglected this history. I don't think they should have—there should have been programs and books about them years ago—but in some ways it's a treasure trove. The neglect of others and the disempowerment of previous generations of Black storytellers means you walk into this treasury of ideas, and nothing's been done. So, in some ways it's an opportunity.

But what's frightening is—and I use the phrase "we," which is that possessive thing the Black community does—we're one Steve McQueen away from not having these stories. Is that not an absolute weakness? I always think we're four or five heartbeats away from being made mute again.

SM: Well, unfortunately, that's the fact. I recently lost a very dear friend of mine, Okwui Enwezor, an amazing academic, a great curator. What's happening now with Black art around the world, that was because of Okwui. And it's like, "Goodness gracious, if he hadn't existed, what would the landscape look like?"

So, I'm hoping that we can inspire other people to do it, because there's been two generations of [Black British] filmmakers that we've lost. They're gone, because they weren't welcome.

DO: Can we talk about the process of making *Small Axe*? These are all films, in different ways, based on real events and real people—or amalgamations of people. Sometimes they're a very faithful telling of history. What was the kind of documentary process of bringing these stories into your writers' room and on to the screen?

SM: At first I wanted to make it about one family through the decades, but then I thought, after doing the research, "No, these have to be individual stories." So, I got this writers' room together because I thought, "Okay, it will be like an episodic TV series, but with different individual stories that are connected."

In some ways, the writers' room became an audition situation for the writers I wanted to work with, who were Courttia Newland [with whom McQueen cowrote *Lovers Rock* and *Red, White and Blue*] and Alastair Siddons [with whom McQueen cowrote *Mangrove*, *Education*, and *Alex Wheatle*]. It was within that process that I decided on the stories I wanted to tell.

The first one was always *Mangrove*. The second was *Lovers Rock*, my aunt's story. *Red, White and Blue* was a very difficult story because I couldn't understand why a Black man [Leroy Logan, played by John Boyega] wanted to be a policeman in the 1980s.

The fourth was *Alex Wheatle*. Alex was one of the writers in the writers' room. One day, I said, "Well, Alex, why don't we do your story?" He was, "What!" Alex was a consultant on all the stories, and was a great asset, because he lived it.

And the last one [*Education*] happened outside the writers' room because it was about my journey. That took a while, just because I was reluctant to go there, but thank goodness I did.

DO: *Education* was the most personal to you?

SM: Absolutely. It's a bit of my childhood.

DO: The music, but also the loving, painstaking re-creation of 1970s/1980s Brixton in *Alex Wheatle*. . . . We're about the same age, and it's a world that we saw as children. I remember record shops like that. I remember some of the posters on the wall—the poster of the Rasta kid with his arms crossed. I kept recognizing things that were part of my childhood, records that I didn't have but longed to have.

SM: I'll never forget going to Brixton for the first time. My mum took me to this church on a Sunday. The service ran for about three hours, so me and my friend Johnny Nicholls were at the back of the church and Johnny said, "Let's go." So, we left, and we went to Brixton! I must have been about fourteen.

DO: Thank God for long services!

SM: Yeah! We went to Brixton and it was amazing, it was the West Indies, it was Africa, it was people being people. My mum [had] moved to the suburbs and it was wonderful to see things that I never got to see. And then we went back to church—they didn't notice that we'd gone!

DO: I remember the first time I read Malcolm X's biography and he talks about being Detroit Red, going to Harlem for the first time. I was brought up in the northeast. My first time in Brixton, I got off the coach from Newcastle, where there were about five Black families, and walked around Brixton with my mouth open.

And I remembered reading Malcolm Little's encounter, and him being the hick, basically—the country boy arriving in Harlem—and that's exactly what I was. All I knew about Brixton was the riots, and suddenly I was in this place. I think part of me must have been scared, part of me must have bought the propaganda that this was the frontline.

I knew some Eddy Grant songs as well [*laughter*].

Another aspect of *Small Axe* that really struck me was, many years later I got to live in Brixton. I spent a year living on Mayall Road, about nine doors down from Darcus Howe, and one of the first things I made as a TV producer was a discussion program with Darcus. I had to argue for him to come on. I don't think anybody I worked with knew who he was.

We knew him from the Channel 4 format *Devil's Advocate*. I knew a very different Darcus at the tail end of his life—he was this ferocious figure. And this film [*Mangrove*] can reframe him. Some people think they understand who Darcus Howe was: he was this Channel 4 guy who had a twinkle in his eye and was a bit of a loose cannon, but *Mangrove* shows him as this remarkable, transnational, highly political, highly articulate legal figure.

SM: That's what art can do: rewrite history in the way it should be written. That's what you do with your TV programs.

I mean, I didn't know about the Mangrove Nine until maybe ten years ago. One of my father's best friends was Rhodan Gordon [one of the Mangrove Nine]. Rhodan used to come to our house all the time, and my father used to go to the Mangrove. But I think what happened was a lot of PTSD after the trial.

Rhodan Gordon, the day after the trial, his leg was broken, his arm was broken, and he was put into prison for possessing a dangerous weapon and assault. Thirty-six months he got. Those people were hounded by the police. And their children had to deal with that and are still dealing with that.

So, the fact that I had no idea who this person was, up until recently, is no real surprise, because it was drama. Now we can celebrate them, now none of the Mangrove Nine men are alive.

DO: I'm trying to work out why I've been so upset by these films. I think it's because you're not messing about with the idea that this stuff is damaging. Sometimes, we like to imagine the blows aren't causing wounds, but particularly in *Mangrove*, but also in *Red, White and Blue*, people are being damaged and you can see them being damaged. And a lot of it is unsaid, which is exactly what we've just been talking about.

SM: That's true. It's unsaid because it hurts so much.

When the George Floyd thing happened, a friend of mine called me and said, "George Floyd, you know George Floyd?" "Oh, yeah, heard about that"—and obviously, I blocked it. And it was only recently when a friend of mine said to me, "Man, I was really hurting," that I realized how much I block these things. Because, how many beatings, how many tortures, how many deaths, and not having any kind of justice? I think instinctively something happens in you, your brain rewires and you move forward, but that can't be healthy, can it?

DO: The ending of *Red, White and Blue* shows Leroy and his father just sitting there, acknowledging without words that they've both been through the mill.

SM: Yeah, he's tried to protect his son, but he couldn't. When you can't protect your own child. . . . And when John Boyega—Leroy—sees his dad beaten up by the police, and joins the police in order to change it from within . . . that's quite a heroic thing to do. But he can't because there's a glass ceiling. And that's when we have that scene with the father and the son.

We shot this before and after John had that situation in Hyde Park [when he made a powerful speech in support of Black Lives Matter during a demonstration]. So I think the process had an influence on him.

DO: So, John Boyega was acting in *Red, White and Blue* at the time of the demonstration in Hyde Park?

SM: He had shot that scene before, and then we went back to reshoot some pick-ups after, but I think the two things are entwined. John is like a Jack

Nicholson in a way. There's something in him that can come out as an artist on screen, just like Nicholson in those movies in the early 1970s.

DO: It came out in real life for the TV cameras in Hyde Park, and—this shows how conditioned I am—I was frightened for him. This guy's a Hollywood actor, and I'm thinking, "My God, are they going to let you work again?" Black people expressing themselves passionately, that feels . . .

SM: . . . I was like, "Man, put your armor on, put your sword up." You saw this guy naked and raw. It was beautiful. It was so bright, it was blinding.

DO: I think people will presume that these films were rushed into existence in response to the murder of George Floyd.

SM: You could never make these films in that time. We were in the middle of it when this unfortunate thing happened with George Floyd. I'll say it again, I wish George Floyd was here today, but all I can say is he didn't die in vain.

DO: No, but there's a terrible risk we'll forget that the catalyst for all of this was . . .

SM: . . . the catalyst was COVID-19, this pandemic. George Floyd being killed, murdered in the most horrific way, plus millions of people on the street. All this has happened for people to say, "Oh, possibly there's a problem with race." Prime ministers coming out and saying, "Oh, this is terrible"; kids out on the street. . . . People all over the world were sat at home because of the pandemic, looking at the TV, and it was undeniable. How many times has a Black person been murdered with a camera on them?

DO: The only thing that's different between this time or Freddie Gray or Breonna Taylor or Trayvon Martin is the pandemic, so it has to come down to that. I was talking to one friend and his argument was that it took the volume being turned down on everything else for people to hear the voices of Black people, and I liked that. You heard these pleas and these screams from the corner for the first time.

SM: It was the pandemic, no ifs or buts. We'd had video after video. People were looking at this at a time when everyone was asking themselves questions. Who am I? What am I going to do?

DO: I think you're right, the new active ingredient was the pandemic. But whatever the cause, it created a moment, and these films are going to be part of the playing out of that moment. They will be seen as part of this unexpected, unpredictable year.

It's interesting to think back to those days immediately after the murder of George Floyd, because there was an awful lot of talk in newspapers and on television in this country and other countries to say: "Look, this is an American issue, this doesn't happen here, we're a different sort of country"—and that attempt to use the political borders to kettle this phenomenon in. But that didn't work. It's a bit like the virus: it didn't obey national borders. The desperate attempts to say that Black people who saw parallels between their life, between the death of George Floyd, and the rise of Black Lives Matter, were somehow deluded.

SM: Well, the evidence was in the streets, the evidence was in the march. That was an amazing thing to see, those young people out marching. It gave me goose pimples, seeing my daughter going out there.

DO: Yes. One of the things that struck me as I was watching, particularly in Lovers Rock, is that here are young Black Britons playing their parents and their grandparents. There's something powerful about seeing this generation of young Black people who have all of these ideas, who are out demonstrating, to see them with the hairstyles and the manmade fabrics of their parents' generation. Black British people playing their own history seems to have a special circularity to it. There's a sense of belonging when you can play your own history.

SM: Absolutely, and there's so much talent. There are these amazing actors who just need to be given the opportunity and, like you say, play themselves. And they need more material to do it.

We've lost geniuses. We've lost our Katharine Hepburns, we've lost our Marlon Brandos, they're all doing other jobs. We never got a chance to see what they were able to do; the films that they weren't able to star in.

That's why it's so emotional, because it's like there's a catharsis about it—like my sister wanting to scream at the screen. I exist.

DO: The making of the films and the content says: "Here is Black creativity, here's what we can do, here's what we can create." I loved the amount of time you gave in *Lovers Rock* to the conversion of a normal London house into a blues party—the getting out of the furniture and the building of the sound system. Here are Black people making something for themselves, people who aren't wanted somewhere else.

SM: For me, it was about ritual. The process is just as important as what it ends up being. To take you on that journey where it gets to a point where it transcends, even beyond the people in the room. It becomes church. Some people say the Holy Spirit or whatever, but you know, it did happen. When I was shooting [the dance scenes in *Lovers Rock*], that was for real. I became invited into that situation. It was an honor to be there. As an artist, you wish to be invited, and that's what happened. I'd never experienced that before.

DO: It reminded me of a scene in *BlacKkKlansman* [2018] that has long lingering shots of dancing and a love of the fashions and the hairstyles. And Spike Lee running shots long to add a celebration.

SM: I'm not sure about that, I think this is something else. It was a spiritual experience. It wasn't performative. Something happened in that room, and we happened to have a camera there to record it. It was Black people seeing other Black people, feeling what they were feeling, and a Black director, a Black cinematographer, and the fact they could see each other and vibe off each other—and be each other, as you rightly said—that's what happened.

DO: That takes me on to the next thing I wanted to ask. You've rightly been vocal about the fact that it was a challenge to crew the films that you've made with Black production staff. Can you tell me about that struggle?

SM: Oh blimey, that was a job! The fact that Black people in this country feel that there's no space for them in the British film industry is a problem. We had four Black heads of department, and then when we moved to Wolverhampton... there was no one. I said, "We've got to do something about this, this is not on. In Wolverhampton, there's no Black people interested in film?" We got one spark, one technician.

It was because people don't feel welcome and it's just not good enough. I had to make a film so you do as best you can, but it's one of those things where, how can I feel comfortable making something like this without a Black crew?

DO: This has been a year where we've had bigger commitments and initiatives in the world of film and television on these issues than ever before. Are you hopeful or skeptical?

SM: I mean, like you said in your speech [the MacTaggart lecture at the Edinburgh TV Festival, which Olusoga delivered in August this year], there's no going back.[1] It's on the powers that be, and people like myself and yourself to make sure the people are doing their job.

DO: Do you think it takes, and I use this word advisedly, "policing," to ensure that there is progress?

SM: Unfortunately, yeah, because if people don't have to do it, they won't. Look what British talent we have, look how wonderful it could be. Look how much revenue could be made. Look how much joy could be brought to so many people. It makes economic and artistic sense.

DO: But my impression is that the liberal arts, the creative arts, all of those sectors have given themselves a free pass. They presumed because they were nice liberal people that this stuff would just happen and that they didn't need to put systems in place. And it hasn't happened, and it didn't happen fifteen years ago. And the reason that you can't have the crew you want, is because people made decisions fifteen, twenty years ago to not give them breaks.

SM: Precisely. I can't remember if it was at the BFI or where. I was a kid, I was like nineteen years old. I said I was interested in the cinematographer Robby

Müller and the person laughed at me. I'll never forget that. They had an impression of what Black people could do or couldn't do.

But I don't care about that, what I care about is the fact that artistic progression for Black people is a progression for everyone, not just for Black people.

DO: But to use the B-word again—burden, that is. We tell Black kids you've got to work twice as hard to get half as far. You do that for twenty, thirty years and you're burnt out. We've internalized this idea that we have to be excellent all the time, but not everyone can be, and those expectations are crushing.

SM: There's no two ways about that, but all I can say is that there is a sense of opportunity here, because the doors are open right now—or closing more slowly—so we've got to get what we can as quickly as possible.

DO: These films are going to be a part of that moment; they're going to have, I think, an incredible impact. These are five brilliant stories plucked from a million Black British stories. What do you hope is the catalytic effect of *Small Axe*?

SM: An awakening. I remember for so long, people would say we've got the best police force in the world. It was only the Black community who knew that it wasn't, and now fifty years later, everyone's catching up.

I hope that people are more inquisitive about the things around them, because these are London stories, these are the untold British stories. People must understand that there are other histories that make up the history of our nation. You've done your bit with your television documentaries. The making of this country has had a profound effect on how British people have lived their lives, if that makes sense.

DO: It does and what's fascinating is, these films span 1968 to 1984, and in them you can see how Black culture and Black music through that time span is becoming more central, more universal. There's that thing that [jazz singer] Lucky Gordon says: "We bought some damn color to this country."

I think young Londoners of all races now, brought up in the most diverse city in the world, are not going to see these as Black stories. These are London stories to them.

SM: Absolutely. It's interesting, I did this project called *Year 3* at the Tate, we took photographs of [London schoolchildren in Year 3], and there are people who walk into the exhibition, who don't know London, and they see how many Black and Brown people are there, and they're freaked out—but that's London.

DO: When I'm appealing to people that we need a history that functions for the country we actually are, I always say, "Go to a London comprehensive." You can't function as a country that has a history that doesn't tell the backstories and the family stories of four out of every ten Londoners. And if you want to see what the future looks like, go to an infant school in London and there's Britain for you. And by transposing it into the Tate, more people saw it than ever, which is exactly what these films are going to do.

We're coming towards the end of a remarkable and unpredictable year. Are you optimistic or fearful for what's going to follow?

SM: I'm optimistic. People have got their head out of the sand. We've been screaming and shouting and all of a sudden, people recognize a reality they were too busy before to see. It is progress, and there's no going back.

DO: And the role of the storyteller, in keeping this momentum up?

SM: Tell the truth, the whole truth, and nothing but the truth. Ugly, hurtful, joyous, painful. . . . Rain or shine, that's how it's got to be.

Note

1. David Olusoga, "James MacTaggart Lecture, Edinburgh TV Festival 2020," YouTube video, https://www.youtube.com/live/XALf10024r8?si=Fs41iPfxIX27WVwC.

"Sometimes the Present Erases the Past, and Sometimes the Past Erases the Present": Steve McQueen on His Cannes-Premiering *Occupied City*

Nicolas Rapold / 2023

From *Filmmaker Magazine*, May 25, 2023. Reprinted by permission.

Tourists in Amsterdam typically stop at the Anne Frank House, but the ever-moving conga line of visitors tends to work against reflecting on the reality of its rooms. Steve McQueen's *Occupied City* opens up a space for contemplation of a hundred-plus houses, buildings, and other sites across Amsterdam that are marked by World War II and the Holocaust in some way, tracing scars and trauma that may no longer be visible, much less widely known.

Informed by an illustrated book by McQueen's partner, Bianca Stigter (who directed *Three Minutes: A Lengthening*), it's a living atlas: scenes of pandemic-era Amsterdam, overlaid with a neutral female voiceover delineating the history of particular addresses and residents. Nazi occupation effectively meant perpetual war on a home population, and so we hear of Jewish families in hiding, German military offices and outposts, Resistance fighters and publishers and artists, and the whole range of appalling, baroque cruelties (such as a guesthouse operated to entrap Jews).

Though highlighting specific events like the 1944 famine known as the Hunger Winter, the achronological nature of survey prevents the viewer from settling into the narrative arc of the 1940s and instead underlines an unsettling simultaneity of these facts of the past and the images of the present. Rather than a facile sense of people today obliviously living on graveyards, what comes across is the fragility of mundane daily routines and the crushing feeling of absence that comes to lurk everywhere (with ready parallels to the civilian battlefields of the present in the Ukraine, Sudan, and elsewhere). For this mapping of past and present, McQueen worked with a Dutch cinematographer, Lennert Hillege, and editor, Xander Nijsten, with a shifting score by British composer and cellist Oliver Coates (*Aftersun*).

In its divergent audio and image, the four-hour film sets up a fraught choice for the viewer, of what to attend to and what not to—one of the more effective such choices in an oeuvre marked by the contrast between extraordinary intimacy and vulnerability, and sometimes severe formal choices that push away and pull in the viewer. I asked McQueen about that and other aspects of the film, which some critics were all too eager to dismiss as a would-be installation (while embracing another stringently conceived WWII work at Cannes, *The Zone of Interest*). McQueen comes to Cannes just after *Grenfell* (about the horrific tower fire) showed at the Serpentine in London, and as he was in postproduction on the WWII London drama, *Blitz*.

Filmmaker: When did you first encounter the book?

Steve McQueen: My wife Bianca wrote the book. I was living in Amsterdam, I'm a Londoner. These stories of the war were all around me. It's a seventeenth-century city. I had this idea of maybe getting some footage from 1940 and then projecting the past onto the present—physically doing that, as some kind of artwork—and seeing the living and the dead. Then I thought, "Bianca's writing this book, maybe the past is text, and the present is the everyday," and I thought I'd put that together. A radical idea: forget archive footage—we can look at the past in the present. That was the starting point. She started writing years ago. I had been mulling this in my head for a while. 2005 was when I first started thinking about it.

F: But it didn't end up being your first feature film (or second). Why now?

SM: I'm the kind of person who plants seeds and sees what comes to fruition, how it grows and matures. Right now I'm living in . . . where am I now? In my head I'm in 2016. Because you plant seeds, and then in seven years, you see, will they come into blossom, will they fade? There's a lot of things that have been planted. The idea is to have time to grow and for things to be consolidated.

F: How did you decide upon a feature film format? I've heard people say that it could be an installation.

SM: It could be.

F: What lent it to a feature?

SM: I shot thirty-six hours of material. The whole book, really. But I wanted to put this into a feature form, a narrative form—well, not narrative, but a form for cinema. That was because I wanted it to be an experience, not a history lesson and not journalistic in that way.

F: Would an installation be more like walking through a museum?

SM: I'm not saying that I won't do that [an installation] in the end as a part of this. But you can do anything you want! There's no rules, as far as I'm aware.

F: In terms of the present (images) and the past (voiceover), I found that my mind couldn't always pay attention to both after a while.

SM: Yes. Great.

F: But for me the film therefore poses an ethical or moral choice, because if I only pay attention to what I'm seeing, I'm ignoring the past.

SM: Sometimes the present erases the past, and sometimes the past erases the present. Sometimes you're just listening to the text but not looking at the images, sometimes you're just looking at the images. And that's fine. It's like being in a classical concert. You can't hold it all in your head. There's also the weight of it, the magnitude. That's why the length is very important because the weight is impossible to hold. That's part of the experience as well.

F: I almost felt guilty that I couldn't hold both past and present in my head at the same time.

SM: Guilty? That's how we're living right now in our every day. This is something that draws from one's own experience in our every day. Again, it's an experience, not a history lesson. Even on the screen visually, there are some kids who are rolling up their spliffs, and they're saying, "Oh, come on with the dead babies now and going to Auschwitz." About people going on about saving the world. They're even saying that visually. They're erasing. That's the part where we talk about the Ten Commandments. No, there's no guilt involved, it's experience. The fact that you drift in and out is beautiful.

F: It's an experience that in a way divides your attention.

SM: Sometimes—and sometimes it consolidates.

F: Interviews have been key to the process of documentation in other films relating to World War II and the Holocaust. What kept you away from that?

SM: Because I just loved the idea of this text and finding someone to deliver it in the way I wanted to deliver it. Someone talking about the facts, what was going on, but not in an incompassionate [*sic*] way. I love the fact that you, the audience, project the emotion and the morality in that.

F: The quality of the voiceover is interesting: neutral but bright.

SM: Exactly! That is beautiful, that word "bright." It's coming from someone who's living in the present rather than living in the past. It's not a dull voice. "Bright" is exactly how I described it: it has to be bright.

F: It reminded me how much a voice conditions how you view what's on screen.

SM: But also how much you involve yourself in it.

F: It's not a sober, litany-like voice. And not a memorial.

SM: No, no.

F: How would you describe the structure of the film? It's not the order of the book exactly.

SM: No. It's as if you were going to the city for the first time and you were walking around. You're going left, you're going right. The structure is not sort of ABCD. The situation is as if you were meandering, from here to there, to here, to here. Because in some ways that's how you discover a city. Amsterdam is a wonderful city to get lost in. You find things, you come back to things. I feel it would have been a bit boring if you had the west, and then the east. You have to be more textual. People are always looking for form, and this has form, of course, but it is one which is textual.

F: When you were putting the order together, did you go on walks yourself?

SM: Yes, and we took a long time to see how and where we were going to start it. One of the most important things about this project is that we shot it on 35mm film. That structure of 35mm disciplines you and how you present it and how you go about your everyday shooting. There's a beautiful ritual which is hugely important for the picture. There's a limitation: it's expensive, it's precious. So therefore every decision was made—I mean, I grew up shooting Super 8 film. So I rattled something off, and oh my God, there's fifty pence! The economy of means of Super 8 taught me how to actually make film, before I actually shot. It gave me a craft in a way that I don't think if I grew up with digital I would have, because I'd just spray a reel with my camera and do it in the edit.

F: It's still a long film.

SM: It is a long film.

F: Sitting down and living with it like that gives you a feeling of the muscle memory of the city.

SM: Yes. I can't imagine making this film for an hour and half. It doesn't have the weight. It would be, "Oh, are you just visiting?" You have to go on a journey and understand the magnitude, and even then after four and a bit hours, you still realize that there's way more out there which is not in the film, which is fine. People and time these days—I think how people see time these days is very different. Sometimes you've got to slow down. The fact is that the means is the process. Addresses: that's what makes the length. It wasn't a case of flexing. And *Shoah*, reading back, was criticized for its length then.

F: Working with your wife's book, what did it feel like having a family connection to this history?

SM: It made me understand Bianca's parents more. Her father died actually while we were shooting it. The movie is dedicated to him, Gerard Stigter. He is a very famous poet and writer in the Netherlands [known under the pseudonym K. Schippers]. He and his wife, Erica, lived through the Hunger Winter [as children]. So it was pretty profound, yeah.

F: What sort of conversations did you have about the history?

SM: We had conversations all the time. There was a friend of theirs who was in hiding. Bianca's grandfather was put in a concentration camp in the Netherlands. He was a poet.

F: Did you feel an added duty to get things right?

SM: No, the duty was to myself because it's my every day, it's what I've been living for the past twenty-seven years. Like I said, sometimes things are right in front of you, it's on your doorstep, it's under your bed. I will never see the city the same as I did when I first got here.

F: What's the significance of the title, beyond the literal meaning? For me, it evokes a sense of being possessed.

SM: In a way you're living with ghosts here. It's a seventeenth-century city, so there's another layer of history on top of it as well.

F: Yes, and you show a ceremony about the centuries of slavery as well.

SM: Yes, it's the perennial past. And the Indonesians.

F: Of the hundreds of historical cases and points in the film, what shocked you the most?

SM: My daughter's school, just because it's personal. My daughter went to that school where kids are putting their rucksacks into their lockers, jostling each other to go into their classroom. That space was where the SS had their interrogation center, where people were tortured and interrogated. And this place is now a jovial environment of kids going to school and learning. They don't have to worry about that! At the same time, it's there, it's how it is. There it is: to have the comparison or not to have the comparison, to erase or not to erase, to listen or not to listen, to see or not to see.

F: It's easy to feel helpless in the face of this history. What can we do with this information?

SM: This is something one could do—make a film. I think the thing for me is not to forget what has been sacrificed for our liberty and our freedom, for me to talk now. It's no small thing. It's real. That's the key, the fact that me and you sitting across the table take it as the norm that we can have these conversations, and it's far from the norm. There were battles fought in the street for it.

F: There are stories of survival, and devastating stories of suicide as well.

SM: Could you imagine to be so hapless that the only way out for you is to take your own life—and also your children's? We take things so much for granted, and with the rise of the far right coming up again, we have to be very mindful of that. I can't fathom that.

F: The film also shows the periods of lockdown in Amsterdam during the COVID pandemic. People protest the lockdown, and the police force (some on horseback) crack down. I don't think it's conflating the lockdown with the occupation, as I'd heard a couple of viewers say. I think it's just showing how the state apparatus of force can be activated.

SM: Yeah, absolutely, what you're saying is making sense. But also in a visual narrative, things can change. You have antivaxxers—which obviously I don't support—on Dam Square at a time in a history when it can change into this military policing, which you can, if you want to, project as the Nazis or not. It's one of those things where I am not supporting that, but again when you put a past on the present, people try and force a narrative on top of the image and make sense of them—and unfortunately make nonsense as well.

F: At one point, when you show hotel workers making the bed and we see them in the mirror, I couldn't help but think of Vermeer.

SM: Sure, sure.

F: A lot of your work has been in dialogue with art history. How is that functioning in the movie?

SM: I'm not very conscious of that, but again these things happen. There you have it. But again people can project what they want or how they think. As a filmmaker, I don't want people to have expectations of who I am or what I do. As my mother said to me, "Don't let your left hand know what your right hand is doing." As an artist, you have to strive to challenge yourself, and that's it. And I think there's a lot of joy in the movie. The ice skating: people are always going to celebrate, people are always going to venture out and do things. As much as it is miserable and mournful, it's celebratory.

F: About a half-hour into the movie, I began to think there should be a hundred movies like this for cities around the world and their histories.

SM: Yes, there should be—there could be! Wouldn't that be amazing? That would be wonderfully beautiful. What happened in *this* location? What would it look like, what would it sound like, what are the contradictions, what are the uncomfortable things?

F: I inevitably thought of your film *12 Years a Slave*. I would love to see this done for, say, South Carolina.

SM: Wouldn't that be great? Please write that in your piece! That would be amazing. That would be kind of frightening and exciting and thrilling.

F: Because the relationship in America to the past is oblivion. One aspect of the idea of the melting pot is to erase the past.

SM: Well, precisely, that is it. And that's why *12 Years a Slave* is interesting for me. I remember these conversations weren't being had.

Interview with Steve McQueen and Bianca Stigter about Their Documentary *Occupied City*

Susan Kouguell / 2023

From *Script Magazine*, December 22, 2023. Reprinted by permission of Sadie Dean, editor-in-chief, *Script Magazine*.

About *Occupied City*: The past collides with our precarious present in *Occupied City*, informed by the book *Atlas of an Occupied City: Amsterdam, 1940–1945* written by Bianca Stigter. McQueen creates two interlocking portraits: a door-to-door excavation of the Nazi occupation that still haunts his adopted city, and a vivid journey through the last years of pandemic and protest.

Steve McQueen is a British film director, film producer, screenwriter, and video artist. His film *12 Years a Slave* received an Academy Award, two BAFTA Awards, and in 2016 the BFI Fellowship. McQueen's critically acclaimed and award-winning films also include *Hunger* (2008), *Shame* (2011), *Widows* (2018), and the anthology series *Small Axe*. Past documentary works include the BAFTA-winning series *Uprising* (2021). For his work as a visual artist, McQueen was awarded with the Turner Prize, and he represented Great Britain at the Venice Biennale in 2009. He has exhibited in major museums around the world. In 2020, McQueen was awarded a knighthood in the Queen's New Year's Honours List for his services to the arts.

Bianca Stigter is a historian and cultural critic. She writes for the Dutch newspaper *NRC Handelsblad* and has published three books of essays. Stigter was an associate producer on *12 Years a Slave* and *Widows*. In 2019, she published the book *Atlas of an Occupied City*. In 2021, she directed the documentary *Three Minutes: A Lengthening*, which premiered in the Giornate degli Autori at the Venice Film Festival and was selected for the festivals of Telluride, Toronto, Sundance, as well as the International Documentary Film Festival Amsterdam (IDFA) and Docaviv. It won the 2022 Yad Vashem Award for cinematic excellence in a Holocaust-related documentary.

There is a haunting quality to *Occupied City*, hearing the emotionless voiceover text about the Nazi occupation of Amsterdam over images of contemporary life in Amsterdam. With encouragement from McQueen and Stigter, I began this interview on a personal note, recounting when I saw the film at a recent press screening. Images of the neighborhood Apollolaan, where my mother grew up, and the text about the Hunger Winter; the countless atrocities, including the many Jews forced into hiding, and the specific identification cards with the letter J stamped on it. My grandmother was among those in hiding, and she too had these documents, which I shared with McQueen and Stigter. I thanked them for allowing me the time to share this with them and expressed that this interview is not about my story, but about their film.

Steve McQueen: It's all of our stories. I don't think you should leave yourself out of this interview; it would not be in service to your readers. It's important to have this transparency. To be honest with you, it's wonderful to add your experience into the interview because you're a survivor of this situation.

Susan Kouguell: Steve, in your interview with curator Donna De Salvo in 2016 at the Whitney Museum, you discussed your installation piece *End Credits* about the Paul Robeson FBI files.[1] The idea/theme of words being redacted brought to mind not only the obvious government censorship but the idea of the literal erasure of history.

There is a thematic correlation between this work *End Credits* and *Occupied City*, and Bianca's documentary *Three Minutes: A Lengthening*. These works are historical investigations, which address the erasure of history, and the fragility of memory and time.

Bianca Stigler: What they also share is that you can find new forms to deal with the past and you don't necessarily have to stick to the strictly well-known feature film or documentary genre. You can try to find a new way to convey history and the erasure of certain histories. And also to make it more of an experience than a history lesson. There's certainly common ground there.

SM: Both of us are very much about the audience and how things can sink in. With *End Credits*, it's much more sculptural than *Occupied City* and *Three Minutes*. It's for an art space due to the nature of its presentation.

SK: *Occupied City*'s length of four-and-a-half hours, including an intermission, requires a type of commitment from an audience. If it was two hours, for example, I don't think the film would have the same impact. Steve, you mentioned that the film had to have the weight of time, the weight of recounting history, and to give the viewer time to reflect.

SM: Once people see the film, the length is never discussed. If anything, when it comes into discussion, people wish it was longer.

BS: People said they lost any track of time. You enter a different zone of time, you don't feel the clock ticking, and you are transported somewhere else. One thing is for sure: you hear so many individual stories and you see so many people that you realize you can't hear everyone's story, [otherwise] the film would have [needed] to be ten thousand times longer. It gives you a certain tension that no matter what you do, you can never know it all.

SM: It's about the practice. It was the whole idea of using Bianca's text, which occurred over nineteen, twenty years of research, and projecting on that every day. We never contemplated it to be shorter. When I was shooting it, I didn't know what it was going to be. I had to find it through the process of filmmaking.

SK: Bianca, in your film *Three Minutes*, you made the decision not to show any contemporary faces except at the very end. We only see the three minutes of footage repeatedly shown and freeze frames of a home movie in 1938 Nasielsk in eastern Poland, months before they were deported to ghettos by the invading Nazis.

With *Three Minutes* and *Occupied City*, you both made some unconventional choices in conveying your narrative, such as avoiding talking heads, and not including—or only including—archival footage from the past.

BS: In *Three Minutes*, it exists only out of archival footage from 1938. Doing things in this way makes you think about time more. With the other forms of documentary, people almost forget there are also forms; here you are asked to think about it.

SK: *Occupied City* was shot over the course of two-and-a-half years on 35mm film, and you had thirty-four hours of footage. With the exterior shots, did people know you were filming them?

SM: Most of the time people knew because the camera was there but sometimes not. It was the case of getting the everyday and wanting to be spontaneous.

SK: Was anything staged? I'm thinking about the scene where the bicyclist hits a woman towards the end of the film.

SM: It just happened. Sometimes you have to predict the unpredictable.

SK: There is a huge responsibility to the history of Amsterdam, the people of the past, and the present. Obviously you cannot include it all so the choices then become what to include or embrace, what to honor, what to leave out. How did you arrive at these decisions in *Occupied City*?

SM: We shot everything in *Atlas of an Occupied City*—over 2,100 addresses. When we had the footage, it was a case of certain things being repeated so, therefore, we could leave that out, and then we decided what was the best for that particular version. What flowed and what didn't. We were fortunate to have this rich footage and situations to make this movie.

BS: When I was writing the book, the most harrowing part was when I couldn't find any information about someone except that he or she was born and murdered, and that was all. If you can keep a little bit by telling about someone, there is at least something left instead of nothing. For me that was difficult to come to terms with; you can't tell everything.

SK: Bianca, I read that you referred to your book *Atlas* as "time machine on paper"—it's a beautiful way to reference it.

BS: For me, it felt like that because you have a lot of history books that deal with the big picture or have the story of one person. What fascinated me was, could you imagine walking through a certain street back in that time so you knew things about the shops and the offices and the people that lived there? That you can get a sense of how something was in a different time and that fascinated me.

The strange thing about Amsterdam, in the city center, the canals, and so on, is that they are very much from the seventeenth and eighteenth centuries. You cannot see the Second World War and what happened there, but you know it happened in the same spots where people were round up or executed, or took their own lives. The book and the film both try to cross that, while at the same time acknowledging that it is uncrossable. There are all kinds of tension between the past and present throughout the whole film.

SK: What questions haven't you been asked in previous interviews that you would like to address about *Occupied City*?

BS: The music; it's very important for movies in general and in this movie, it is especially important.

SM: What composer Oliver Coates brought to the table was so transcendent; it brings another layer into the narrative, another echo in the audio sense.

BS: It makes it more abstract in a way, but also grounds it very much.

SK: What was then and what is now repeats for me. Ending with the bar mitzvah rehearsal and then the actual bar mitzvah was quite moving.

SM: We were invited to our friends' son's bar mitzvah. We thought it would be a good idea to shoot it. It was one of those things that everything in this movie is about our city; it's about where we live, where our children go to school. We talked to the rabbi for permission.

In a way, it was to say that after all that, the Nazis didn't win. There is a Jewish life that continues and exists in Amsterdam today. It was a very personal way to end the film. It's about our family and our friends, and all of our futures.

BS: It's beautiful and hopeful. It's something fragile of course. We see and hear the boy's voice trying to read the old words—it is very touching for me. It was also about not showing just the bad things but also the good things.

SK: What has been the response to *Occupied City* from the Dutch audience?

BS: We had the Dutch premiere in the most beautiful cinema in the world, the Tuschinski theatre. The original owner was murdered in Auschwitz during the war.

SM: It was extremely special to have the premiere there, and we dedicated it to him. It was a packed theater. You could feel the atmosphere was special to put this movie in this cinema.

BS: To see it in Amsterdam or another cinema, when you walk outside, I think one will have the feeling, I'll look differently at my city now. In a funny way, of course, people realize yes, that it's very extremely local but it also has something universal. One can imagine this film in Paris or in London or New York. One can imagine the film anywhere.

SK: Indeed. It is universal.

SM: Your background and history is amazing, and thank you for sharing it with us.

Note

1. Steve McQueen, interview by Donna De Salvo, *Whitney Museum of Art*, June 14, 2016, https://whitney.org/media/78.

Additional Resources

Books

Austin, Thomas, ed. "ReFocus: The Films of Steve McQueen." Edinburgh: Edinburgh University Press, 2023.
I Want the Screen to Be a Massive Mirror: Lectures on Steve McQueen. Basel, Switzerland: Schaulager Basel and Steudler Press, 2013.

Journal Articles

Alexander, Karen. "Recasting History: The Transformative Cinema of Steve McQueen and Raoul Peck." *Afterall: A Journal of Art, Context and Enquiry*, no. 46 (Autumn/Winter 2018): 138–48.
Cobb, Jasmine Nichole. "Directed by Himself: Steve McQueen's *12 Years a Slave*." *American Literary History* 26, no. 2 (Summer 2014): 339–46.
Demos, T. J. "The Art of Darkness." *October*, no. 114 (Autumn 2005): 61–89.
El-Khairy, Omar Assem. "Snowflakes on a Scarred Knuckle: The Biopolitics of the 'War on Terror' through Steve McQueen's *Hunger* and Kathryn Bigelow's *The Hurt Locker*." *Millennium: Journal of International Studies* 39, no. 1 (August 2010): 187–91.
Evans, David. "War Artist: Steve McQueen and Postproduction Art." *Afterimage* 35, no. 2 (September/October 2007): 17–20.
Garfield, Rachel. "Peggy Ahwesh, Steve McQueen and Russell T. Davis: Reflections on the 1980s Under Lockdown." *Moving Image Review & Art Journal*, no. 9 (September 2020): 270–75.
Gifney, Noreen. "The Look of *Shame*: Sex as Excavation." *Studies in Gender and Sexuality* 16, no. 2 (June 2015): 103–9.
Goarzin, Anne. "Seeing 'Seeing' in Steve McQueen's *Hunger*." *Nordic Irish Studies* 13, no. 2 (2014): 79–97.
Horton, Zach. "Can You Starve a Body without Organs? The Hunger Artists of Franz Kafka and Steve McQueen." *Deleuze Studies* 6, no. 1 (February 2012): 117–31.
Kaisary, Philip. "The Slave Narrative and Film Aesthetics: Steve McQueen, Solomon Northup, and Colonial Violence." *MELUS* 42, no. 2 (Summer 2017): 94–114.
Lynch, John. "*Hunger*: Passion of the Militant." *Nordic Journal of English Studies* 13, no. 2 (2014): 184–201.
McNamee, Eugene. "Eye Witness: Memorialising Humanity in Steve McQueen's *Hunger*." *International Journal of Law in Context* 5, no. 3 (September 2009): 281–94.

Melvin, Adam. "Sonic Motifs, Structure and Identity in Steve McQueen's *Hunger*." *The Soundtrack* 4, no. 1 (August 2011): 23–32.

Mitchell, Michael. "With Covered Eyes: Amerindians and the Arts of Seeing in Wilson Harris and Steve McQueen." *Literature, Critique, and Empire Today* 39, no. 3 (September 2004): 107–18.

Robinson, Joel. "On Steve McQueen's *Giardini* and the Follies of Nations." *Visual Culture in Britain* 16, no. 1 (2015): 86–102.

Stadtler, Florian. "Theatres of Memory: Un-silencing the Past—Steve McQueen's *Small Axe* Anthology." *Transnational Screens* 13, no. 2 (May 2022): 129–40.

Vogt, Naomi. "Small Monuments: Recording and Forgetting in the Work of Steve McQueen." *Third Text*, no. 29 (2015): 123–40.

Wanzo, Rebecca. "How Long, Not Long: A Take on Black Joy." *Film Quarterly* 74, no. 4 (Summer 2021): 51–55.

Wynne-Walsh, Rebecca. "Troubled Boundaries: Corporeal and Territorial Transgression in *Hunger* (Steve McQueen, 2008) and *'71* (Yann Demange, 2015)." *Gothic Studies* 25, no. 1 (March 2023): 77–92.

Artist Monographs

Demos, T. J., ed. *Steve McQueen: Giardini—Notebook*. London: British Council Visual Arts Publications, 2009.

Kim, Clara, and Fiontán Moran, eds. *Steve McQueen*. London: Tate Publishing, 2020.

Krystof, Doris, ed. *Steve McQueen*. Vienna: Kunsthalle Wien, 2001.

Matsumara, Madoka, and Yuka Uematsu, eds. *Steve McQueen: Caresses*. Kagawa, Japan: Marugame Genichiro-Inokuma Museum of Contemporary Art, 2006.

Meschede, Friedrich, ed. *Steve McQueen: Barrage*. Cologne: Verlag der Buchhandlung Walther Koenig, 2000.

McQueen, Steve. *Breakaway Mechanics*. Nantes, France: Capricci, 2023.

McQueen, Steve. *Queen and Country*. London: British Council Visual Arts Publications, 2010.

McQueen, Steve. *Speaking in Tongues*. Paris: Editions des musées de la ville de Paris, 2003

McQueen, Steve. *Works*. Chicago: Art Institute of Chicago, 2012McQueen, Steve, and Jean Fisher. *Caribs' Leap/Western Deep*. London: Artangel, 2002.

Newman, Michael, ed. *Steve McQueen*. London: ICA; Zurich: Kunsthalle Zürich, 1999.

Todolí, Vicente, ed. *Sunshine State*. Venice: Marsilio Arte, 2022.

Wallis, Clarrie, and Nathan Ladd, eds. *Steve McQueen: Year 3*. London: Tate Publishing, 2021.

Interviews with Steve McQueen

Adams, Sam. "*Widows* Director Steve McQueen on Why He Wanted to Adapt a 35-Year-Old TV Series." *Slate*, 20 November 2018, slate.com/culture/2018/11/steve-mcqueen-interview-widows-director-trump-metoo.html.

Adams, Tim. "Eyes on the Prize." *The Observer*, 10 October 1999, p. 30.

Aspden, Peter. "Interview: Steve McQueen on Telling the Truth in Hollywood." *Financial Times*, 3 October 2014, www.ft.com/content/5a07b594-49bb-11e4–80fb-00144feab7de.

Bazaar. "Exclusive Interview with Steve McQueen," 1 November 2018, bazaar.town/widows-steve-mcqueen-interview.

Bickers, Patricia. "Let's Get Physical." *Art Monthly*, December 1996–January 1997, www.artmonthly.co.uk/magazine/site/article/steve-mcqueen-interviewed-by-patricia-bickers-dec-jan-96–97.

Blazwick, Iwona. "Oh My God! Some Notes from a Conversation with Iwona Blazwick, Jaki Irvine, and Steve McQueen." *MAKE: The Magazine of Women's Art*, no. 74 (February/March 1997): n.p.

Boltin, Kylie. "*Shame*: Steve McQueen and Michael Fassbender Interview." *SBS*, 7 February 2012, www.sbs.com.au/whats-on/article/shame-steve-mcqueen-and-michael-fassbender-interview/7d0xeunvu.

British Council France, "Un entretien avec Steve McQueen," 6 December 2011, www.britishcouncil.fr/blog/un-entretien-avec-steve-mcqueen-artiste-britannique-et-realisateur-de-hunger-et-shame.

Clarke, Donald. "Steve McQueen: 'Calling Me a Political Director Is Like Calling Me a Male Director.'" *The Irish Times*, 27 February 2021, www.irishtimes.com/culture/film/steve-mcqueen-calling-me-a-political-director-is-like-calling-me-a-male-director-1.4489633.

Daley, Michelle, and Mike Lambert. "Steve McQueen: 'We Want Meaningful Change—So Let's Get on with It.'" *Inclusion Now*, 16 July 2021, www.allfie.org.uk/news/inclusion-now/inclusion-now-59/steve-mcqueen-we-want-meaningful-change-so-lets-get-on-with-it.

Ebony. "The *Slave* Director's Narrative: Steve McQueen [Interview]," 18 October 2013, www.ebony.com/the-slave-directors-narrative-steve-mcqueen-interview.

Elkann, Alain. "Steve McQueen." *Alain Elkann Interviews*, 7 April 2024, www.alainelkanninterviews.com/steve-mcqueen.

Fennessey, Sean. "Steve McQueen on *Widows* and Reinventing the Heist Movie." *The Big Picture*, 19 November 2018, podcasts.apple.com/us/podcast/steve-mcqueen-on-widows-and-reinventing-the-heist/id1439252196?i=1000424135728.

Ford, Rebecca. "Steve McQueen on Expectations: 'I'm Happy to Defy Them.'" *Vanity Fair*, 20 May 2023, www.vanityfair.com/hollywood/2023/05/steve-mcqueen-occupied-city-interview-cannes.

Funzine. "An Interview with Steve McQueen" [2008], funzine.hu/en/eng/an-interview-with-steve-mcqueen-2.

Gates, Henry Louis, Jr. "*12 Years a Slave*: A Conversation with Steve McQueen." *Transition*, no. 114 (2014): 185–96.

Girish, Devika. "Steve McQueen on *Occupied City*." *The Film Comment Podcast*, 20 May 2023, www.filmcomment.com/blog/the-film-comment-podcast-steve-mcqueen-on-occupied-city.

Goodsell, Luke. "Interview: Steve McQueen and Chiwetel Ejiofor Talk *12 Years a Slave*." *Rotten Tomatoes*, 17 October 2013, editorial.rottentomatoes.com/article/interview-steve-mcqueen-and-chiwetel-ejiofor-talk-12-years-a-slave.

Graham, Bill. "*Shame* Star Michael Fassbender & Director Steve McQueen Talk Addiction in Us All and the Business of Storytelling." *The Film Stage*, 2 December 2011, thefilmstage.com/interview-shame-star-michael-fassbender-dire . . . ve-mcqueen-talk-addiction-in-us-all-and-the-business-of-storytelling.

Greenstreet, Rosanna. "Q&A: Steve McQueen, Artist and Film-Maker." *The Guardian*, 22 November 2008, www.theguardian.com/lifeandstyle/2008/nov/22/steve-mcqueen-interview.

Gritten, David. "*Shame*: Steve McQueen Interview." *The Telegraph*, 14 January 2012, www.telegraph.co.uk/culture/film/filmmakersonfilm/8994878/Shame-Steve-McQueen-interview.html.

Kapadia, Asif. "Transcript + Podcast: *Small Axe*—Steve McQueen in Conversation with Asif Kapadia." *Directors UK*, 4 June 2021, directors.uk.com/news/podcast-small-axe-steve-mcqueen-in-conversation-with-asif-kapadia.

Knegt, Peter. "*Shame* Director Steve McQueen: 'We Have to Keep Cinema Alive.'" *IndieWire*. 16 September 2011, www.indiewire.com/news/general-news/shame-director-steve-mcqueen-we-have-to-keep-cinema-alive-52275.

Kohn, Eric. "Steve McQueen Justifies His 4.5-Hour Documentary on the History of Nazi-Occupied Amsterdam." *IndieWire*, 16 May 2023, www.indiewire.com/features/interviews/steve-mcqueen-interview-occupied-city-1234863193.

Lee, Dan P. "Where It Hurts: Steve McQueen on Why *12 Years a Slave* Isn't Just about Slavery." *Vulture*, 8 December 2013, www.vulture.com/2013/12/steve-mcqueen-talks-12-years-a-slave.html.

Levy, Emanuel. "*Hunger*: Interview with Director Steve McQueen." 13 November 2008, emanuellevy.com/interviews/hunger-interview-with-director-steve-mcqueen-2.

Loughrey, Clarisse. "Steve McQueen Interview: 'Men Are a Little Bit Tone Deaf to Certain Aspects of Feminism.'" *The Independent*, 5 November 2018, www.independent.co.uk/arts-entertainment/films/features/stev...een-widows-interview-feminism-director-shame-12-years-a8614621.html.

Matt, Gerald. "Steve McQueen." In *Interviews*, edited by Gerald Matt, 232–37. Cologne: Kunsthalle Wien and Verlag der Buchhandlung Walter König, 2007.

McCracken, Kristin. "Interview: Steve McQueen Talks *12 Years a Slave*, *Django Unchained*, Pitt & Fassbender & More." *IndieWire*. 11 September 2013, www.indiewire.com/features/general/interview-steve-mcqueen-talks-12-years-a-slave-django-unchained-pitt-fassbender-more-93822.

McQueen, Steve. "What's There Left to Say about Kanye West?" *Interview*, 14 January 2014, www.interviewmagazine.com/music/kanye-west.

Medina, Joseph Jammer. "Interview: Steven McQueen on His Captivating New Movie *Shame*." *LRM Media* [2011], lrmonline.com/news/2011-11-interview-steven-mcqueen-captivating-movie-shame.

Mende, Doreen. "Conversation autour de *End Credits*." *Issue*, 11 July 2023, issue-journal.ch/flux-posts/conversation-autour-de-end-credits-2.

Mendez, Paul. "'These Stories Needed to Be Told': Steve McQueen and the Golden Age of Resistance." *Esquire*, 1 October 2020, www.esquire.com/uk/culture/a34217348/steve-mcqueen-interview.

Mitchell, Elvis. "Steve McQueen." *Interview*, 1 October 2013, www.interviewmagazine.com/film/steve-mcqueen-1.

Mitchell, Elvis. "Steve McQueen: *Shame*." *The Treatment*, 7 December 2011, www.kcrw.com/culture/shows/the-treatment/steve-mcqueen-shame.

Montagne, Renee. "*12 Years a Slave*: 160 Years Later, a Memoir Becomes a Movie." *NPR*, 17 October 2013, www.npr.org/2013/10/17/235486707/12-years-a-slave-160-years-later-a-memoir-becomes-a-movie.

Movies.ie. "*Hunger* Interview Steve McQueen" [2008], www.movies.ie/hunger-interview-steve-mcqueen.

Neglia, Matt. "Interview with *Occupied City* Director Steve McQueen & Producer Bianca Stigter." *The Next Best Picture Podcast*, 8 November 2023, nextbestpicture.com/the-next-best-picture-podcast-interview-with-occupied-city-director-steve-mcqueen-producer-bianca-stigter.

O'Hagan, Sean. "Steve McQueen: 'Black People Are Weirdly Missing from the Narrative.'" *The Observer*, 15 November 2020, www.theguardian.com/tv-and-radio/2020/nov/15/steve-mcqueen-black-people-are-weirdly-missing-from-the-narrative-small-axe-mangrove-viola-davis-idris-elba-bernardine-evaristo.

O'Hagan, Sean. "Steve McQueen: 'It's All about the Truth, Nothing but the Truth. End Of.'" *The Observer*, 26 January 2020, www.theguardian.com/culture/2020/jan/26/steve-mcqueen-interview-tate-modern-retrospective.

O'Hagan, Sean. "Steve McQueen: The Interview." *The Observer*, 12 October 2008.

O'Hehir, Andrew. "Interview: Steve McQueen Talks Naked Bodies and *Shame*." *Salon*, 1 December 2011, www.salon.com/2011/12/01/interview_steve_mcqueen_talks_naked_bodies_and_shame.

Okundaye, Jason. "Black Men Deserve to Grow Old: Sir Steve McQueen on the UK's Stark Health Inequalities." *The Standard*, 19 January 2022, www.standard.co.uk/lifestyle/steve-mcqueen-embarassed-interview-es-magazine-b970787.html.

Pometsey, Olive. "Steve McQueen: 'We Have an Idea of Who We Like to Be, but I'm Interested in Who We Actually Are.'" *GQ*, 6 April 2021, www.gq-magazine.co.uk/culture/article/steve-mcqueen-interview-2021.

Radish, Christina. "Michael Fassbender and Director Steve McQueen *Shame* Interview." *Collider*, 29 November 2011, collider.com/michael-fassbender-steve-mcqueen-shame-interview.

Robertson, Emma. "Steve McQueen: 'It's about What's Right, Not What Fits.'" *The Talks* [2018], the-talks.com/interview/steve-mcqueen/.

Rochlin, Margy. "The Grim Truth." *DGA Quaterly Magazine*, Summer 2013, www.dga.org/Craft/DGAQ/All-Articles/1303-Summer-2013/Independent-Voice-Steve-McQueen.aspx.

Ryan, Mike. "Steve McQueen on *Widows* and Why He Ignored a 'Warning' that an Actor Was 'Difficult' to Work With." *Uproxx*, 11 September 2018, uproxx.com/movies/steve-mcqueen-interview-widows-michelle-rodriguez.

Searle, Adrian. "Artist Talk: Steve McQueen." *Schaulager: Laurenz Foundation*, 24 May 2013, schaulager.org/en/schaulager/video-archive/video/12.

Sepinwall, Alan. "'It's about a Certain Kind of Blackness': Steve McQueen on the Making of *Small Axe*." *Rolling Stone*, 18 December 2020, www.rollingstone.com/tv-movies/tv-movie-features/small-axe-steve-mcqueen-interview-1104952.

Solomons, Jason. "Film Weekly: Steve McQueen." *The Guardian*, 16 October 2008, www.theguardian.com/film/audio/2008/oct/16/podcasting.

Sooke, Alastair. "Venice Biennale: Steve McQueen Interview." *The Telegraph*, 29 May 2009, www.telegraph.co.uk/culture/art/venice-biennale/5394613/Venice-Biennale-Steve-McQueen-interview.html.

Stidhum, Tonja Renée. "Steve McQueen on the Blackest *Soundtrack of America* and Music's Impact on His Filmmaking." *The Root*, 7 June 2019, www.theroot.com/steve-mcqueen-on-the-blackest-soundtrack-of-america-an-1835322715.

That Shelf. "Interview: Steve McQueen, John Ridley & Henry Louis Gates," 16 October 2013, thatshelf.com/interview-steve-mcqueen-john-ridley-henry-louis-gates.

TimeOut. "Steve McQueen on *Shame*: Interview," 30 November 2011, www.timeout.com/film/steve-mcqueen-on-shame-interview.

Tonet, Auréliano. "J'aimerais que *Shame* fasse sur son public un effet semblable à celui du sifflement du maître sur son chien." *Trois Couleurs*, 19 April 2023, www.troiscouleurs.fr/article/shame-steve-mc-queen-interview.

Ugwu, Reggie. "Steve McQueen and Viola Davis on Hollywood, Race and Power." *The New York Times*, 15 November 2018, www.nytimes.com/2018/11/15/movies/steve-mcqueen-viola-davis-widows.html.

Utichi, Joe. "Steve McQueen 'Saw the Matrix' When He Visited the FBI for *Widows*." *Deadline*, 19 December 2018, deadline.com/2018/12/widows-steve-mcqueen-oscars-directing-interview-1202519741.

Williams, Kam. "The *12 Years a Slave* Interview: Steve McQueen." *The New Journal and Guide*, 3 February 2014, www.thomasdanegallery.com/usr/documents/press/download_url/383/smq-the-new-journal-feb-2014.pdf.

Young, Kirsty. "Steve McQueen." *Desert Island Discs*, 21 September 2014, www.bbc.co.uk/programmes/b04hml41.

Zemler, Emily. "Steve McQueen on His New *Small Axe* Films and Why No One Tells Him What to Do." *Observer*, 20 November 2020, observer.com/2020/11/steve-mcqueen-small-axe-interview.

Video Resources

"The Artist's Voice: Steve McQueen—Institute of Contemporary Art/Boston." YouTube video, 1:22:13, posted by "ICA Boston," 9 November 2017, www.youtube.com/watch?v=J4X3x7GFFh8.

"An Evening with Steve McQueen." YouTube video, 47:34, posted by "Kunsthistorisches Museum Wien," 27 April 2020, www.youtube.com/watch?v=4cGiK3CqPg8.

"Steve McQueen and Bianca Stigter on *Occupied City*—NYFF61." YouTube video, 28:38, posted by "Film at Lincoln Center, 5 October 2023, www.youtube.com/watch?v=AR9zhVbiDNw.

"Steve McQueen Dialogue with Stuart Comer." YouTube video, 1:53:45, posted by "Walker Art Center," 31 January 2014, www.youtube.com/watch?v=-KM_5z9WvUc&t.

"Steve McQueen in Conversation with James Lingwood." YouTube video, 1:01:15, posted by "Artangel," 4 May 2020, www.youtube.com/watch?v=O9eRrf3OTgQ.

"Simon Mayo Interviews Steve McQueen and Bianca Stigter." YouTube video, 5:48, posted by "Kermode and Mayo's Take," 8 February 2024, www.youtube.com/watch?v=OF6qmRfNLlo.

"Talk: Steve McQueen—IFFR 2023." YouTube video, 58:05, posted by "International Film Festival Rotterdam," 14 February 2023, www.youtube.com/watch?v=C1TCATsSH40.

Index

Academy Awards (Oscars), viii, xvii, 70, 72, 114–15, 122
Adderley, Cannonball, 78
addiction, xvi, 66–67, 114, 125
Alex Wheatle (McQueen), xviii, 147, 151
"All Day" (West), xvii
All God's Chillun Got Wings (O'Neill), 111
Amsterdam, the Netherlands, x, xiv–xvi, xix, 4, 6, 8, 13, 39, 74, 84, 108, 159–60, 163–69
Angels with Dirty Faces (Tricky), 13
antivaxxers, 164
Apocalypse Now (Coppola), 83
architecture, 46, 67, 128–29
archival footage and materials, xix, 34, 38, 41, 167
Art Institute of Chicago, xvi–xvii, 74
art school, 76, 88, 140. *See also* Goldsmiths, University of London
Artist, The (Hazanavicius), 67
Ashes (McQueen), 85–86, 132
Atlas of an Occupied City (Stigter), xix, 160, 162, 165, 167–68
audio. *See* sound

Bach, Johann Sebastian, 9
Baldwin, James, viii, 95, 111
Baltimore, Maryland, 103–4, 108
Barrage (McQueen), xiv
Basel, Switzerland, xvi
Bass (McQueen), xix
BBC, xviii, xix, 122, 127, 137

Bear (McQueen), xiii, 4, 57, 76, 132
Beckett, Samuel, 34
Belafonte, Harry, xvii, 93–94, 99, 102
Belfast, Ireland, 41, 43, 52, 57, 91
Bergman, Ingmar, xiii
Beyoncé, 100
BFI, 29, 156, 165
Björk, 20, 22, 30
Black artists, ix, 4, 7, 24, 30, 98–99, 114, 151
Black British experience, 147–49, 151, 155, 157
Black church, 103, 111, 143–44, 155
Black Freedom Movement, 107
Black Lives Matter, xviii, 112, 137, 142, 147, 153, 155
Black Panther Party, 94
Black People's Day of Action, xix
Black Police Association, xviii
black-and-white film, xiv, 80, 144
BlacKkKlansman (Lee), 155
Blitz (McQueen), xviii, xix, 160
Blowback (Tricky), xiv
blues (music), 13, 22, 97, 103, 143, 147, 149, 155
Blues Before Sunrise (McQueen), xvi
bodies/the body/embodiment, ix, xiv, 4, 18, 21, 34, 44, 48–49, 52, 56–57, 59–60, 82, 91, 100, 112, 127, 132, 142. *See also* physicality
boredom, 6, 11, 60, 81, 132
Bovell, Dennis, 143
Boyega, John, xviii, 142, 147, 151, 153

Brecht, Bertolt, xin10
Brit Awards, 13
Britain. *See* United Kingdom
Brixton riots, xix, 41, 127, 152
Broken Column (McQueen), vii–viii, xvii
Brown, Michael, Jr., 112
burden of representation, 150, 157

Cahiers du cinéma, 59
Caméra d'Or, xvi, 44, 53, 57
cameras and camerawork, ix, xiv, 4, 19, 21, 35–36, 42, 46, 50, 53–57, 62, 67, 76–81, 85, 88, 97, 128–29, 134, 143, 154, 156, 162, 167
Cannes Film Festival, xvi, xix, 44, 53, 91, 160
capitalism, 105, 117
Carib's Leap/Western Deep (McQueen), xv, 57, 82, 85–86
Catch (McQueen), viii, xiii, 57
Catholicism, 15, 52, 59, 62–63, 85
celebrity age, 26
Charlotte (McQueen), xv, 81
Chicago, Illinois, 122–24, 133
Chinatown (Polanski), 126
Christianity, 35, 100, 118
cinéma-vérité, 33
Citizen, The (Hamilton), 128
class, 14, 120, 133
close-ups, 59, 62, 68, 79, 81
Coates, Oliver, 160, 168
Codes of Conduct (McQueen), xvii, 114
Cold Breath (McQueen), xiv
coltan, xv, 82
communism, 116, 117, 120
Congo, 82
Couch (Warhol), xin2, 40
COVID-19 pandemic, x, xix, 145, 154, 163, 165
"Cross, The" (Prince), 100

Crowdus, Gary, 57–65
Current (McQueen), xiv, 6

dance and dancing, 40, 143, 155
D'Angelo (musician), 21
Davis, Miles, 7, 9–10, 17, 25, 78, 95
Davis, Viola, xviii, 122, 124
de Antonio, Emile, 75
De Salvo, Donna, 73–92, 94, 166
Deadpan (McQueen), xiv, 3, 6–7, 52, 66, 77, 132
death and dying, vii, xvii, 52–54, 58, 60–61, 63, 74, 85, 87, 91, 98, 118, 128, 153, 155
"Defense of Poetry, A" (Shelley), 98
Desert Island Discs (radio program), ix
Devil's Advocate (television program), 152
dialogue, 42–46, 54–55, 61–62, 65, 67, 70–71, 77, 87, 91, 118, 127–29, 140
digital media, 36, 82, 162
documentary film and media, vii, ix, x, xv, xix, 33, 36, 37, 57, 80, 131, 134, 151, 165–67
Drumroll (McQueen), xiv, 3, 4, 53, 77–78, 82
Du Bois, W. E. B., 94, 99, 103, 105, 107, 111
dub music, 143
Dunn, Jamie, 66–69
Durrant, Sabine, 6–9

Eames, Ray and Charles, 38
education, 138, 147–51
Education (McQueen), xviii, 142, 147–50
Elizabeth II (queen), xviii, 123
Ellwood, Gregory, 122–26
Emperor Jones, The (O'Neill), 111, 113
Empire (Warhol), 79
Empire State Building, 79

End Credits (McQueen), x, xvii, 73–74, 77, 116, 119–20, 166
England, 14–16, 18, 22, 24, 29–30, 43, 47, 90
Enwezor, Okwui, 85, 151
Europe, 18, 90, 108
Europe, James, 97
evidence, viii, ix, 6, 9, 71, 75, 155
excrement, 48–49, 58, 60–61
exhibitions, vii, xvi, xvii, xviii, 3, 4, 32, 34, 38–40, 57, 157
Exodus (McQueen), xiii
experimentation, xiii, 36, 38, 57, 76, 88
Eyes Wide Shut (Kubrick), 66

Face, The (magazine), 24
Fassbender, Michael, vii, xvi, 43–45, 56, 59, 66, 68, 71, 91, 129
Faul, Denis, 59, 63
FBI, x, xvii, 7, 74, 101, 103, 116–17, 123, 166
fear, 15, 22, 67, 101, 117–19, 132–33, 137, 140, 158
Fela (McQueen), xvi
fiction, 37, 59, 63, 125
film school, 8, 46, 88. *See also* New York University (NYU)
film scores, 28, 60, 72, 160, 168
Five Easy Pieces (McQueen), xiii, 4, 35
Five Easy Pieces (Rafelson), 4
Floyd, George, xviii, 145, 147, 153–55
Flynn, Gillian, xviii, 123, 133
France, 23
Franklin, Aretha, 100, 107, 111
funding, 43, 46
funk, 4, 100

Game of Thrones (television series), 116
Gaye, Marvin, 21, 101, 106, 107
gender, 133–34, 139
genre, ix, 122, 131, 134, 143, 166

Ghost Dog (Jarmusch), 28
Giardini (McQueen), xvi, 83–84
Gilroy, Paul, 108, 136–46
Girlfight (Kusama), 125
Girls Tricky (McQueen), 33
God, 34–35, 100, 111
Godard, Jean-Luc, xiii, 61, 90–91
Godfather, The (Coppola), 126
Goethe, Johann Wolfgang von, 102
Gordon, Lucky, 157
Gordy, Barry, 106
Grant, Simon, 127–30
Gravesend/Unexploded (McQueen), xv, 39, 82, 83
Great Britain. *See* United Kingdom
Gregg, Ronald E., 132
Grenada, 85–86
Grenfell (McQueen), xix, 160
Grenfell Tower fire, xix, 160
Guardian, The, viii

Hairy Ape, The (O'Neill), 111
Hansberry, Lorraine, 99, 105, 107, 117
Hathaway, Donny, 111, 118
H-Blocks. *See* HM Prison Maze (Long Kesh Detention Centre)
heist movies, xviii, 122, 124–25, 133
Hendrix, Jimi, 15, 79
Here I Stand (Robeson and Brown), 94, 109
hip-hop, 16, 20, 22, 24, 29, 118
history, viii, 44–45, 49, 61, 71–72, 76, 89, 91, 98, 104, 110, 117, 124, 130–32, 136, 138, 139, 145, 147–52, 155, 157, 159–60, 162–64, 166–67, 169
Hitler, Adolf, 12, 110
HM Prison Maze (Long Kesh Detention Centre), xvi, 44–46, 50, 57–58, 60, 63–66, 91, 127
Hollywood, 46, 70, 94, 113, 154

180 INDEX

Holocaust, xix, 61, 159, 161, 165
Howe, Darcus, 144–45, 148, 152
H3 (Blair), 58
Hunger (McQueen), vii, xvi, 39, 41–66, 70–71, 87, 90, 114, 127–30, 134, 137, 165
hunger strikes, 59, 61, 64, 114, 125, 127
Hunger Winter (1944), 159, 162, 166
Hurricane Katrina, 98, 118

"I Like the Girls" (Beastie Boys), 29
"I Like the Girls" (Tricky), 29
Illuminer (McQueen), xiv, 35–36, 80, 132
improvisation, 33–35, 45, 55, 78, 142
IRA (Irish Republican Army), 44, 48–49, 52, 57–58, 63–64, 66, 127
Iraq, xv, 39, 80. *See also* Second Gulf War
Ireland, 15, 43, 46, 59
Island Records, 10, 23
Israel, 17–18

Jamaican English, 19
jazz, 7, 34, 40, 95, 157
Jazz Singer, The (Crosland), xix
Jelinek, Elfriede, x, xin10
Jim Crow laws, 109–10
Johannes Vermeer Award, xvii
Johnson, Jack, 95
Jones, Claudia, 117
Jones, Jonathan, 3–5
Jones-LeCointe, Altheia, 144–45
Jubilee Singers, 97
Jump Cut (journal), 131
Just Above My Head (McQueen), xiii, 57
justice and injustice, 105, 110, 137–38, 145, 153

Keaton, Buster, xiv, 3–5, 52, 66, 77, 132
King, Martin Luther, Jr., 94, 101, 103, 107, 109–11, 117, 120
Kouguell, Susan, 165–70

"Kung Fu Fighting" (Douglas), 143
"Kunta Kinte" (the Revolutionaries), 143

La Plante, Lynda, 123
Lemercier, Fabien, 41–43
Léon (Besson), 28
Leopold II (king), 82
"Let Paul Sing" (Robeson concert), 107
Leturcq, Armelle, 44–47
light and lighting, xv–xvi, xix, 21, 38, 42, 50–51, 55, 62, 79–81
Logan, Leroy, xviii, 140, 142, 151, 153
London, xiii–xiv, xviii, 11, 13, 15, 27, 40–41, 57, 66, 86, 97, 107–8, 122–23, 142, 147, 155, 157, 160, 169
Lost Weekend, The (Wilder), 68
love, 8, 11, 17–18, 97, 100, 119, 125, 132–33, 139, 140–42, 150
Lovers Rock (McQueen), xviii, 142–43, 147, 149, 151, 155
Lovesexy (Prince), 100
lynching, 89, 107
Lynching Tree (McQueen), xvi

Maids, The (Genet), 125
Mangrove (McQueen), xviii, 137, 144–45, 147–49, 151, 153
Mangrove Nine, xviii, 138, 144, 147, 149, 153
March on Washington, 105
Marcus (McQueen's cousin), 32–35, 81
martyrdom, vii, xin1, 49, 58
Massive Attack, 11, 15, 19–20, 22, 29
masturbation, 35, 60, 66–67
Maxinquaye (Tricky), 12, 15, 22, 29
Maxwell (musician), 21, 25
May, Theresa, 137
Mayfield, Curtis, 105–6, 118
Mees, After Evening Dip, New Year's Day, 2002 (McQueen), xv

melodrama, xvi, 134
Melody Maker (magazine), 24
Metropolitan Police, 141–42
military, xv, 35, 159, 164
Milton (McQueen's neighbor), 73, 93
Monet, Claude, 63, 81
Moonlit (McQueen), 79, 81
Morrison, Toni, 9, 34
"Mother's Child" (Prince), 100
Müller, Robby, 85, 87, 156–57
Mulligan, Carey, xvi, 68
Murder in the Cathedral (Eliot), xiin1
Murmurs of the Earth (Sagan), 37
music, vii, xvi, xvii, 9, 10–31, 33, 35, 40, 42, 47, 56, 60, 64, 78, 95–98, 106–8, 111, 118–19, 138, 142–43, 157, 168
music videos, xvii, 21–22, 26, 30
musicals, 3, 72, 119
My Bed (Emin), xiv
My Favorite Things (Coltrane), 106
"My Funny Valentine" (Rodgers and Hart), 33

narrative, vii, x, xviii, 39, 41–42, 44, 53, 58, 60–63, 82–83, 71, 103, 123, 128, 133, 159–60, 164, 167–68
Nauman, Bruce, 5, 78–79
Navy Seals, 80
Nazism, x, 110, 159, 164, 166, 168
Nearer to God (Tricky), 13
New Regency, 123
"New York, New York" (Sinatra), 68
New York City, New York, 15, 39–40, 75–78
New York University (NYU), 4, 88
Nicholls, Johnny, 152
Nicholson, Jack, 4, 153–54
Nikita (Besson), 28
Nil by Mouth (Oldman), 27
NME (magazine), 24

Northern Ireland, 39, 43–44, 46, 52, 57, 60–61, 66, 114, 127
Northup, Solomon, vii, xvi, 71–72, 89, 132, 134
nudity and nakedness, xiii, 8, 48, 67, 80–81, 86, 154
Nyong'o, Lupita, 71

Obama, Barack, 103, 118
Obrist, Hans Ulrich, 32–38
Occupied City (McQueen), viii, x, xix, 159–64, 165–69
Oldman, Gary, 26–28
Olusoga, David, 147–58
Once Upon a Time (McQueen), 32, 34–38
O'Neill, Eugene, 111
Open Plan (exhibition), x, 73, 75

Pacino, Al, 27
paint and painting, 5, 7, 25, 33, 38, 40, 46, 63, 76, 79, 85, 128
Palmer, Julian, 10, 15
Paradise (Morrison), 34
Paris, France, xiv, 18, 41, 80, 96, 108, 110, 169
Paris Peace Conference, 110
Parkes, Shaun, 148
parks, 84
Parks, Gordon, 134
Patterson, William, 94
performance, 6, 52, 55, 62, 66, 100, 156
permutation (McQueen's term), 132, 134
Perry, Tyler, 113
physicality, ix, xviii, 4–5, 34, 40, 46, 48–50, 58, 63, 76, 79, 160
Pitt, Brad, 70–71
Plan B (production company), 71

Plato, 98
Player, The (Altman), 55
poetry, xiv, 34, 44, 46, 60, 88, 98, 103, 162, 163
police, 58, 64, 104, 141–42, 153, 163
politics and politicians, viii, xviii, 29, 48–50, 64–65, 93, 122–24, 129–30, 133, 147, 171
Portrait of an Escapologist (McQueen), xv
post-traumatic stress disorder (PTSD), 138, 153
poverty, 37, 101, 104, 123, 125
Pre-Millenium Tension (Tricky), 12–13, 22
Prey (McQueen), xiv, 6, 7
Prince (musician), 12, 17, 21, 95, 98–101, 108
Prosser, Gabriel, 112, 118
protests and demonstrations, xviii, 48–49, 58–59, 67, 137, 142, 144, 147, 153, 163, 165
Pulley, Frank, 145
Pursuit (McQueen), xv

Queen and Country (McQueen), xv, 37
queer cinema, 134
queer theory, 131, 132

race and racism, xviii, 4, 14–17, 29–30, 105, 111, 123, 125–26, 133–34, 136, 141, 143, 148, 150, 157
radio, ix, 10, 15, 23, 58, 65, 106, 119
Raging Bull (Scorsese), 4
Rainer, Yvonne, 78–79
Rampling, Charlotte, xv, 81
Rapold, Nicolas, x, 159–64
realism, 67, 131
reality, 14, 33, 42, 67, 90, 117, 128, 138, 149, 158–59
Red, White and Blue (McQueen), xviii, 139–40, 142, 147, 151, 153
rhythm, xiv, 35, 42, 67
ritual, 33, 127, 155, 162
Robeson, Ben, 102

Robeson, Eslanda "Essie," 102, 105
Robeson, Maria Louisa, 94
Robeson, Paul, x, xvii, 73–74, 93–121, 166
Robeson, William Drew, 94, 111
Rodriguez, Michelle, xviii, 122, 125
Rolling Stones, 22
Roosevelt, Franklin Delano, 96
Roots (television series), 148
Rouch, Jean, 33
rubber, 82
Running Thunder (McQueen), vii, xvi
RZA, 16, 28

Saint Lucia (island), 86
Samarin, William, 34
Sands, Bobby, xvi, 41–42, 44–45, 48–49, 52–61, 65, 90–91, 127–30
Sauteurs, Grenada, 86
Scarface (De Palma), 27
Schaulager (museum), xvi, 73, 77
Scherf, Angeline, 32–38
Schippers, K. (Gerard Stigter), xiv, 162
sculpture, vii, xvii, 5, 40, 77, 79–80, 165
Second Gulf War, xv, 39
Second World War, xviii, 159–61
Sedgwick, Eve Kosofsky, 131
Semprun, Jorge, 59
Serpell, C. Namwali, 131
Serpentine Gallery, xix, 160
7th Nov. (McQueen), vii, xiv, 32–34, 81
sex, 8, 66, 67, 68
Shakespeare, William, 33, 65
Shame (McQueen), vii, xvi, 66–71, 77, 87, 132, 165
Shelley, Percy Bysshe, 98
Shoah (Lanzmann), 162
Siddons, Alastair, 145, 151
silent cinema, xiii, xiv, 3, 57, 67, 77
"Silly Games" (Kay), 143
Simmons, William J., ix, 131–35

Singin' in the Rain (Kelly and Donen), xin2
slapstick, 3, 5, 39
slavery, vii, viii, xvi, xvii, 70–71, 87, 89, 95, 97–98, 100, 104, 111–12, 114, 120, 122, 125, 132–34, 163–65
Sleep (Warhol), 132
Small Axe (McQueen), viii, xviii, 136–58, 165
Smith, Zadie, 29
social realism. *See* realism
socialism, 63, 106, 111
Soho, London, 6, 18
Some Mother's Son (George), 58, 64
Something Old, Something New, Something Borrowed, Something Blue (McQueen), xiv
Sorrow of Young Werther, The (Goethe), 102
sound, xiv, xv, xix, 11, 18–19, 22, 34, 36, 40, 45, 60, 64, 74, 76, 77, 81, 91, 98, 103, 108, 119–20, 142–43, 155, 160, 164, 168
Soviet Union, 109, 117
Speaking in Tongues (exhibition), 23
speaking in tongues (glossolalia and xenoglossia), 34–35
Specials, the, 19, 21, 29
spirituality, 14, 100–101, 111–12, 114, 155, 156
spirituals, 97, 108
Spruell, Sam, 145
Stalin, Joseph, 109
Star Wars (film franchise), 142
Static (McQueen), xvi, 132
Steamboat Bill, Jr. (Reisner), 52
Stigter, Bianca, x, xiv, xix, 159–60, 162–63, 165–70
storytelling, 82, 103, 126, 157–58, 166–67
suicide, 49, 59, 101, 103, 163
Sun, The, 30

Sunday Mirror, The, 30
Sunshine State (McQueen), xix
Super 8 film, 86, 162
surveillance, 75, 101, 103, 119
Synge, J. M., xin1

Tate Gallery, xiv, xviii, 6, 127, 157, 158
television, 19, 30, 35–36, 80, 90, 113, 116, 118, 120, 123, 128, 132, 138, 145, 149, 151–52, 154, 156–57
terrorism, 49–50, 58, 63
Thatcher, Margaret, 50, 58–59, 64, 90, 129
35 mm film, 44, 54, 62, 162, 167
Thomas Dane Gallery, x, 39
3D (Robert Del Naja), 19–20
Three Minutes (Stigter), xix, 159, 165–67
thrillers, xviii, 122
Tinkham, Chris, 52–56
Tisch School of the Arts. *See* New York University (NYU)
Toomey, Matthew, 70–72
Trading Twelves (Ellison and Murray), 95
Trainspotting (Boyle), 68
trauma, 63, 138–41, 159
Tricky, xiv, 10–31, 33, 37, 40
Trinidad and Tobago, xiii, 138
Troubles, the, 39, 57, 58
Trump, Donald, 104
"Turn Out the Light" (the Investigators), 143
Turner Prize, viii, xiv, 5, 6, 53, 66, 165
Tuschinski theatre, Amsterdam, 169
12 Years a Slave (McQueen), vii, viii, xvi, xvii, 70–72, 87, 89, 98, 120, 122, 124, 132–33, 164–65
Twelve Years a Slave (Northup), vii, xvi, 132–34

United Kingdom, xix, 8, 13, 30, 40, 57–59, 85, 91, 122, 136, 138, 142, 145, 147, 157

United States of America, 13–15, 24, 30, 75, 78, 89, 92, 103, 108, 110, 154, 164
University College London (UCL), 136, 145
Untitled (Fingers) (McQueen), xv
Uprising (McQueen and Rogan), xix, 165
urine, 48, 60, 61, 90, 112

van Gogh, Vincent, 65
Venice Biennale, xv–xvii, 39, 43, 47, 83–85, 165
victims and victimization, 49, 58, 120, 137, 141
video, 46, 66, 76, 81, 132, 154
Vietnam War, 101, 107, 110
Vigo, Jean, viii, xin2, xiii, 39, 43
voice, 8, 11–12, 20–21, 50, 65, 74, 90, 96–97, 129, 138, 147, 154, 161, 168
voiceover, xix, 36, 159, 161, 166
Voyager space probes, xv, 32, 36, 37

Wales, 43, 46, 73, 94
Walikale, Congo, 83
Walsh, Enda, xin1, xvi, 41, 42, 52, 59, 60–61, 91
Warhol, Andy, vii, viii, xin2, xiii, 4, 40, 79, 132
Weight (McQueen), viii, xvii
West, Cornel, viii, 93–121
West Indies, 80, 86, 93, 139
Westerns, 62, 123, 145
"What's Going On" (Gaye), 106
What's Going On (Gaye), 106
"What's Happening Brother" (Gaye), 107

Wheatle, Alex, 148, 151, 152
whirling dervishes, 35
Whitaker, Forest, 28
White, Charles, 99
White House Correspondents' Association Dinner, 118
white people and whiteness, 3, 4, 14–15, 19, 30, 31, 34, 83, 95, 96, 99, 104, 110, 112, 117–18, 120, 132–34, 140, 150
Whitney Museum of American Art, viii, x, xvii, 39, 73–74, 92, 93, 166
widescreen formats, 3, 60, 63
Widows (McQueen), xviii, 122–26, 131, 165
Widows (television series), 122, 131, 132, 133
Wilmore, Larry, 118
Wimbledon (tennis tournament), 54, 62
Wind That Shakes the Barley, The (Loach), 58, 64
women, 18, 30, 122–25, 133, 143
Wu-Tang Clan, 16

X, Malcolm, 94–95, 97, 103, 106, 107, 109, 111, 117–18, 152

Year 3 (McQueen), xviii, 157
Yeats, W. B., xin1
Young, Kirsty, ix

Z (Gravas), 59
Zéro de conduite (Vigo), xin2, 39–40, 43
Zimmer, Hans, 72
Zone of Interest, The (Glazer), 160

About the Editor

Photo by Lachlan Brooks

Geoffrey Lokke is a PhD candidate in theatre and performance at Columbia University. His work has appeared in such publications as *PAJ: A Journal of Performance and Art*, *TDR: The Drama Review*, and *Textual Cultures*. He is editor of *Gaspar Noé: Interviews*, published by University Press of Mississippi.

www.ingramcontent.com/pod-product-compliance
Lightning Source LLC
Chambersburg PA
CBHW022100160426
43198CB00008B/297